WHAT SHOULD WE THINK ABOUT
ISRAEL?

J. RANDALL PRICE

General Editor

HARVEST HOUSE PUBLISHERS
EUGENE, OREGON

What Should We Think About Israel?
Copyright © 2019 by World of the Bible Ministries
Published by Harvest House Publishers
Eugene, Oregon 97408
www.harvesthousepublishers.com

ISBN 978-0-7369-7779-1 (pbk)
ISBN 978-0-7369-7780-7 (eBook)

Library of Congress Cataloging-in-Publication Data

Names: Price, Randall, editor.
Title: What should we think about Israel? / J. Randall Price, general editor.
Description: Eugene : Harvest House Publishers, 2019. | Includes
    bibliographical references and index.
Identifiers: LCCN 2019004515 (print) | LCCN 2019011435 (ebook) | ISBN
    9780736977807 (ebook) | ISBN 9780736977791 (pbk.)
Subjects: LCSH: Palestine--In Christianity. | Israel (Christian theology)
Classification: LCC BT93.8 (ebook) | LCC BT93.8 .W44 2019 (print) | DDC
    956.9405--dc23
LC record available at https://lccn.loc.gov/2019004515

Printed in the United States of America
19 20 21 22 23 24 25 26 27 / BP-GL / 10 9 8 7 6 5 4 3 2 1

In memory of
Dr. H.L. Willmington

Lover of Zion
and its prophetic hope

Contents

PART 1: WHAT SHOULD WE THINK ABOUT ISRAEL'S POLITICS?

PART 2: WHAT SHOULD WE THINK ABOUT ISRAEL'S PROBLEMS?

PART 3: WHAT SHOULD WE THINK ABOUT ISRAEL'S PROSPECTS?

Contributors

Mark L. Bailey, PhD, Dallas Theological Seminary, is the president and senior professor of Bible exposition at Dallas Theological Seminary. For more than 40 years he has served in theological education, pastored various churches, led many tours to Israel and the Middle East, and contributed to numerous books, including *Israel, the Church, and the Middle East* (Kregel, 2018). He has served on the board of Jews for Jesus since 2009.

David Brickner, MA in Missiology with a concentration in Jewish Evangelism/Judaic Studies, Fuller School of World Missions, has been executive director of Jews for Jesus since 1996. He is the author of numerous books and publications on Israel and the Jewish people, including *Jewish Family Matters* (1996), *Christ in the Feast of Tabernacles* (2006), and *Christ in the Feast of Pentecost* (2008).

Michael L. Brown, PhD, New York University, is founder of ICN Ministries and has taught Old Testament and Jewish apologetics at Trinity Evangelical Divinity School and Fuller Theological Seminary. Dr. Brown hosts the television program *Answering Your Toughest Questions* and the animated online series "AskDrBrown" and is the author of numerous books and articles. He is considered to be the world's foremost Jewish apologist, having debated Jewish rabbis, agnostic professors, and activists on radio, TV, and college campuses internationally.

Arnold G. Fruchtenbaum, PhD, New York University, is executive director of Ariel Ministries, San Antonio, TX, where he serves as an international teacher and conference speaker. He is author of numerous books on Israel and the Jewish people and commentaries on the Old and New Testaments.

Steven Charles Ger, ThM, Dallas Theological Seminary, grew up in a Jewish family. He was educated in both church and synagogue due to his distinctive heritage as a Jewish Christian. He is the founder and director of Sojourner Ministries, has served as adjunct professor of Jewish studies at Criswell College and taught at Tyndale Seminary. He currently serves as senior pastor at messianic congregation Beth Sar Shalom (Plano, TX). He is the author of numerous books and commentaries on the Bible, including *The Book of Acts: Witnesses to the World* (AMG, 2005) and *The Book of Hebrews: Christ Is Greater* (AMG, 2009).

Mitch Glaser, PhD, Fuller Theological Seminary, is the president of Chosen People Ministries. He speaks and writes widely on Jewish evangelism and messianic Judaism. He is coeditor with Darrell Bock of four academic volumes published by Kregel Publications and has authored numerous books and articles.

Mark Hitchcock, JD, Oklahoma State University, PhD, Dallas Theological Seminary, is an associate professor of Bible at Dallas Theological Seminary and senior pastor of Faith Bible Church, Edmond, OK. He is an international conference speaker and the author of more than 30 books related to end-time Bible prophecy that, combined, have sold more than one million copies.

Thomas Ice, PhD, Tyndale Theological Seminary, is the cofounder and executive director of The Pre-Trib Research Center and professor of Bible and theology at Calvary University in Kansas City, MO. He is the author or coauthor of numerous books and articles and is an international conference speaker.

Walter C. Kaiser Jr., PhD, Brandeis University, is the former president and Colman M. Mockler Distinguished Professor of Old Testament at Gordon-Conwell Theological Seminary in South Hamilton, MA. For more than 20 years he was the academic dean and professor of Old Testament at Trinity Evangelical Divinity School. Dr. Kaiser is the author of numerous books and articles on subjects related to Israel and biblical interpretation.

Meno Kalisher graduated from the Friends of Israel Institute of Biblical Studies and is currently pursuing a DMin at The Master's Seminary. He is a native-born Israeli and founding pastor of the Jerusalem Assembly House of Redemption. He is the author of several books on biblical and prophetic studies and has produced commentaries on the books of Galatians and James.

Justin Kron studied at the Moody Theological Seminary in Chicago and is the cocreator and producer of *Hope in the Holy Land: Delving Beneath the Surface of the Israeli-Palestinian Conflict* (www.hopeintheholyland .com). He is the founding coordinator of the Kesher Forum, an interdenominational gathering for those who are interested in learning more about Jewish culture and building bridges with their Jewish friends and neighbors, and is the founding director of Experience Israel, a short-term ministry and spiritual pilgrimage program for young adults sponsored by Chosen People Ministries.

Jim Melnick, MA degrees from Harvard University in Russian studies and Harvard Law and Business Schools and from the US Naval War College in National Security and Strategic Studies. A retired US Army Reserve colonel in military intelligence, he served as a Russian affairs analyst at the Department of Defense at the Pentagon during the final years of the Cold War, with his last assignment in the Office of the Secretary of Defense. After leaving government, he worked in the computer security industry, developing expertise on Russian and Chinese hackers. In 2005, *Business Week* cited his cyber threat work as "some of the most incisive analysis in the business, particularly about Russian hackers." Since 2013 he has been active in ministry among both Israeli messianic Jewish and Palestinian Christian pastors and leaders and now serves as the international coordinator of the Lausanne Consultation on Jewish Evangelism (LCJE) and the editor of the *LCJE Bulletin* and as a tentmaker missionary with Life in Messiah International and president of Friends of Russian Jewry, Inc., where he publishes a global Russian-language messianic newspaper. He is author of *Jewish Giftedness and World Redemption: The Calling of Israel* (Messianic Jewish Publishers, 2017).

Olivier J. Melnick was born in France to Holocaust survivors. He graduated from Moody Bible Institute and serves with Chosen People Ministries and on their French board of directors. He is an international speaker on modern and postmodern anti-Semitism and is author of *End-Times Antisemitism: A New Chapter in the Longest Hatred* (HFT, 2017).

John Piper, ThD, University of Munich is the pastor emeritus of Bethlehem Baptist Church and chancellor of Bethlehem College & Seminary in Minneapolis, MN. A prolific author, many of his books have received the ECPA Christian Book Award.

Randall Price, PhD, University of Texas, is Distinguished Research Professor of Biblical and Judaic Studies at Liberty University, Lynchburg, VA, and founder and president of World of the Bible Ministries, San Marcos, TX. He has worked as an archaeologist in Israel for 20 years and is the author of numerous books on biblical subjects and the Middle East conflict. Dr. Price serves on the board of the Friends of Israel Gospel Ministry.

Imad N. Shehadeh, PhD, Dallas Theological Seminary, post-doctoral studies Theological Faculty, Leuven, Belgium and the University of Edinburgh, is the founder and president and senior professor of theology at Jordan Evangelical Theological Seminary (JETS), Amman, Jordan. He is the author of numerous academic journal articles and publications in English and Arabic.

Tim M. Sigler, PhD, Trinity International University, Israel scholar-in-residence for CJF Ministries and provost and dean at Shepherd's Theological Seminary in Cary, NC, and served with distinction at the Moody Bible Institute for 18 years, most recently as professor of Hebrew and Biblical Studies. He has provided educational opportunities and nonprofit consulting in Israel, Jordan, Egypt, and other international contexts. He is a contributor to *The Moody Bible Commentary*, *The Dictionary of Daily Life in Biblical and Post-Biblical Antiquity*, and other publications.

Michael J. Vlach, PhD, Southeastern Baptist Theological Seminary, professor, The Master's Seminary, CA, and editor of *The Master's Seminary Journal*. He has authored several books on biblical and theological subjects related to Israel, including *Has the Church Replaced Israel?: A Theological Evaluation* (B&H Academic, 2010) and *He Will Reign Forever: A Biblical Theology of the Kingdom of God* (Lampion Press, 2017).

Paul Wilkinson, PhD, University of Manchester, England. He has studied at the International School of Holocaust Studies at Yad Vashem in Jerusalem and is an international conference speaker and contributor to Christian broadcasting in the UK. He is the author of *Israel Betrayed: The Rise of Christian Palestinianism* (Ariel, 2018).

Andy Woods, JD, Whittier Law School, PhD, Dallas Theological Seminary, president of Chafer Seminary, and senior pastor of Sugarland Bible Church, Sugarland, TX. He has several books on Israel, including *The Coming Kingdom* (Grace Gospel Press, 2016).

Tuvya Zaretsky, DMiss, Western Seminary in Portland, OR. He is one of the founders of the Jews for Jesus ministry and chairs the board for the Jews for Jesus branch in Tel Aviv, Israel. He currently serves as president for the International Coordinating Committee of the Lausanne Consultation on Jewish Evangelism, a networking body of Jewish mission agencies. He was a contributing author to *Israel the Land and People* (Kregel Publishers, 1998).

Foreword

These are dangerous days in which we live! The storm clouds are gathering. The lightning is flashing—and the lightning rod is Israel. Christians cannot deny or ignore the significance of the nation of Israel...The eyes of the entire world are upon the tiny state of Israel, and your eyes need to be there too, because the Jews and Israel are the people and the land of destiny. As the Jew goes, so goes the world. Israel is God's yardstick. Israel is God's measuring rod. Israel is God's blueprint. Israel is God's program for what He is doing in the world.

ADRIAN ROGERS, *UNVEILING THE END TIMES IN OUR TIME*

The eyes of the world are on Israel, and our eyes need to be there too. Whatever your denomination, affiliation, or theological background, you should care about what the Bible says about Israel's present and future in God's plan for the ages. Israel is mentioned more than 2,500 times in the Bible. After almost 2,000 years of dispersion to more than 70 nations, the modern state of Israel was founded in 1948, and the Jewish people are still being regathered to their ancient homeland.

What Should We Think About Israel? That's not an easy question to answer because there are so many other questions connected to it—about the Arab-Jew relations, the Temple Mount, anti-Semitism, and more. Unfortunately, the answers to these questions are often buried underneath piles of politics, personal opinions, preconceptions, prejudice, and provocation. Historical revision clouds the past and confuses the present. Discussions about Israel often generate great heat but little light. More and more today, Israel is demonized at every turn—even by evangelical

Christians. Who and what are we to believe? Where can we get more light? *What Should We Think About Israel?*

Finally, there is a balanced book that passionately, yet objectively and carefully, examines the biblical evidence to answer this question and provide sound, well-researched conclusions. The authors of this book share a simple, straightforward approach—they interpret the text of Scripture through the lens of a consistent, literal method of interpretation. Using this approach, they capably guide us through the modern maze of confusion surrounding today's important questions about the Jewish people and the land of Israel.

While I have studied this subject extensively, I have learned a great deal from this book. In fact, it's the best book I've read on this topic. I cannot recommend it highly enough.

This book will challenge you. It will connect you with God's plan for the Jewish people. It may even convince you. But most importantly, it will call you to recognize the covenant-keeping God who is faithful to every one of His promises, including those made to the people of Israel.

Dr. Mark Hitchcock
Senior Pastor, Faith Bible Church, Edmond, OK
Associate Professor of Bible Exposition, Dallas Theological Seminary

What Should We Think About This Book?

RANDALL PRICE

In the mass of publications about the Middle East, this book is different. It exposes the key issues of conflict and controversy, provides objective facts, and allows readers to examine their own belief systems and opinions on the matters presented. The contributors come from American, European, Jewish, and Arab backgrounds, live in various countries of the Middle East as well as Europe and the United States, and represent different academic, religious, and political disciplines. Most have published previously on their topics and some are recognized leaders in their field. The unifying goal is for this to serve as a practical resource that helps readers not only know what to think, but to do so in a fully informed way.

When one hears the word *Israel*, what should he think? One blog site states,

Israel. The very name means different things to different people. It is a geographic place: the ancient land of the Israelites as well as a modern Mediterranean nation. It is a people: practitioners of Judaism who see themselves as descended from Biblical Jacob. It is a hot-button political topic, a homeland, a vacation destination and—perhaps most significantly—it is the place where three of the world's major religions converge, creating a palimpsest of history that is one of the richest and most complex in the world.[1]

With so many options regarding one place, it might be thought impossible to even suggest what someone should think about Israel! But, that is the purpose of this book, and in it we want to connect ancient Israel (the place and the people) and the ancient promises made to the Jews (in distinction from the other two religions that have staked their claim there) with modern Israel (again, the place and the people) and the controversies and conflicts that exist as a result of the Jewish people's return to the Land.

This Book's Focus

Our primary focus will be on Israel's role in the Middle East conflict and the theological and practical controversies that have resulted. In each chapter, this book will ask a question about how we should think about Israel and certain specific issues that touch the lives of millions of people in the Middle East as well as those who live in the West. While Israel remains our subject, we have not forgotten the Arab population living within Israel as fellow citizens with the Jewish people, the Palestinian population that shares Israel's borders, and the greater Arab world that shares a concern for how the rest of the globe, especially the West, thinks about Israel. Within the scope of what our subject allows, we have sought to address the issues related to the Arab people and their plight, yet with an appeal to them to understand the biblical worldview we adopt and why it makes a difference for all of our futures.

There are, of course, hundreds of books that have already been published on Israel (many of the contributors to this book have written some of them), but where does one go to separate fact from fiction in this plethora of literature written from diverse and often opposing perspectives? Are we truly getting the facts on these matters of international importance, or just spin from agenda-driven sources? Mike Evans, a bestselling author and the founder of the Friends of Zion Museum in Jerusalem, underscores this problem. He reports that he once asked a joint chief of staff what determines when wars begin and end. He said this official whispered in his ear, "The media."[2]

Today we hear accusations being made from the highest office in the US concerning "fake news," stories that are largely fiction created to serve a private (usually political) agenda. The problem with such "fake news" is that the average person who depends on the internet or television or even the newspaper (yes, some still read them) to give him or her daily information on the affairs of state has no reason to suspect he or she is being manipulated by misinformation. The problem, however, as the ancient Greek philosopher Thucydides noted, is that "most people do not take pains to get at the truth of things but believe the first thing they hear." The public cannot be faulted for this because many people are not equipped to recognize fake news, nor do they have the means within themselves to counter it.

Sometimes the problem is not fake news, but no news at all on matters of significance. I often find more important news running on the ticker tape at the bottom of some televised news broadcasts than in their planned programming. Even when the news is delivered accurately, it is still presented selectively so that the full picture of events, especially in the Middle East, go unreported by the press and therefore unknown by the public. A historical example of this is the Jewish persecution that took place in Arab countries and the subsequent expulsion and dispersion of 850,000 Jewish refugees from those lands as a consequence of the UN partition vote in 1947.[3]

Many publications have focused exclusively on a similar situation that has existed for Arab people in the Middle East, and while their plight should be made known, the forced Jewish exile should not be overlooked. The present-day media spotlight is often focused on Gaza and Palestinian resistance to Israeli occupation (despite the fact that in 2005 Israel disengaged from Gaza and that Gaza has had Palestinian autonomy under an elected Palestinian government since 2006), while just up the coast near Damascus, Syria, we come to Yarmouk, the site of the largest Palestinian refugee camp in the Middle East. There, a population of some 200,000 Palestinians have been bombed, driven from their homes, and starved to death by the Syrian army and Islamist groups. As of 2018, the population of the camp is between 100–200 Palestinians.[4] The suffering in this literal death camp is a humanitarian "catastrophe" (Arabic *nakba*, the term used by Palestinians for Israel's declaration of a state in 1948), yet it has scarcely been heard of by the international community.[5]

Similarly, it has been observed that the death toll in a single day of the Syrian conflict is more than that of all the wars and conflicts between Israel and the Arab world combined! Yet such comparisons are never made in the mainstream media because the problem is not strictly a humanitarian concern but a political agenda against the Jewish state, and it is deemed politically correct to depict Israel and Israel alone as the root cause of all conflict and suffering in the region.

In our time, there has also arisen an "online intifada" of terrorists and hate groups that use social media to incite violence against Israel and the Jewish people worldwide. This has become a problem that is difficult, if not impossible, to monitor, one that has influenced terrorist acts against Israel and the Jewish community and has affected the perceptions that Millennials and Generation Z have toward Israel as a negative and even hostile entity. Many believe that the widespread acceptance of the BDS (Boycott, Divestment, Sanctions) movement on university campuses is due to its promotion via the online intifada.[6]

So where can we go for objective reporting on the Middle East conflict and the controversies that emerge from it—or any news, for that matter? First, we should take the idea of complete and unbiased objectivity off the table. Within a democratic society, especially one that values its right to free thinking and free speech per the guarantees in the US Constitution, everyone has a right to their opinion and feels the right to advance it for the good of their cause. Where opinions differ, the politically correct virtue is to keep an open mind. This was often stated when Supreme Court justice Brett Kavanaugh underwent his 2018 confirmation hearing. Congressional inquirers repeatedly asked him if he could approach decisions impartially and "with an open mind." What his questioners wanted to know was whether his religious, political, or personal views could sway him in his judicial decision making.

Kavanaugh replied that he would base his decisions on the law (an objective standard outside himself)—and in that sense, he would be open to whatever the law would allow. This in itself constitutes a decision (rather a presupposition) that the law is an acceptable and objective standard, even though it was forged out of the strong opinions of this nation's forefathers, who were reacting to the tyranny they had experienced under British rule. Yet without a presupposition of something, we all lack a starting point. As one humorist said, "If you have too open a mind, your brains may fall out!" We may argue about our differing presuppositions, but we all have them. The question will then be this: Which presupposition is the best starting point for dealing with the complex political, social, and emotional issues surrounding the Middle East conflict?

This Book's Contributors

As mentioned earlier, the contributors in this book come from Arab, Israeli, Jewish, European, and American backgrounds. Their different cultures affect their daily perspectives and decisions, yet they are united by a common conviction that they must weigh their views and actions by a higher standard that supersedes their diverse backgrounds. That is the presupposition that guides them: They interpret the events and issues that form the Middle East conflict (much of which they have experienced firsthand) from a presupposition that the Scripture (the Bible, containing the Old and New Testaments) is authoritative. You may not share their biblical conviction, but you are invited to give them a hearing and compare your own standard of evaluating facts in the process.

Read the biographies of these contributors, and you will see that many live in the context of the current conflict and have a passion for justice and a compassion for those who suffer from injustice. In fact, they would say that their biblical worldview compels them to think, feel, and act in this way. Some Jewish contributors lost family members in the Holocaust yet try to reconcile with those who were once perceived as enemies in order to promote peace. They will say that such peace is only possible, despite conflicting political persuasions, if hearts can be united by a common conviction and allegiance to God. Throughout the Middle East today there is such spiritual reconciliation taking place, though it's happening underground due to local persecution and therefore it goes unseen and unreported. Such a change of heart is the only means of achieving a change of mind when lives have been shattered by religious and national conflict.

This Book's Audience

This book is for anyone who may feel either uninformed of the biblical teaching concerning Israel or who may feel confused by the negative climate that surrounds Israel's role in the Middle East conflict and what they have heard from the media or other sources. Statistically, many younger people today view the subject of Israel with increasing disinterest if not disdain. Others who have watched the news headlines over recent decades often wonder how to make sense of the frequently conflicting information that's out there.

Most of us who are contributors to this book have experienced the dramatic changes that have occurred in the Middle East over multiple decades and are able to speak with firsthand knowledge about things that are little known today. We grew up in an era when the events in the Middle East, and especially in Israel, forced us to reconsider the ancient texts of the Bible and to become more aware of how these events were part of a divine plan for the ages. With that in mind we offer facts from our lifetimes of evaluating the evidence from the biblical worldview. We believe it is necessary to share this knowledge at this juncture in history because we have observed that younger generations have often adopted perspectives based on the perceived ill-treatment of others (injustice) as stated in popular reporting, and have consequently championed their cause without accurate knowledge of key facts that all too often are overlooked.

While we, too, advocate justice for the oppressed, we are aware that some of what is called oppression is actually the result of political agendas and is not entirely based on the real attitudes of the resident populations. In fact, those often deemed the "oppressors" from a politically correct perspective have been part of a greater history of oppression in which they themselves have suffered injustice and continue to do so on an unparalleled scale. Therefore, it is necessary to separate the sentiments that may at times result from fictitious reports (fake news) from a proper passion for justice and reconciliation based on an accurate assessment of the facts.

In addition, polls taken among young evangelical Christians have shown a decided move away from traditional support for Israel and a disinterest in biblical prophecy, which is largely Israel-centered. Some of the contributions in this book seek to encourage balanced thinking in this area.

Because we want to allow for self-expression and structured thinking on the topics presented, we have provided a means for you to journal your personal responses after each chapter. We trust this will enable you to engage more actively with the issues we address and retain a record of your thoughts as they continue to form on these important matters.

Finally, it is our hope that people will recognize that the issues connected with the Middle East conflict will only escalate in days to come, and that a lasting solution is unattainable from the political process alone. The peace that is longed for in this world must start within, rather than from without. Only an understanding of the real cause of the conflict and its continuance can provide the proper basis for the greater appeal to the One who governs these events and has His own plan to resolve them in perfect peace.

INTRODUCTION

Why Should We Think About Israel?

MARK L. BAILEY

When I consider what one should think about Israel, four things come to mind: a Bible, a newspaper, a church, and a telescope. The Bible is where we find out what God thinks about Israel. The newspaper brings the contemporary conflict of the Middle East to our attention. The church comes to mind because it is somewhat divided as to its view of the Jews and the nation of Israel. And last, the function of a telescope is to see more clearly what is far away—in this case, the unknown future. Is God finished with Israel, or does the nation have a future in His plans?

The Bible—What Does God Think About Israel?

God refers to Israel as a people of His "own possession" (Deuteronomy 7:6); His "special treasure" (Psalm 135:4), and even the "apple of His eye" (Zechariah 2:8). The psalmist affirms that God's affectionate choice has not been set on any other nation (Psalm 147:20). With Deuteronomy 7:6-10 as a central text detailing the purposes for which God chose Israel, along with other passages that speak to this, one can summarize that God chose Israel to be the channel through which the Messiah would come, a light to the nations and a repository of the truth.

Channel of the Messiah

The family tree of Jesus the Messiah begins with the very first promise that one would come through the human race and bring victory over the enemy (Genesis 3:15). Out of all the nations of the world, God chose one, via a covenant with Abraham, through which He would bring the One who would bless the world (Genesis 12:1-3). God further determined He would come through the tribe of Judah (Genesis 49:8-10), and more specifically, from the family of David—to whom the throne, a house, and a kingdom were promised, all of which would never be taken away (2 Samuel 7:13-17). The village in which the Shepherd-King of Israel would be born was identified as Bethlehem (Micah 5:2). Even the male gender of the Messiah was identified 700 years before His birth (Isaiah 9:6). While it may be typological from the Old Testament angle, the miracle of the virgin-born Son of God brought the Messiah incarnate into the world in fulfillment of prophecy (Isaiah 7:14; Matthew 1:23) at just the right time to deliver people from the curse of sin though His substitutionary death (Galatians 4:4). In the seminal passage regarding the Abrahamic covenant, the promised "seed" of Abraham are the recipients and the conduits of blessing. They are to be blessed as descendants of Abraham, and they are called to be a blessing to the rest of the world (Genesis 12:2-3). As the Bible states, how people respond to this chosen nation will determine whether they are blessed or cursed by God (Genesis 12:3).

Light to the Nations

As promised in the Abrahamic covenant, it is through the seed of Abraham that blessing will come to the world. God's mission has always been for the world to know Him as God. Isaiah 42:6-7 records these words spoken to Israel:

> I am the LORD, I have called You in righteousness, I will also hold You by the hand and watch over You, and I will appoint You as a covenant to the people, as a light to the nations, to open blind eyes, to bring out prisoners from the dungeon and those who dwell in darkness from the prison.

Then in Isaiah 49:6 God said, "It is too small a thing that You should be My Servant to raise up the tribes of Jacob and to restore the preserved ones of Israel; I will also make You a light of the nations so that My salvation may reach to the end of the earth." God's saving activity in Israel was designed to transform the people into His servants through whom the world could hear the good news and be saved.

Malachi 1:1-5 reveals that God's elective love of Israel in contrast to Edom was so that the Lord would be magnified beyond the borders of Israel. This is a repeated theme throughout the Hebrew Bible. In the Exodus narrative, Moses told Pharaoh that God was sending the plagues "in order to proclaim My name through all the earth" (Exodus 9:16). God informed Moses that He would establish Israel so that "all the peoples of the earth will see that you are called by the name of the LORD" (Deuteronomy 28:10). Joshua told Israel that God dried up the waters of the Jordan "so that all the peoples of the earth may know that the hand of the LORD is mighty" (Joshua 4:24). David challenged Goliath that the results of his death would be "that all the earth may know that there is a God in Israel" (1 Samuel 17:46).

Solomon prayed that God's attention to the prayers of the aliens who lived within the borders of Israel would be a testimony "in order that all the peoples of the earth may know Your name, to fear You, as do Your people Israel" (1 Kings 8:43). The psalmist prayed that "all the ends of the earth will remember and turn to the LORD" (Psalm 22:27), "that Your way may be known on earth, Your salvation among all nations" (67:2), and that "all nations will be blessed through him" (72:17 NIV). In Isaiah, God said, "I will…make You a light of the nations…that My salvation may reach to the end of the earth" (49:6). Jeremiah forecast a time when "the nations" would hear of all the good God does for Jerusalem and, as a result, will exhibit fear and trembling (33:9). The choice of Israel was not redemptive solely for Israel, but also missional in messaging the possibilities of blessing to the nations.

Repository of the Truth

God revealed Himself in the Law, the Prophets, and the Writings of the Hebrew Scriptures, all of which were designed to lead people to Jesus the Messiah (Luke 24:44). All three portions record the words and works of God in His dealings with Israel as unique among the nations. As the chosen people of God, Israel was an advantaged people "entrusted with the oracles of God" (Romans 3:1-2). Paul, in his treatise on the purposes of God for Israel, wrote, "…Israelites, to whom belongs the adoption as sons, and the glory and the covenants and the giving of the Law and the temple service and the promises, whose are the fathers, and from whom is the Christ according to the flesh, who is over all, God blessed forever. Amen" (Romans 9:4-5). Israel was not chosen to serve merely as a depository to hold the truth, but as a repository to relay the truth to her own people as well as all others. Gerald McDermott, in his discovery of the role of Israel, wrote,

> One of my "Aha!" moments was the day I started to see a pattern to the biblical story in both Testaments. The pattern moves from the particular to the universal. God uses the particular (a particular person or people) to bring blessing to the universal (the world). In the Old Testament, God uses a particular man (Abraham) and his people (the Jews) to bring blessing to their neighbors and to the world (the universal).[1]

God wanted a people who would be a showcase for both His redeeming grace and His righteous judgment. I love how our friends at One for Israel put it on their website: God wanted a "flagship" nation that was an example to the world—not of how they behave, but of how He behaves.[2]

Newspaper: What Is the Ongoing Conflict in the Middle East?

States and governments emerging out of wars often struggle for legitimacy at home and abroad. One does not need to listen long or read very widely to be exposed to the competing narratives for identity, legitimacy, and security on the eastern coastal territory of the Mediterranean. The modern narrative can be briefly summarized as follows.

The claims to the land by Israel are religiously rooted in the promise to Abraham and his descendants. This promise was outlined in passages such as Genesis 15:18-21; Numbers 34:1-12; and Joshua 1:4. That land was also the site of the ancient kingdoms of Saul, David, and Solomon, which later divided into the two kingdoms of Israel and Judah. Along with the argument of historical possession and continuity come the political arguments, which include the natural right of self-determination—the need for a Jewish homeland for the preservation of a people, their language, culture, protection, and international recognition, specifically the Balfour Declaration of 1917 and UN Resolution 181 in 1947.

Those who are called Palestinians claim the land has been theirs by virtue of their continuous residency and the fact they were the demographic majority until the war of 1948. Whereas Israel uses the Balfour Declaration of 1917 in support of their legitimacy in the region, the Palestinians argue the Declaration was not implemented as conditioned and parts of it were ignored by Israel, specifically the section that reads as follows:

> His Majesty's Government view with favour the establishment in Palestine of a national home for the Jewish people, and will use their best endeavors to facilitate the achievement of this object, it being clearly understood that *nothing shall be done which may prejudice the civil and religious rights of existing non-Jewish communities in Palestine* or the rights and political status enjoyed by Jews in any other country.[3]

The Palestinians' religious argument also goes back to Abraham—they argue that because Ishmael was the firstborn, the right of inheritance should be theirs. Other voices in the Arab world trace their origins to the ancient Philistines of Bible times, who existed in the region before the Israelites conquered the Promised Land.

Since the War of Independence in 1948, Israel has secured its borders through successive wars, including the Six-Day War in June 1967, during which Israel gained control of the Sinai Peninsula, the West Bank, Gaza Strip, and the Golan Heights. In the 1973 Yom Kippur War, Israel took over more territory in Syria and Egypt. There remains a continuing conflict between the Jews and the Arabs over Israel's right to existence and its boundaries, and whether a one- or two-state solution is more ideal.

The two-state solution, which would provide for independent Israeli and Palestinian states in the region, has been the favored option since the days of the British Mandate. However, history has shown that a two-state solution seems to be a nonstarter because of the persistent Arab opposition to the idea of an independent sovereign Jewish state, as well as the lack of consensus over

- where to establish the border lines
- who would control Jerusalem
- what rights the Palestinian refugees would have
- how many Jewish settlements are permitted in disputed territories
- the military security necessary for Israel's survival

The one-state solution proposes resolving the conflict by establishing a confederated Israeli-Palestinian state encompassing all the territories of the region—territories that are presently divided. Two different versions have been advanced: The first is a single true democracy wherein the Arab Muslims would outnumber the Jews, effectively eliminating the Jewish state. The second suggests that Israel annex the region and either force vast numbers of Palestinians to leave or deny them the right to vote. Most reject this solution as seriously violating the inhabitants' civil rights. That's why neither the one- or two-state solution has prevailed. The conflict continues, often resulting in isolated or more highly organized acts of aggression with the expected defensive responses from those who are under attack.

The Church—Why Is There Such a Difference of Opinion?

A recent 2017 LifeWay Survey measuring evangelical attitudes toward Israel and the Jewish people reveals a shifting landscape.[4] While the results are generally favorable, there is concern that some in the younger generation may not be as positive toward Israel as their parents. This may be because the Holocaust and rebirth of modern Israel in 1948 are further in the rearview mirror for the younger generations.

At the press conference releasing the results of the survey—held on December 4, 2017, at the National Press Club in Washington, DC—Joel Rosenberg made the following statement:

> Millennials are sending the Church a sobering message. At the moment, they're not against Israel. Not at all. But the survey

makes it clear that many of them really don't understand Israel's place in the biblical narrative. Thus, their support for Israel is nearly twenty points less than their parents and grandparents. Now, extrapolate that going forward. Unless the Church gives younger believers a healthy, balanced, solidly biblical understanding of God's love and plan for Israel, overall Evangelical support for the Jewish State could very well plummet over the next decade as Millennials represent an ever-larger percentage of the overall Church body.[5]

With the widespread perception that Israel has managed to decisively win its wars and establish itself as a first-world economy, concerns for the plight of the Palestinians has gained much press coverage and garnered sympathy that assumes the Palestinians are a misplaced and persecuted people. Part of the purpose of this book is to provide a biblical perspective of Israel— her past, present, and future—and, at the same time, advance a biblical perspective of justice, righteousness, and peace for everyone. Whether Jewish, Arab, or of some other ethnicity, every person has been created in the image of God and is the object of God's love, and therefore is a candidate for the gospel.

Undoubtedly the shift in perception has also been fueled by a growing influence of replacement theology, or supersessionism. This is the view that the New Testament church supersedes, replaces, or fulfills Israel's place in God's plan. Michael J. Vlach, in his book *Has the Church Replaced Israel?* (see also chapter 13 of this book), writes,

> Supersessionism…appears to be based on two core beliefs: (1) the nation Israel has somehow completed or forfeited its status as the people of God and will never again possess a unique role or function apart from the church, and (2) the church is now the true Israel that has permanently replaced or superseded national Israel as the people of God. In the context of Israel and the church, Supersessionism is the view that the NT Church is the new and/or true Israel that has forever superseded the nation Israel as the people of God.[6]

In response, the contributors of this book agree with Scot McKnight's conclusion that "replacement theology is an unbiblical doctrine that violates clear statements in both the Old and New Testaments that teach and affirm a national salvation and restoration of Israel."[7]

Supersessionists spiritualize the land promises made to Israel and make them applicable to the worldwide church. While the mission of the church certainly includes all the nations, that does not have to invalidate the particular and special meaning of the land for Israel. The silence of the New Testament about land promises is not conclusive evidence in support of those who hold that the land is not a factor in the New Testament era. Noteworthy is the fact that 80 percent of those surveyed today believe that God's promise to Abraham includes the preservation of the Jewish people, including their ultimate right to the land given to them.[8]

Telescope: Is There a Future for Ethnic Israel?

In contrast to the supersessionist view, the contributors to this book will argue that the term *Israel*, whether in historical or prophetic Scripture texts, always refers to ethnic Israel. While the first section of this chapter dealt with the nature and purposes of God's choice of Israel historically, this final section looks to the future. Replete throughout the Bible are passages that present Israel and especially Jerusalem as the geographical center of end-time events. Those events include the regathering and restoration of Israel, the second coming of Christ, and His earthly messianic reign.

The Regathering of Israel

What God has planned for Israel's future is in keeping with His continuing self-revelation to the nations. According to Isaiah 11:12, a reunification and regathering of Israel was anticipated: "He will lift up a standard for the nations and assemble the banished ones of Israel, and will gather the dispersed of Judah from the four corners of the earth." Likewise, Jeremiah 30:3 promises, "'Behold, days are coming,' declares the LORD, 'when I will restore the fortunes of My people Israel and Judah.' The LORD says, 'I will also bring them back to the land that I gave to their forefathers and they shall possess it.'"

God's promise of a future for the people and land of Israel did not mean the inhabitants would dwell there without interruption. In fact, multiple Bible passages present God's warning that disobedience could mean servitude to foreign nations and even extended periods of exile and dispersion.[9] Yet with the warning of discipline came God's reassuring covenant commitment as exemplified in Leviticus 26:44-45: "In spite of this, when they are in the land of their enemies, I will not reject them, nor will I so abhor them as to destroy them, breaking My covenant with them; for I am the LORD their God. But I will remember for them the covenant with their ancestors, whom I brought out of the land of Egypt in the sight of the nations, that I might be their God. I am the LORD."

Some maintain the regathering of the Jewish people from Babylon was the fulfillment of these prophecies. However, two observations should be made. First, Isaiah 11:11 says they will be gathered "the second time." The regathering from Babylon was the first time they came back to the land. And second, Isaiah 11:12 says they would be gathered "from the four corners of the earth." That cannot refer to the regathering from Babylon, which was from only one country. So a future event was in mind. The preservation of Israel during their dispersions was also prophesied—in Jeremiah 31:35-37, God said the Jewish nation would remain intact as long as the sun, moon, and stars were around.

Promises of a final return are also recorded in multiple passages,[10] and they clearly include the land as part of the restoration. For example, Ezekiel 11:16-17 states, "Thus says the Lord GOD, 'Though I had removed them far away among the nations and though I had scattered them among the countries, yet I was a sanctuary for them a little while in the countries where they had gone.' Therefore say, 'Thus says the Lord GOD, "I will gather you from the peoples and assemble you out of the countries among which you have been scattered, and I will give you the land of Israel"'" (see also Amos 9:14-15). Amazingly, Ezekiel 39:27-28 promises that not one Israelite would be left behind when God accomplishes the final regathering of His people.

Ezekiel 37:11-14 leaves no question that the Jewish people will be gathered from all over the world to the land of Israel before the Spirit is placed within them. Thus Israel's current lack of faith in God is in perfect harmony with the condition described in Ezekiel 37. However, Ezekiel went on to declare that a bright day is coming for the people of Israel, spiritually and physically—a day when she will be redeemed from all of her wanderings (Ezekiel 11:17-21; 36:24-28). She will return her focus upon her Lord, and the purpose for which she was originally set apart—to lead the other nations to a knowledge of the Lord—will take center stage (Zechariah 12:10).

The Salvation of Israel

In the New Testament, Romans 11:28-29 is a key passage indicating the continuing status of the Abrahamic covenant and its promises for Israel. "From the standpoint of the gospel they are enemies for your sake, but from the standpoint of God's choice they are beloved for the sake of the fathers; for the gifts and the calling of God are irrevocable." Even in their unbelief Israel remains the chosen, and the blessings that came with that choice are permanent. In Romans 11, Paul affirmed that the rejection of Israel is not complete on account of a remnant of believers (verse 5). That rejection is not final; there is coming a day when all Israel will be saved (verse 26).

The hardness and the blindness of the nation was partial because not every Israelite refused to believe (verse 25). In addition, the Jews' rejection of Jesus is temporary in that it will last until the fullness of the Gentiles is accomplished (verse 25). Paul argued on the basis of Isaiah 59:20-21 that the conversion of Israel would come though faith in the Messiah, who will come from Zion and save them in keeping with the covenant He has with them (verses 26-27).

Seeking Greater Clarity

It is important to think about Israel because of why God chose the people, preserved them, and made promises to them. Has He cancelled His covenants? Has He fulfilled them in Jesus Christ? Or has He transferred the covenants to the church? Are there cohesive arguments in response to those who believe that last scenario is the case? Does Israel have a legitimate right to possess the land even in their unbelief? Who should have the rights to govern Jerusalem today? How should a believer respond to the political climate surrounding the Middle East? What is the righteous response to both the Jews and the Palestinian Arabs in the region, and what responsibility does one have to the believing communities of both? Do ethnic traditions retained in the congregations of believers help unite or tend to divide the church?

These are just a few of the topics we will cover in the chapters to follow. May we together pray for the peace of Jerusalem (Psalm 122:6) and proclaim Jesus Messiah as Lord (2 Corinthians 4:5) and ourselves as the servants of others for the sake of our Savior!

PART 1

What Should We Think About Israel's Politics?

1

What Should We Think About the Zionist Movement?

THOMAS ICE

Zionism is both maligned and misunderstood in the mainstream media. In the Middle East it is equated with racism and occupation, yet in the West, many Christians identify themselves as Christian Zionists. What is the basis for Zionism, and how have its tenets historically influenced political action on behalf of the Jewish people and the state of Israel?

For nearly 2,000 years, the Jewish Passover ritual has concluded with the statement, "Next year in Jerusalem!" Regardless of what one may think about the Zionist movement, it was the instrument God used to bring about the reestablishment of the modern Jewish state of Israel. It enabled Jews to realize the dream of "next year in Jerusalem."

The Zionist movement refers to "the movement whose goal was the return of the Jewish people to Erez Israel"[1] and "the creation and support of a Jewish national state in Palestine, the ancient homeland of the Jews, the Land of Israel."[2]

The History of Zionism

The modern Zionist movement arose in Europe during the late 1800s because of the renewed persecution of the Jewish people simply because they were Jews. Earlier it was thought by many Jews that the secularization of Europe would result in their being accepted into society in general on the basis of merit—they believed that by this time, their ethnic distinctive had been minimized, but that was not the case. The direction in which culture grew led to the rise of a secular rather than religious basis for Gentile anti-Semitism.

It was in the context of anti-Semitism that the Zionist movement was born. "The Jewish national revival which took place in the nineteenth century, culminating in political Zionism, was preceded by a great many activities and publications, by countless projects, declarations and meetings; thousands of Jews had in fact settled in Palestine before Herzl ever thought of a Jewish state."[3] Theodor Herzl (1860–1904) recognized where history was headed and organized and put into motion a vision that resulted in the reestablishment of the modern state of Israel about fifty years later. "As historic movements go, Zionism had a speedy passage from inception to realization, whether we consider it to have begun with the meteoric appearance of Herzl in 1896, or with the upsurge of *Chibat Zion* in 1881."[4]

There has always been a Jewish presence in Jerusalem for more than 3,000 years, even though at times there was only a small, suppressed remnant. The modern surge of Jews returning to the land in an effort to resettle Eretz Israel is thought to have begun in 1881—the year pogroms began under the "iron czar" Nicholas I in Russia, leading to an effort by some Eastern European Jews in the Pale to make alijah to Israel.[5] However, there is evidence that "the cause, the concept of Zion, has been present throughout Jewish history."[6]

Before the rise of the enlightenment in Europe (early 1700s), virtually all Jews were part of what we would think of today as the Orthodox community. Before the beginning of the nation-states in Europe, Gentiles were thought to be members of the broader Christian or Islamic empires. As nationalism arose across Europe, many Jewish businessmen became prosperous and became part of the growing upper class and had hoped to achieve acceptance within society. Yet anti-Semitic outbreaks continued to occur all throughout Europe, causing many Jews to realize they would never be accepted into the mainstream of European life.

The Divine Purpose and Zionism

Theodor Herzl, an Austrian newspaper correspondent in Paris, was the instrument God used to draw many other similarly concerned Jews together to form a coalition that would lead to the reestablishment of the modern state of Israel on May 14, 1948. I believe, with all of its perceived faults, Zionism arose in the fullness of time in order to bring into existence the modern state of Israel. After all, the ancient Jewish prophets had written of a future seven-year tribulation, the salvation of Israel, and the return of Christ to planet Earth—prophecies that, in order to be fulfilled, required Israel to exist as a nation again.

Herzl was the driving force in the rise and organization of the Zionist movement, especially in relation to its political developments. Because he was not a devoutly religious Jew, his motivation for the resurrection of the Jewish state was to create a place of safety in the midst of a rising tide of anti-Semitism. Herzl's instincts proved to be right as illustrated by all that took place to bring about the conditions that made the Holocaust possible. Thus, in the Zionist movement we see a merging of the theological belief in a future restoration of the Jews to Israel as part of the end-time drama with the more practical desire to protect the Jewish people from Gentile persecution.

That Herzl had a sense of foreboding about the future—about the possibility of persecution on the scale of the Nazi Holocaust appears evident from Herzl's response to a writer of his time. This response is brought to our attention by Israeli prime minister Benjamin Netanyahu:

> Herzl wanted to hear from Nordau's reaction to his thesis that the Jews of Europe were being placed in unprecedented danger by the rise of anti-Semitism. This would produce Jewish activists for Communism, he suspected, and further grist for the anti-Semites. Such developments, Herzl believed, would lead to catastrophe, not only for the Jews but for Europe as a whole. The only solution was the immediate establishment of a Jewish state and the exodus of the persecuted Jews to it.[7]

Anti-Semitism and Zionism

Anti-Semitism was the primary factor that motivated the Jews to return to their homeland in the Middle East. The *Encyclopedia Judaica* defines anti-Semitism as "denoting all forms of hostility manifested toward the Jews throughout history."[8] The modern expressions of Jew-hatred certainly qualify as anti-Semitism. By the time of Augustine in the early 400s, it was widely believed that Christianity had conquered and totally replaced Judaism. "Their existence was further justified by the service they rendered to the Christian truth in attesting through their humiliation the triumph of the church over the synagogue."[9] Such thinking within Christendom paved the way for a millennium and a half of horrific treatment by many—including by those within the church—culminating in the Holocaust. Today's greatest threat against the Jews comes from Islam because Arabs believe that the land Israel occupies should be under their rule. And with the rapid growth of Muslim populations all across Europe, we are seeing a corresponding reawakening of anti-Semitism in Europe.

Over the last 300 years, the world has become increasingly secular. This trend has even manifested itself within Jewish and Christian circles. Before modern times, cultures were molded primarily by the religious values of a community. From the time the Jews were scattered after the destruction of the Temple up to the enlightenment and the rise of the modern day, the Jewish community existed primarily under Orthodox influence because of almost universal persecution. During this time, the overwhelmingly dominant view within the Jewish community was a focus on a promised Messiah who would come and make possible their return to the Promised Land. This is still a widely held perspective among a number of Orthodox communities, including those that are present in Israel today. But it was largely in the less religious Jewish communities that Zionism grew and made a concerted effort to encourage Jews to return to Israel.

The Bible and Zionism

Clearly it was the secular leadership of the Zionist movement—which includes Chaim Weizmann (1874–1952), the first president of Israel, and David Ben-Gurion (1886–1973)—that spearheaded the foundation of the modern state of Israel. However, the Bible (both the Old and New Testaments) contains a future agenda for the Jewish people as the nation of Israel. If the Bible is one's authority, one must conclude that it was almighty God who scattered His chosen people, preserved them as a distinct entity, and still has yet-unfulfilled plans for them individually and corporately. That God has a plan in place for the Jewish people is all the more plausible when one considers that the Jews are the only people group in the history of the world who have been kicked out of their land, scattered across the globe, and yet maintained their ethnic identity and returned to their national homeland.

A look at Scripture shows there are a significant number of prophecies yet to be fulfilled for God's elect nation and the world as a whole. As stated earlier, for these prophecies to become reality, Israel must exist as a nation. This is why Israel is considered God's "super sign" of the end times. The fact that God has recalled His chosen people to their homeland appears to be a prophetic indication that He is on the verge of moving to the next stage of history, transitioned by the rapture of the church, followed by the seven-year tribulation, and culminating in Christ's return and reign on planet Earth for 1,000 years.

A number of Old Testament passages predicted Israel's state of unbelief during her time of global dispersion (Leviticus 26:42,44-45; Deuteronomy 4:25-31; 28:64-68; 32:20-22). However, many more passages speak of an end-time regathering back to the land in relation to events that will lead to the nation entering a time of right relationship with the Lord their God, resulting in great blessing to Israel and the world. The outline of Israel's history and future blessing begins in Genesis and is expanded upon in Leviticus and Deuteronomy. The book of Revelation, which looks to the future, displays a glorious climax not only for Israel, but for all the world. This time of future blessing is mentioned and expanded upon by every prophetic book in the Old Testament except Jonah.[10] Further, many passages in the Old Testament look forward to a glorious future for the nation of Israel. Among them are Genesis 12:7; 13:14-15; 15:18; 17:8; 28:1; Leviticus 26:33,43; Deuteronomy 26:9; 30:1-11; Joshua 24:20-28; 2 Samuel 7:11-16; Ezra 4:1-3; and Psalm 102:13-20.

Prophetic Interpretation and Zionism

Today it is said about 43 percent of the world's Jewish population

resides in Israel (6.5 million Jews, about 75 percent of the total population).[11] When the nation was founded on May 14, 1948, the Jewish population in the land was about 650,000.[12] Of course, we will not know what
percentage of the Jewish people will be in the land and what percentage
will remain in the diaspora once the seven-year tribulation commences.
With the ratio of the dispersion of Jewish people worldwide and in the
land each approaching 50 percent, it appears we are seeing the stage be set
for tribulation events.

The rise of the Zionist movement not only gave birth to the modern
state of Israel, it also excited those Christians who take Bible prophecy literally. The events of the Reformation began to pave the way for a return of
awareness within Protestantism of a future for Jewish Israel, which was a
stark contrast to more than a millennium of anti-Semitism within Christendom, usually led by the church itself. "Neither Luther nor Calvin saw a
future general conversion of the Jews promised in Scripture; some of their
contemporaries, however, notably Martin Bucer and Peter Martyr, who
taught at Cambridge and Oxford respectively in the reign of Edward VI,
did understand the Bible to teach a future calling of the Jews."[13] It appears
that near the end of the Reformation there was some movement toward a
belief in the conversion of the Jews, which would eventually grow into the
belief of a national restoration of the Jews to their land. This movement
would grow and flourish, especially among the Puritans, and give rise to
today's widely held belief among Bible-believing Christians in a future for
national Israel and the Jewish people.

Even though the Reformation laid the groundwork for a proper recognition of the biblical teaching about Israel, Reformers like Martin
Luther (1483–1546) carried Rome's anti-Semitism into some aspects of
Protestantism. Early in his ministry Luther spoke favorably of the Jews
in an effort to convert them, but when they did not respond positively,
he turned against them with a vigor that would have made any Catholic
medievalist proud. Andrew Robinson summarizes Luther's ungodly rants
against the Jews:

> Luther frequently referred to the Jews as "idle and lazy," "useless,"
> "impenitent, accursed people," "consummate liars," "boastful

arrogant rascals," "bloodhounds," "murderers," and the "vilest whores and rogues under the sun." He accused them of poisoning wells, assassination, ritual murder, branding them collectively as "venomous serpents and devil's children." He attacked "their accursed rabbis, which wantonly poison the minds of their poor youth and the common man, to divert them from the truth."[14]

It is not surprising that 400 years later, the German people followed a leader like Adolph Hitler, who quoted favorably from Luther three times in his book *Mein Kampf.*

In England, sentiments toward the Jews followed a different track. Thomas Brightman (1552–1607), likely a postmillennialist, wrote concerning the Jews, "What, shall they return to Jerusalem again? There is nothing more certain; the prophets do everywhere confirm it."[15] In America, one of the standout advocates of the restoration doctrine was Increase Mather (1639–1723), the son of Richard and father of Cotton. Increase wrote more than 100 books and was a president of Harvard College. His first work, *The Mystery of Israel's Salvation*, went through about a half dozen revisions during his life.[16] His support of the national restoration of Israel to her land in the future was typical of American Colonial Puritans and was generally widespread. Carl Ehle notes:

> The first salient school of thought in American history that advocated a national restoration of the Jews to Palestine was resident in the first native-born generation at the close of the seventeenth century in which Increase Mather played a dominate role. The men who held this view were Puritans…From that time on, the doctrine of restoration may be said to have become endemic to American culture.[17]

Why such a sea change after hundreds of years of vehement Jew hatred within the church? The main gift of the Reformation was that of the Bible in the language of the people. "The reformation opened men's eyes to the Scriptures," notes Gruber. "Its entire thrust was to turn away from the traditions of men which had nullified the Word of God, and to examine the Word itself."[18] When one is influenced by what the Bible itself says, then one will no doubt see a future for Israel in both testaments. Michael Pragai explains:

> The growing importance of the English Bible was a concomi-
> tant of the spreading Reformation, and it is true to say that the
> Reformation would never have taken hold had the Bible not
> replaced the Pope as the ultimate spiritual authority. With the
> Bible as its tool, the Reformation returned to the geographic ori-
> gins of Christianity in Palestine. It thereby gradually diminished
> the authority of Rome.[19]

Christianity and Zionism

The simple provision of the Bible in the native tongue of the people, which gave rise to their ongoing reading and familiarization of it, espe-cially the Old Testament, was the soil in which Christian Zionism could flourish. The Reformation not only restored the gospel but also reestab-lished the literal hermeneutic by which to properly read Scripture. It was a short step from a near-consensus belief in the conversion of the Jews to the widely held view among post-Reformation Puritans in the restoration of Israel to her covenant land. Many Puritans of the seventeenth century taught the restoration of the Jews to the Holy Land.

In this way Protestant Christianity accomplished the great task of turn-ing many segments of Christendom away from the Jew-hatred of Roman-ism and Greek Orthodoxy to philo-Semitism over a 300-year period to become the dominant view within evangelicalism in our day. Israel and the Jews were seen once again as the heroes and keys to the understanding of the Bible and the future. It is also important to note that within God's plan for history, it was the pro-Israel nations that went on to grow in stat-ure and play a role in the reestablishment of the land of Israel as the home-land of the Jewish people. One might think God favored those nations at that time, at least in part, as a means of restoring Israel.

In Anticipation of What Is to Come

The Zionist movement, though largely secular, combined with a

Protestant return to the literal reading of the term *Israel* in the Bible, served the means our sovereign Lord used to regather the Jewish people and reestablish the state of Israel. This nation has been an important cog in God's plan as history moves forward. The Zionist movement has not been flawless or consistently biblical; however, through God's sovereign oversight, it has put into place the things that are necessary for the Bible's end-time prophecies to be fulfilled. Israel's current situation has God's chosen people on the precipice to fulfill hundreds of prophecies that will come into play after the rapture of the church, during the seven-year tribulation, and up to the rescue and salvation of Israel at Jesus' second coming. The stage is now set, and the church awaits the lifting of the curtain via the rapture of Christians worldwide. For now, the church's task is to faithfully preach the gospel, teach God's Word, and serve the Lord—with one eye on the eastern sky in anticipation of the rapture.

CHAPTER 1
READER RESPONSE

What Should We Think About the Zionist Movement?

WHAT DO *YOU* THINK?

I agree with the author on

I disagree with the author because

What was news to me?

How does this change the way I think about Israelis and the Zionist movement?

2

What Should We Think About the Modern State of Israel?

STEVEN CHARLES GER

The modern state of Israel is often differentiated from ancient Israel as a nation. Is this distinction legitimate in terms of the people group who claim historic rights in the land? Is there evidence for historic continuity between the ancient and modern people who comprise Israel, and has the history of Israel revealed a special purpose for the Jewish people?

As long as in the heart within the Jewish soul yearns,
And toward the eastern edges, onward, an eye gazes toward Zion.
Our hope is not yet lost, the hope that is two thousand years old,
To be a free nation in our land, the Land of Zion, Jerusalem.
Hatikvah (The Hope), national anthem of Israel

Rare is the individual without an opinion regarding the modern state of Israel. The legitimacy of Israel's formation in 1948 and its very *raison d'etre* as the world's sole Jewish state continue to evoke passionate and often diametrically divergent views. It is not uncommon for people to fail to grasp the fundamental matters with regard to differentiating between the Jewish people, the ancient nation of Israel, and the modern state.[1]

In an effort to clarify how we might think about the modern state of

Israel, this chapter will address the relationship between the land of Israel and the Jewish people in two specific areas. First, the *history* of the Jewish people will be traced in relation to the land of Israel. This will be followed by an exploration of the Jewish people's unceasing national *hope* regarding the land. The historical and genealogical continuity between ancient *Israelites* of biblical times and modern *Israelis* currently populating the nation will be patently evident.

The Land in the People of Israel's History

At the establishment of the modern Jewish state on May 14, 1948, the Jewish People's Council approved the nation's declaration of independence, which begins, "The Land of Israel was the birthplace of the Jewish people. Here their spiritual, religious and political identity was shaped. Here they first attained to statehood…After being forcibly exiled from their land, the people kept faith with it throughout their Dispersion and never ceased to pray and hope for their return to it and for the restoration in it of their political freedom."

Beginning with the Bible, Israel's ancient foundational Scriptures, the record shows that the people and the land of Israel are inextricably connected. That tenacious connection linking a specific people to a specific land can be traced over a period of four millennia. The origins of this connection began with highly specific promises of land possession from God to the forefathers of the Jewish people, Abraham,[2] Isaac,[3] and Jacob.[4] The connection continues during the nation's absence from their land during the formative sojourn and servitude in Egypt[5] and extends through their fourteenth-century BC return and conquest of the land.[6] The ties between people and land are further strengthened under Israel's period of monarchy, particularly following David's appointment of Jerusalem as the national capital and his heir Solomon's construction of the Temple.[7]

Following a civil war, for the next two centuries, the nation was divided into northern and southern kingdoms. In 722 BC, the northern kingdom was destroyed by the Assyrians and its population deported. The southern kingdom, known as Judah,[8] remained free and independent for another century. As the sixth century BC dawned, Judah was conquered by the Babylonian Empire, with most of Judah's inhabitants forced into captivity and dispersed throughout the empire's territories. Following Persia's conquest of Babylon seven decades later, a minority of the exiled Judean populace were permitted to return home to rebuild their ruined Temple along with their capital, Jerusalem. For roughly the next 2,500 years, the status quo of the Jewish people was to be geographically divided, with a substantial remnant residing within the land of promise and the remainder distributed throughout various nations.

By the close of the fourth century BC, Judah came under a new world power as Persia yielded to Greece.[9] The Greek occupation of Judah, now known as Judea, created religious and cultural tensions that fueled the Maccabean revolt against Greece.[10] A remarkable Jewish victory led to a triumphal return to national self-determination under the Jewish Hasmonean dynasty and a geographic expansion of borders reminiscent of the glorious era of David and Solomon.

Following a century of independence, the ascendant Roman Empire inaugurated a new occupation of Judea in AD 63. Even so, Roman technology enabled the scattered diaspora Jews to return regularly for festival worship at Jerusalem's Temple, reinforcing the people's ties to the land.[11]

The Jews staged two lengthy, violent, and costly revolts against their Roman occupiers. The first, from AD 66–73, resulted in the sacking of Jerusalem and destruction of the Jewish Temple. The result was more than one million Jews killed and 100,000 enslaved and deported.[12] Defeat notwithstanding, the Jewish population in the land still numbered more than a million, with cities and towns largely remaining intact.[13]

Six decades later, the Jewish population recovered sufficiently to stage a second revolt that took place AD 132–135. This conflict against Rome resulted in wholesale Jewish casualties, enslavement, and enforced deportation numbering into the hundreds of thousands.[14] Rome renamed Jerusalem *Aelia Capitolina*, exiling Jewish residents from their holy city and redistributing them elsewhere in the land. The province of Judea was merged with its neighboring province, Syria, and renamed *Syria Palestina*. This new name, a humiliating reference to the ancient archetypal foes of Israel, the Philistines,[15] was to serve as a continual reminder of Judea's disgrace and defeat. Thereafter, from AD 135 until 1948, Palestine was the acknowledged name of the ancient Jewish homeland. This marks the terminus of the first Jewish nation-state's fifteen-century-long existence. This event punctuates the start of an eighteen-century period when the territory now known as Palestine became a subordinate province subject to the rule of a succession of several world empires.

These seismic events caused the Jewish population's center of gravity to shift from Judea to the diaspora. Yet substantial Jewish population centers remained throughout Palestine and retained majority status for centuries.[16] Certain regions, such as the Galilee, served as influential nuclei of Judaism's theological development for centuries. For 1,800 years, Palestine was never absent a significant, albeit minority, Jewish population. By the middle of the fourth century, Jerusalem had regained its name and the Jews of Palestine once again had permission to reside in their holy city.

The Roman Empire gave way to that of the Byzantine, which in turn gave way in the seventh century to conquest by Islam. Under Islam, substantial numbers of Jewish people, while subjugated, remained protected within their promised land, notwithstanding the imposition of Islam's humiliating and restrictive dhimmi system.[17] Arguably, the Jews who were forced to endure the oppression of dhimmi status under Islam were better off than their brethren dispersed throughout Christendom. For the crime of being Jewish, those communities were regularly subjected to intensive bouts of persecution, including capricious torture, massacre, or exile.

Beginning in 1095, Crusaders were commissioned by European Christendom to liberate the Holy Land from the control of Islam. Over a period of two centuries, successive waves of Crusaders washed over the Holy Land, and control of Palestine fluctuated between Christians and Muslims. Often crushed in the middle were those Jewish communities situated en route from Europe to Palestine. Crusaders repeatedly massacred entire communities of Jews for their refusal to forcibly convert to Christianity.

Later, as the intensity of the Crusades waned, conditions became more favorable in Palestine as it remained under Crusader rule.[18] In the Crusaders' wake came large numbers of European Jews who were eager to permanently relocate back to Palestine so they could escape inquisitions, exiles, persecutions, forced conversions, and other European torments.[19]

In 1571, as the Ottoman Empire expanded, the Turks gained control of Palestine. This provided four centuries of political stability to the region.

During this century the Ottoman ruler Sultan Suleiman the Magnificent rebuilt the city walls upon the remains of the ancient walls. In the centuries that followed, the Turks treated the province of Syria Palestine as a faraway backwater with little political significance and paid the region scant attention. In his classic 1867 travelogue of Palestine, *The Innocents Abroad*, Mark Twain relayed in prodigious detail his impressions of the land's stark desolation and sparse habitation, with the exception of Jerusalem and a few other areas,[20] remarking that Palestine "sits in sackcloth and ashes," "desolate and unlovely."[21]

By this time, the population of Jewish communities within Palestine was a fraction of what it had been in past eras.[22] Persecution, poverty, epidemics, and earthquakes all played roles in decimating the populace. Still, during the 400 years of Turkish rule, it was generally safe to be Jewish. This was not the case throughout many regions of Europe and North Africa, and immigration to Palestine continued as Jews fled intensified persecution. Palestinian Judaism thrived throughout the land, particularly in majority Jewish cities like Jerusalem, Sfad, Tiberius, and Hebron, the four holy cities of Judaism.[23] Palestine's Jewish population began experiencing an exponential uptick that would see the people increase from 24,000 in 1882 to 85,000 as the twentieth century dawned.[24]

The Land in the People of Israel's Hope

In an ancient psalm composed by Babylon's Jewish exiles some 2,600 years ago, we read of the inextricable links between the land of Israel and Jewish identity and origins: "How can we sing the LORD's song in a foreign land? If I forget you, O Jerusalem, may my right hand forget her skill. May my tongue cling to the roof of my mouth if I do not remember you, if I do not exalt Jerusalem above my chief joy" (Psalm 137:4-6). The connection spoken of by the psalmist is so profoundly fundamental to the Jewish psyche that it can neither be severed nor reduced even during periods of the people's physical absence from their land. Jewish history records only three periods of absence in whole or in major part: a four-century duration of Egyptian sojourn, seven decades of the sixth-century Babylonian exile, and the eighteen-century diaspora that concluded in May 1948. The sustained use of the term *diaspora*—that is, "those dispersed from their land," illustrates the point.

None of those periods diminished the Jewish people's ongoing dream to one day return to their God-given homeland. History reveals that intermittent remnants of exiles, when presented with an opportunity to return, did so.[25] As for those generations who tenaciously embraced their ancestral land while experiencing discriminations and adversities, their aspiration to once again live within a free and autonomous Jewish nation had neither wavered nor receded.[26] Whether separated from or resident in their homeland, both communities successfully met the challenge of maintaining their Jewish identity.

Many nations witnessed vast population shifts in the closing decades of the nineteenth century.[27] In particular, Jewish immigration accelerated as the Jews of Eastern Europe and Russia fled persecution. While some sought refuge in the Americas, many yielded to Israel's ancient hope and fled to Palestine to join the burgeoning Jewish communities there. For the next 60 years, Jewish refugees purchased tracts of land in western Palestine from Turkish and Arab owners, many of whom were speculators and lived elsewhere.[28] Much of this land was considered nonarable, worthless desert or malaria-infested swampland, which explains why it was enthusiastically sold to the Jews, often at vastly inflated prices. By the time of the 1947 UN partition, the Jewish people owned legally procured deeds to almost 9 percent of Palestine (687.5 square miles of a possible 7,912 square miles).[29]

Over time and with considerable effort, the newly arrived immigrants succeeded in draining the swamps and making the desert bloom. This led to economic opportunities and a marked improvement in the region's quality of life, which in turn attracted an influx of Arab and Bedouin migrants from eastern Palestine and surrounding countries. These migrants included Egyptians,[30] Turks, Syrians, Lebanese, Greeks, and many other ethnicities.[31]

In the years preceding the first world war, the idea of restoring a Jewish state in Palestine was an idea whose time had come. Following the publication of his 1896 book *The Jewish State,* the European Jewish intellectual Theodore Herzl became an activist for the Zionist cause. The following year, he convened the first of several annual Zionist Congresses in Europe.

These summits catalyzed an energetic movement in the diaspora,[32] a movement Herzl tirelessly promoted until his premature death in 1904.

The twentieth century's initial two decades saw a new and momentous wave of Jewish immigration as thousands fled the horrors of Russian pogroms. These Jews were integrated within Palestine's expanding Jewish communities, which were developing economically and becoming more politically organized. Communal innovations such as the *kibbutzim*, farming collectives, added to societal bedrock. The Hebrew language, which had not been the people's mother tongue since the biblical era, was revived. Through no small effort, what had been relegated for millennia as merely the language of Holy Scripture, documents, and prayers had rapidly become the lingua franca of the Palestinian Jews. It became clear that with continued immigration, a numerical critical mass could be achieved for autonomy. At last, there was a realistic hope of reestablishing a Jewish state within Palestine.

The end of the first world war saw the defeat of the Ottoman Turks and an accompanying division of its empire by victorious Western powers. Control of Palestine fell to Britain for the next three decades. During that period, a series of international documents (the Balfour Declaration in 1917, the 1922 congressional resolution declaring a Jewish national homeland in Palestine, the League of Nations' 1923 recognition of the Jewish people's historical connection to Palestine and right to self-determination, and the UN's partition plan of 1947, among others) established the legitimacy of Israel's right to a homeland in Palestine by incontrovertible international law.

Alongside these victories came crushing disappointments as well. In 1922, Britain carved off from Palestine all territory situated east of the Jordan River, 80 percent of the whole. This initial nation-state in partial Palestine became the state of Transjordan, accommodating a population of some 320,000 Palestinian Arabs and specifically excluding Jews by law and design.[33] This was followed by the 1947 UN Partition Plan's truncated territorial allotment for the Jewish homeland in the remaining 20 percent of Palestine west of the Jordan. Jewish territorial allotment was limited to three barely contiguous areas: the Negev Desert, a narrow strip along the coastline, and a band of territory along the Sea of Galilee. This comprised just over 50 percent of what remained of Palestine, sans Transjordan.[34] Jerusalem, Judaism's holiest city, which had a longstanding, overwhelmingly Jewish population, would become a separate internationalized zone.[35]

Most tragic of all was Britain's restrictive imposition of quotas on Jewish immigration to Palestine during the years leading up to and including the Holocaust.[36] The sanctuary that Hitler's desperate victims needed, and of which so many thousands might have availed themselves, was expressly made inaccessible and remained unattainable until the end of the British Mandate.

Even so, the Palestinian Jewish people were by that point 650,000 strong and were not about to curtail their ancient hope of returning to their homeland on account of being offered only a tenth of Palestine for their own. Although the Palestinian Arabs rejected the November 1947 UN partition plan, the Palestinian Jews gratefully accepted it. At the conclusion of the British Mandate on May 14, 1948, the Jewish people declared the establishment of the Jewish state of Israel.

The Land in the People of Israel's Heart

After an eighteen-century absence from the world stage, the descendants of the first Jewish nation-state inaugurated the second in the same territory, an unprecedented reunification of land and people. Within three years, streams of immigrants flooded Israel from 70 different countries, adding 687,000 more Jews and more than doubling the infant nation's population. More than a third of the Jewish communities from Islamic countries such as Egypt, Libya, Morocco, Algeria, Iraq, Syria, Tunisia, and Yemen came as refugees.[37]

With a population today of 6,600,000, the modern state of Israel has now surpassed the United States[38] as the nation with the single largest Jewish community[39]—from 6 percent in 1948 to an estimated 41 percent of world's Jewish population today.[40] The land of Israel is once more the heart and center of world Jewry; the Jewish people's center of gravity continues to shift toward home.

CHAPTER 2
READER RESPONSE

What Should We Think About the Modern State of Israel?

WHAT DO *YOU* THINK?

I agree with the author on

I disagree with the author because

What was news to me?

How does this change the way I think about the modern state of Israel?

3

What Should We Think About Christian Support for Israel?

IMAD N. SHEHADEH

Historically, Christians have not supported the Jewish people or their aspirations for a homeland. However, in modern times, a significant segment of the Christian population now identifies as Christian Zionists. The new bond between evangelicals and Israel has led to concerns that a political agenda underlies this relationship. What is the reason for Christian support, and how does it affect the direction of Middle East peace negotiations? How, too, should Arab Christians understand such support for Israel in light of biblical statements and the realities of the Islamic world in which they live?

In view of the complexities of the question being addressed, it is important to understand the assumptions that underlie this chapter. First, the Bible is the only divinely inspired, inerrant, and authoritative Word of God, and the source of ultimate truth. Second, the truth of a doctrine is determined by its adherence to Scripture and not how late or early it appeared in history. Third, any theological position is welcome at the scholarly table as long as it is arrived at from proper exegesis of Scripture and not based on a certain political bias. Fourth, the positive theological contributions of the West on the East and vice versa are not to be ignored, but rather examined to help improve communicate between the two. Fifth, it is not what is expedient for ministry, for missions, or for contextualization that gives warrant to a particular interpretation. Sixth, one's eschatological position may or may not have a bearing on his or her political aspirations. For example, an amillennialist could be pro-Zionist and a dispensationalist could be anti-Zionist. Seventh, in scholarly dialogue, one assumes that deductions are made based on one's evaluation of the data of Scripture, with freedom of expression as well as openness to critique and being critiqued in Christian love and civility. In all these assumptions, hermeneutical consistency is a test of veracity.

This short presentation covers the conditional elements of God's covenants with man followed by the unconditional elements. Then a harmony between the two will be stated at the theological and political levels.

Conditional or Unconditional?

Beginning with Genesis 12:1-3, God promised Abraham a land, a posterity, and a blessing. This expanded into a covenant with Moses, a covenant with David, and the new covenant. Both conditional and unconditional elements are found in these covenants.

The Conditional Elements

The conditional elements in God's promises to Abraham are seen in four major areas: in the original call of Abraham, in the development of the call, in the Mosaic covenant, and in the history of Israel.

First, let us consider the conditions present in the original call of Abraham. There is a difference between the promises given to Abraham beginning in the original call (Genesis 12:1-3) and the covenant made later on with Abraham (Genesis 15:1-21). The former covers the conditional aspect, while the latter covers the unconditional. The conditional aspect of the promises given to Abraham is first seen in his original call (Genesis 12:1-3), which is composed of six promises built around two commands. Each command is followed by three promises.

The first command given to Abraham is that he was to "go" (Genesis 12:1). Abraham's obedience to this command will bring about the fulfillment of three promises: God will make him a great nation; God will bless him; and God will make his name great. If Abraham had not obeyed the command to leave his home, he would not have received the three promises.

The second command given to Abraham is that he was to be a blessing. In Genesis 12:2, God said, "I will make you a great nation, and I will bless you, and make your name great; and so you shall be a blessing." The implication is that God would enable Abraham to carry out this command (for similar examples, see Genesis 20:7; 42:18). For Abraham to be a blessing meant for him to be rightly related to God in a way that would qualify him to be both an example as well as a channel of blessing to the whole world.

This second command is followed by three promises: God will bless those who bless Abraham; God will curse those who despise Abraham; in Abraham all the families of the earth will be blessed. While the first set of promises are about Abraham being blessed, the second set are about him being a blessing. In the former, Abraham is the focus; in the latter, the world is the focus. According to this second set of promises the people of the world can determine the nature of their relationship with God on the basis of their relationship with Abraham. Thus, Genesis 12:1-3 reveals the missionary heart of God to the whole world.

Next, let's consider the conditions in the development of the call of Abraham. The promises given to Abraham were of a developing nature. Each time a new version of the promise appeared, it was after some act of obedience on Abraham's part. This occurred after Abraham had travelled by faith (Genesis 12:7); after he, by faith, separated from Lot (Genesis 13:14-17); after he rescued Lot (Genesis 15:1-21); after the trial with Ishmael (Genesis 16:2-6; 17:18; 21:10-11); and after the trial of being asked to give up Isaac (Genesis 22:16-17).

We must also consider the conditional aspects of the Mosaic covenant, which came after the Abrahamic covenant in the form of a Suzerain-vassal treaty (Exodus 20–31; Deuteronomy 1–32). The conditionality of this covenant promised blessing for obedience and curses for disobedience. This hinges on the conditional "if" that is prevalent in the terminology of this covenant (Deuteronomy 4:25; 28:1) beginning in the section on the blessings, and in Deuteronomy 28:15, which begins the section on the curses.

Finally, we need to consider the conditions reflected in the history of Israel. The history of the nation clearly demonstrates the conditional nature of God's relation to the people. The history of Israel is an application of the Mosaic covenant. It clearly shows that God was willing to fulfill His promises to a particular generation of Israelites only when certain conditions were met.

The Unconditional Elements

Though God's promises to Israel contained conditional elements, the promises of a land, a posterity, and a blessing were all unconditional, as evidenced in the Abrahamic covenant, the Davidic covenant, and the new covenant.

First, let's look at the unconditional elements present in the Abrahamic covenant. This covenant is found in Genesis 15:1-21, and the fact it is unconditional is made clear by several main points: the Abrahamic covenant was unilaterally expressed through a divinely ordered ritual (Genesis 15:7-21), communicating that the fulfillment of the covenant depended on God and not on Abraham or his seed; it is confirmed by the New Testament (cf. Hebrews 6:13-18); it is said to be eternal (Genesis 17:7,13,19); it is made with no conditions whatsoever; it is made to the seed of Abraham (Genesis 15:18; 28:12-13; 50:24); and the promise that Israel would continue to exist forever is repeated later in a time of apostasy (Jeremiah 31:35-37). It's important to note that though both Isaac and Ishmael were promised blessing, only Isaac was promised to be a blessing—the chosen line of blessing was through Isaac.

Second, let's look at the unconditional elements present in the Davidic covenant. That it was unconditional is seen in the confirmation of the seed promised to Abraham; in the Davidic king—called "anointed"—being promised the throne and who anticipates "*the* anointed," that is, the Messiah; in the use of the word "eternal"; and in being emphasized in the angel's words to Mary, promising that her Son will sit on this throne forever (Luke 1:32-33).

Finally, the new covenant includes unconditional elements as well. This is seen in the fact it is called an eternal covenant (Isaiah 24:5; 61:8; Jeremiah 31:36,40; 32:40; 50:5); that it is entirely dependent upon the "I will" of God for its fulfillment; that it amplifies the third great area of the original Abrahamic covenant, the area of blessing; and that it is largely occupied with the matters of salvation from sin and the impartation of a new heart.

A Theological Harmony of the Conditional and the Unconditional Elements

The conditional elements reflect God's justice and holiness, while the unconditional elements reflect God's grace and faithfulness. Extremism occurs when we emphasize one at the expense of the other. There are several suggestions as to how the two can be harmonized.

The Unconditional Elements

First, though many aspects of the Abrahamic, Davidic, and new covenants have been partially fulfilled in Israel's history and in the church, complete fulfillment is yet in the future. For the first time, a regenerated nation of Israel, in the midst of other nations likewise regenerated, will serve as the kingdom of priests (Exodus 19:6) and will be an example and a channel of blessings. Second, the unconditional elements ultimately relate to the eschaton. While the promises of the new covenant can be experienced by individual Jews and Gentiles, its acceptance on a national level will take place at a future time. The unconditional elements speaking of everlasting blessing will confront each generation (of faith) as a future certainty.

The Conditional Elements

First, the conditional elements serve to make participation in the unconditional elements a historical possibility. Participation is conditioned on obedience. The conditional elements only act as the means by which each individual Israelite, as well as any generation of Israel (which would constitute the nation at any particular time in history), may participate in God's eschatological promises. In other words, they are the means through which any generation of Israel could realize the promise of blessing in their own day.

Second, the conditions to be met do not determine whether some promises are fulfilled, but *when* they are fulfilled, and *who* will participate in them. Even classic dispensationalists agree on this point.

Third, obedience to certain conditions set by God demonstrates faith—not as a merit to inherit the promises, but as a readiness to receive them. To say that the experience of a promise is conditional is not to deny God's loyalty, but rather, to declare the importance of a heart ready to receive it.

Fourth, no generation of Israelites can claim to be the eschatological Israel. Only God will determine that. The sole responsibility of each generation of Israelites is to respond to God in faith and obedience in order to participate in the promises in their time.

A Political Harmony Between the Conditional and Unconditional Elements

As in the case of seeking theological harmony, the key to a resolution to the present Arab-Israeli conflict is to maintain a balance between the conditional and unconditional aspects of God's relationship to Israel. The West, emphasizing the unconditional aspects, tends to support the state of Israel. The East, emphasizing the conditional elements, tends to oppose the state of Israel. Consideration of the following cautions is helpful.

Pro-Israeli Imbalance

Western Christians who unconditionally support the present state of Israel should be careful not to ignore the conditional elements of God's covenants. Ignoring these conditional elements communicates wrongly that the God of the Bible is unjust. This imbalance translates into a blind support to everything that the current state of Israel does when this state is called upon to walk in the stipulations of the Mosaic covenant. Every generation of Israelites has the responsibility to walk in accordance with the clear stipulations of the Mosaic covenant. While Western Christians should not be anti-Semitic, they also must be anti-sin.

Stanley Ellisen, a dispensational premillennialist professor who has spent his career studying the Palestinian issue, concludes that in spite of the remarkable achievements of the Jewish people and any human or international rights to the land, "she falls far short of her covenant obligations. To put it bluntly, she has no biblical right to the covenant land."[1] [Editor's note: Other scholars (see the next chapter) argue that Israel does have a biblical right to the land of Israel based on the explicitly unconditional nature of the land promise to Abraham and his descendants. They say that conditions within the unconditional covenant only affect how long and how well the nation enjoys the land but also understand that Israel's present condition as unregenerate and under divine discipline does not excuse it from acting justly toward a foreign people in its midst nor its neighbors and that acknowledging this biblical right to the land does not permit Christians to disregard social and political offenses.] Taking this further, and in looking at the political situation in the Middle East, because neither Jew nor Arab today are "in Christ" (as nations), the best recourse to follow is one of equity and justice. All efforts must be pointed at achieving peace in the Middle East, taking into consideration the human rights of each party. It is not enough to consider only the sufferings and rights of the Jewish people; we must also keep in mind the sufferings and rights of the Arab Palestinians.

Moreover, in this system of pro-Israeli imbalance, unqualified equations are often made of present world scenes with eschatological realities not yet fulfilled. In addition, this pro-Israeli imbalance also deemphasizes God's heart for the whole world. God's goal in the Abrahamic covenant has always been blessing to all the nations of the earth. The pro-Israeli imbalance communicates a God who imposed a nation to be established by arms in total disregard for other nations. This is not the heart of God. Also, when speaking about Israel as the chosen people, Western Christians should stress that the promise of the land to the Jews is in accordance with the loyal love of God. The Jews do not deserve the land; it is a gift based on no merit but the grace of God alone. It belongs to God, and the Jews are residing aliens (Leviticus 25:23) as Abraham was. Thus the Christian message should emphasize the *Chooser* rather than the chosen—God's *grace* rather than their privilege.

This pro-Israeli imbalance often projects a one-sided view of eschatological Israel on present Israel. The overemphasis on the land has almost totally ignored the nature of a regenerated nation, in which each Jew would be so humbly aware of God's grace that he would invite his Palestinian friend to share the land. Thus the pro-Israeli imbalance gravely ignores the spiritual component. Though the Jews may return to the land of Palestine in unbelief, the divine promises of regathering Israel to the land are conditioned on the national repentance of Israel, which coincides with the second coming of Christ. In addition, these promises are in the context of God's will to bless all the nations of the earth. The extremism expressed by some can easily foster the incorrect assumption that it is God's will to impose one nation on a particular geographical region through military might.

As a result, Western Christians must direct Israel toward kind treatment of non-Jews (Exodus 22:21; 23:9; Leviticus 19:34), granting to them as well the privileges of Sabbath rest, festivals, social welfare, and legal rights. Jews must be careful not to treat others in the same way they were treated before their arrival in Palestine. Israel today is unlike before—it is a major Middle East power and it should shun the victim mentality of its founding years. It now has an obligation to exercise justice humbly. The nation does not have a divine right to rid the land of non-Jews.

Pro-Arab Imbalance

Arab Christians must be careful not to ignore the unconditional elements in God's covenants. Doing so would communicate that the God of the Bible is unfaithful and ungraceful. Arab Christians must consider the Jews as beloved for the sake of the ancestors (Romans 11:28-29). Accordingly, Arab believers must put away all political bias and recognize that the fulfillment of His covenants reflects His grace and faithfulness and will occur in His own way and time, according to His perfect attributes. It is also important to be careful and use consistent hermeneutics (principles of interpretation) when studying the Bible. There is a common tendency to apply a literal hermeneutic on all of Scripture except the eschatological passages. Also, people are prone to arrive at theological conclusions that serve their political aspirations. Doing this is inconsistent with trusting God's wisdom and plan. Some Arab Christians have great difficulty with the occurrence of the name *Israel* in the Bible, yet it is impossible to sidestep the multitude of references to it. One's hermeneutics will determine how one interprets the references to Israel throughout the Bible. What a believer interprets as a result of objective and inductive study of Scripture should be communicated with wisdom and skill. Every person has the privilege and responsibility to share personal opinions in a way that does not cause misunderstanding or faction, especially with regard to eschatological matters that can be easily and mistakenly tied to political matters.

Arab Christians should also not confine themselves to Western theology but must be innovative and create their own expressions of theology. No one should be under any obligation to use such terms as *dispensational, premillennialism, amillennial,* etc., to define their own personal views. In fact, Arab Christians have the challenge to coin new terms and develop new systematizations of eschatological truth from an Eastern perspective. In light of developing a theology, Arab Christians who think that they must not speak of Israel in order not to offend Muslims must remember that the Qur'an speaks of Israel in shocking ways, a fact often ignored (cf. Qur'anic surahs *Al-A'raaf* 7:159-160; *Al-Alisraa'* 17:2,4-7; *Al-Maida* 5:13-14,22-29,122; *Al-Baqara* 2:40,47; *Al-Jathiah* 45:16-17a; *Al-Tah* 20:80). Also, because the Arab Christian church is largely based within Muslim lands as a minority population, much of the thinking of those within that church regarding the nation Israel has been shaped to some degree by Islamic perspectives. Some Arab Christians can end up becoming so anti-Israel that they become pro-Islamic!

Arab Christians must remember the grace of God that is reflected in the Mosaic covenant. The Qur'an agrees up to a certain point about the conditions of a covenant made with Israel (Surah 20:80; 2:40; 5:12-14). It speaks of a Mosaic-like covenant that promises reward for obedience and punishment for disobedience. However, the Qur'an knows no other covenant but a conditional one. It is also anthropocentric with regard to salvation. Everything depends on man's merit.

Though the Mosaic covenant and the Qur'anic covenants are conditional, there is a big difference between them. This is evident in five main ways: (1) The conditional Mosaic covenant comes *after* the unconditional Abrahamic covenant and *before* the unconditional Davidic and new covenants. The Qur'an does not speak of the Abrahamic, Davidic, or new covenants. (2) When God gave the Mosaic covenant, He showed to Moses the need for a regenerated heart to enable the individual and the nation to obey His precepts: "So circumcise your heart, and stiffen your neck no longer" (Deuteronomy 10:16); "yet to this day the LORD has not given you a heart to know, nor eyes to see, nor ears to hear" (29:4); "the LORD your God will circumcise your heart and the heart of your descendants, to love the LORD your God with all your heart and with all your soul, so that you may live" (30:6). This was fulfilled in the new covenant (cf. Jeremiah 31:31-34 and New Testament fulfillment in the church). The Qur'an knows no such bestowal of grace. (3) The Mosaic covenant is a revelation of the nature and holiness of God, whereas the Qur'anic covenants are a declaration of the will and power of God. (4) The Mosaic covenant seeks to establish a relationship between man and God, whereas the Qur'anic covenants seek subservience of man to God. (5) Blessing is assured in the first case but not guaranteed in the second. (6) The Bible points to man's need for a regenerated heart and a new nature, while the Qur'an points to the need for Shari'ah law. Thus Arab Christians must be careful not to conceive of God as having no room to act in grace. They should remember that if God were not to fulfill His promises to the nation, there would be no assurance that He would fulfill His promises to the church. Assurance of fulfillment in the former guarantees assurance of fulfillment in the later.

Some Arab Christians have also allowed themselves to show hatred and to justify eye-for-an-eye retribution. Some rarely condemn terrorist acts that are carried out against the Jews and give lip service to the love and forgiveness they are called to exhibit as Christians, celebrating with their fellow Arabs when Jews are hurt or even killed. In addition, Arab Christians tend to maintain a victim mentality, and with it a constant fault-finding in the other side. In this state of affairs the truth is often not sought out, with the Arab side being presented as right and the Israeli side as wrong. Examples of this abound. Finally, sometimes Arab Christians are so affected by the thinking around them that they become closed to how God might do His work. The challenge for them is to trust God to fulfill His plans, which they might not agree with.

The Ultimate Focal Point

A careful look at Scripture shows that balance needs to be maintained between the conditional and unconditional elements of God's promises to the nations, beginning with Israel. Ultimately, the Bible is not about Israel but about Christ, who chose the nation to be an example of receiving blessing and to be a channel of blessing to all nations. In time and space,

God took on human nature with the purpose of paying for man's sin on the cross and bestowing His righteousness and life upon all who believe. After His death, He rose again to give assurance of the veracity of His purposes and promises. No one can look at the cross and doubt His love for all people as expressed in His promises. And no one can look at the empty tomb and doubt His power to fulfill His promises.

CHAPTER 3
READER RESPONSE

What Should We Think About Christian Support for Israel?

WHAT DO *YOU* THINK?

I agree with the author on

I disagree with the author because

What was news to me?

How does this change the way I think about the way Christians support Israel?

4

What Should We Think About Israel's Right to the Land?

WALTER C. KAISER JR.

Some Christians say modern Israel has no right to the land on a biblical basis—they claim Jesus changed the land promise to extend to the world and transferred it from Abraham to the church. Israel claims a right to its land on the basis of the Bible, political promises, outcomes of war, and for humanitarian reasons. How strong is this claim in comparison with the claims of others?

It's not easy to know how we should think about the land of Israel. On the one hand, the Bible records that God gave it to the Jewish people in ancient times. On the other hand, the land has been occupied and claimed by other peoples and nations in both the past and present. The rightful ownership of the land remains the greatest point of contention in the political negotiations that have involved the three world religions that have staked their claim there. In particular, Christian debate on the matter has affected political attitudes and actions toward the Jewish people and the state of Israel.

Some Christians, while conceding that God promised the land of Israel to Abraham and his descendants in Genesis 12:1-3 and 15:1-6, have asserted that Messiah's first coming changed this. Instead of maintaining that God still plans to faithfully fulfill the original promise to Abraham, they contend that when Jesus gave the "great commission" (Matthew 28:19) and sent His disciples into all the world and not just Israel, He enlarged the original land promise to include to all the peoples on Earth. Their support for this view is based on one statement in Jesus' beatitudes: "Blessed are the gentle, for they shall inherit the earth" (Matthew 5:5).

"Surely this meant," some carelessly argue, "that God had rescinded His ancient promise of the land of Canaan to Israel and instead was giving it to 'the gentle,' who will 'inherit the earth.'"[1] Proponents of this view argue that the New Testament should be interpreted in a spiritual sense and say that God is no longer concerned about a distinct ethnic group (the Jewish people) or a marginal parcel of land called Canaan. Instead, God is now working on a cosmic scale. It is said that Jesus came to start a new religion (Christianity) consisting of a new group of people. God's earlier gift of the land to the Jewish people is said to have been abrogated because of Jewish unbelief, and Jesus started over with all the people of the world and transferred the promise to the "gentle" among them who would "inherit the earth."

This view, however, does not agree with the teaching of Scripture, which clearly states that God promised "on His very life" (see Genesis 15:10,17-21) to give the land of Canaan to Abraham and his ethnic descendants forever (Genesis 13:15; cf. Isaiah 60:21; Jeremiah 7:7; 25:5; 33:26)—a truth reaffirmed in the New Testament (Romans 9:4-5).

The Prominence of the Land Theme in the Bible

In the Old Testament, the land—in reference to the geographical region of Israel—is mentioned more than 1,000 times. Two hundred of these references are directly to Israel and appear some 70 times in the book of Deuteronomy alone. As the Old Testament scholar Gerhard von Rad summarized it, "Of all the promises made to the Patriarchs it was that of the land that was most prominent and decisive."[2] To put it another way, the Old Testament theme of the land is more common than the mention of covenants, which many scholars regard as fundamental to the message of the Bible.

In fact, the term *land* that many readers of the Bible assume is a nonessential detail is one of the central aspects of the covenant. Gerald R. McDermott observed that while the topic of the covenant is fundamental to the biblical narrative, "in more than 70 percent of the places where 'covenant' appears, it is linked to the land promise."[3] McDermott went on to note that he had never realized how central the land was to God's covenant in all of his previous reading of the Bible, for up to that point he had regarded the land as merely another piece of cultural baggage in the Bible—much like the food laws of the Old Testament. Therefore, he had concluded that the land was irrelevant to Christians. Yet because God's promise of the land *is* a central concern in Scripture, it must have relevance for Christians.

However, it is important to notice that the land of Canaan was never a guaranteed possession to Israel; instead, the land was owned by God alone. Only Israel's occupation of the land was promised by God, conditioned on Israel's obedience. Thus Israel could not count on any of the generations that followed Abraham continuing to occupy the land if they indulged in corrupt behavior forbidden in Scripture—such as child sacrifice to false gods, prostitution and various forms of sexual misconduct, and other offenses. Disobedience would result in God cursing the land (Deuteronomy 28:15-68) and the nation being exiled from it. Yet the final fulfillment of the land promise was unconditional, for it depended on God's faithfulness rather than Israel's actions.

The Abrahamic Covenant: An Unconditional, Eternal Covenant

Abraham was called by God and divinely promised that his descendant (a "seed") would be given the land of Canaan and a blessing would flow through him to all the families of the earth (Genesis 12:2-3). God validated this promise through a ritual described in Genesis 15:1-17.

Abraham followed the ritual as prescribed by God, arranging the cut-in-half heifer, goat, and ram, along with the undivided dove and pigeon, to form an aisle. Abraham then entered into a deep sleep. Next, God Himself, as "a smoking oven and a flaming torch," passed between the pieces[4] (verse 17), thereby taking upon Himself an oath of death if He did not fulfill the promises made in this covenant. This unique act by God made the Abrahamic covenant both unconditional and unilateral, a crucial point in understanding the larger promise-plan of God.[5]

This point, however, has been much debated. For example, Wheaton College professor Gary M. Burge argues,

> Possessing the land was contingent on Israel's consistently living by God's righteous standards…The nation Israel is promised possession of the land as an everlasting gift, but this promise is conditional; it depends on Israel's fidelity to the covenant and its stipulations.[6]

Yet that is *not* what the biblical text said. God initiated and would maintain the covenant by Himself, and those who would live to enjoy its benefits and participate in this gift would do so only by faith in Messiah[7] and by their subsequent obedience to His Word. This can be seen in the three subparts of the Abrahamic covenant: (1) the seed of the woman, (2) the land of Canaan, and (3) the blessing that would come to all the nations of the world through the promise made with Israel. The promise came from God to Abraham, Isaac, and Jacob, with more promises given to David. Yet in every case these promises were to be fulfilled by God alone.

The Davidic Covenant: An Everlasting Rule and Reign

One thousand years after the Lord cut His covenant with Abraham, He continued to unpack His promise-plan as embodied in His stream of covenants. God called a young shepherd boy, David, and made a covenant with him through the prophet Nathan. To the preceding ancient promise-plan God added that He would give to David a "house," a "kingdom," and a "throne" that would endure "forever" (2 Samuel 7:16). As with the Abrahamic covenant, no conditions were added to the Davidic covenant (Genesis 13:15; 17:7-8; 2 Samuel 7:13-16).

The Abrahamic and Davidic covenants were connected, reiterating some of the same foundational promises and employing the distinctive and unique name for God—viz. Adonai Yahweh (Genesis 15:2,8; 2 Samuel 7:18-19 [twice],20,23,28), a name for God rarely used in the Old Testament except in these two covenants. To the Abrahamic-Davidic covenants God added a final covenant, the new covenant.

The New Covenant: Universal Peace and the Knowledge of God

In the heart of the prophetic messages came the continuation of God's plan, known as the new covenant (Jeremiah 31:31-34). This covenant was made exclusively with the entire nation of Israel, called in this text "the house of Israel and…the house of Judah." It did not replace the Abrahamic or Davidic covenants, but it did make an important contrast with the Mosaic covenant. Because the Mosaic covenant, unlike the unconditional covenants with Abraham and David, was conditional, Israel could break it and had "broken" (Hebrew, *heperu*) it (Jeremiah 31:32; see also Genesis 17:14). For this reason, the Mosaic covenant was not a direct part of the ongoing promise-plan of God on which Messiah's salvation and future reign rested.

The connection of the new covenant with the Abrahamic and Davidic covenants can be seen in the fact that 70 percent of its contents repeat the previous covenants. However, it also included several new items, such as (1) a universal knowledge of God (Jeremiah 31:34), (2) a universal peace in all of nature (Isaiah 2:4; Ezekiel 34:25; 37:26), (3) a universal prosperity for all people (Isaiah 61:8; Jeremiah 32:41; Ezekiel 34:26-27), (4) a new sanctuary (and priesthood, Jeremiah 33:18) built in the midst of Israel (Ezekiel 37:26,28; 40–48), and (5) a universal outpouring of the Holy Spirit on every believer (Joel 2:28-32), forming those "in Christ" (1 Corinthians 12:1-13) into His church.

What is important here is that this new covenant was not made with the people or leaders of the New Testament church, as if they were the "new Israel"; instead, it was made with the houses of Israel and Judah (Hebrews 8:8). While the church partook of the blood of the new covenant in the Lord's Supper (Matthew 26:28; Mark 14:24) and its ministers were "ministers of a new covenant" (2 Corinthians 3:6; see also Romans 11:27), the covenant was not made directly with the church, but with Israel and Judah. This being the case, some may ask, "Of what use, then, were the Abrahamic, Davidic, and new covenant to the rest of the world beside the Jewish people? What benefit could the Gentile church gain from this covenantal promise-plan of God?" Finding the answer to this helps us to realize the continuing nature of the land promise in the New Testament.

Should the Promise of Land Be Spiritualized in the New Testament?

Replacement theologians contend that any literal prophecies about Israel's return to the land were fulfilled in the past during the postexilic period and therefore offer nothing with respect to a literal future restoration of the nation.[8] This understanding relegates any New Testament text concerning future restoration to a spiritual interpretation and, working backward, reinterprets "restoration to the land" texts in the Old Testament as having an ultimate spiritual fulfillment in Christ. Therefore, the oft-repeated promise of the land in the Old Testament is seen as a metaphor designed so God could eventually urge His people to bring the whole world into submission to Christ's healing and saving reign. However, there is no biblical text that gives any hint that the term *land* was a figure of speech or that it had a spiritual interpretation rather than its natural or literal meaning. If a symbolic meaning were intended, shouldn't this be more obvious in the text?

Instead, the Bible stresses repeatedly that the land was a physical reality and that it was a gift from God to Israel (Leviticus 25:23) in order to fulfill His promise to Abraham (Deuteronomy 1:8). Some Christian scholars, however, view the New Testament through the lens of progressive revelation, saying that the climax of God's revelation came in the person of Jesus Christ. They argue that every Old Testament promise to Israel has its fulfillment in the church. Claiming that because the name *Jesus* (*Yeshua* in Hebrew) is linguistically the same as the name *Joshua*, they view Jesus as the "new Joshua" who achieved something infinitely greater and different than Joshua's territorial achievements when Israel entered the Promised Land. In this light the New Testament book of Acts is seen to correspond to the book of Joshua, revealing that the real intent of Joshua was not the conquest of the land of Canaan but a message concerning the spread of the gospel to the world (Acts 1:8). The life of Jesus is viewed as a type of filter through which one can reinterpret the Old Testament statements about the land and avoid the issues surrounding modern Middle Eastern real estate.

While these alleged correlations between Jesus and Joshua and between the book of Joshua and the book of Acts are interesting, there is no evidence that such correlations (if they exist) correspond to the actual meanings of the Scripture text. We cannot justify on textual or hermeneutical grounds a Christocentric reinterpretation of the Old Testament by the New Testament.

Because the land of Israel was the place where God revealed Himself, Jerusalem was the place where the Temple was built, and the Temple was the place where God's purpose was brought into sharper focus, replacement theologians claim these connections between the land, Jerusalem, and the Temple show that these three centers of the Old Testament formed the center for the entire world and cosmos of the New Testament. On this basis, it could be argued that everything that the Old Testament said about the literal land was intended to yield to the greater spiritual meaning of the land.

From this perspective, the prophet Isaiah's hyperbolic language describing a restoration of the desolate land to extreme productivity (Isaiah 35:1, 3-6,8) concerns more than a people's return to a piece of land. In like manner, Jeremiah's linkage of Israel's return from Babylonian captivity to the land with themes such as the knowledge of God, repentance, and the covenantal relationship (Jeremiah 24:5-7) is said to argue for a spiritual, rather than literal, interpretation. Likewise, whereas Ezekiel's prophecy of the dry bones (Ezekiel 37:1-14), which describes the national resurrection of Israel, clearly states "these bones are the whole house of Israel" (verse 11), replacement theologians reinterpret this through the Christocentric lens to teach this is what Christ will do for the whole human race (that is, a symbol of the redemption of humanity).

For these reinterpreters of the Old Testament, the former locale of God's redemptive work in the land has been transferred and expanded in the New Testament to embrace the entire cosmos. National Israel, which previously lived in the land, has now been replaced by a universal community that has no territorial attachments whatsoever. In other words, the land has now been "christified" so that to be "in Christ" means to be "in the land" with the further understanding that the entire world is the new land!

What was Jesus' understanding of the land? Some claim that He reinterpreted the promise of the literal land of Israel to apply to the cosmic sphere. One way replacement theologians argue this is by citing what Jesus said in the Sermon on the Mount: "Blessed are the meek, for they will inherit *the earth*" (Matthew 5:5). They contend that Jesus expanded the idea of a limited "land" in Israel by using the more comprehensive term "the earth." However, the Greek word translated "earth" (*ge*) can also mean "land," and here it should be given an eschatological sense to mean "the land of promise." Jesus appears to have drawn His reference from Psalm 37:11: "The meek [Hebrew, 'anavim] will inherit the land" (Hebrew 'aretz). In this context, God's future earthly kingdom is promised to those in a right relationship with Him. In verse 9, "those who hope in the LORD" and "inherit the land" are contrasted with "those who are evil" and will be cut off (from the Lord and the land). Jesus, recognizing this psalm's echo of the Abrahamic covenant, did not reinterpret the land promise so as to give away what God had promised to Abraham.

Another passage used by the "new Israel interpreters" is the one cited by Jesus when He began His public ministry. He read from Isaiah 61:1-2 in the synagogue in Nazareth (Luke 4:17-21) and proclaimed at the conclusion of His reading that "today this scripture is fulfilled in your hearing" (verse 21). These scholars argue that this was Jesus' method of taking Old Testament passages that looked to a future regathering of the Jewish people and applying them to the ingathering of the Christian community from all over the world. Again, nothing in this text or any other text supports such a reinterpretation.

The Unsupported Case for a Conditional Abrahamic Covenant

The case made thus far for the unconditionality of the Abrahamic covenant has been that in the covenant ritual depicted in Genesis 15, Abraham was passive while God was active, taking upon Himself the obligation to fulfill the covenant or suffer the consequences. But not all interpreters are satisfied with this description of what took place. Some have argued that the covenant was conditioned on Abraham's obedience because the ritual required him to slaughter and arrange the sacrificial animals. Because he was an active participant, did this not make the covenant conditional? No—Abraham was active in the *preparation* for the ritual, not the ritual itself. The *provision* of the covenant was clearly separate from the *participation* and *participants* in the covenant.

Yet it is further argued that any participation in a covenant that includes conditions requires the covenant to be conditional.[9] For example, the command in Genesis 12:1—"Now the LORD said to Abram, 'Go forth from your country...to the land I will show you'"—is viewed by some interpreters as a clear obligation imposed on Abram. However, the text does not say, "If Abram leaves Ur and goes to the place God will show him, *then* he will receive the divine blessings that follow." Rather, the text says for Abram to "go forth *and* I will…" Abram's "going forth" is the first in a sequence of events that will occur as God works out His previously announced unconditional covenant. Therefore, Abram's obedience to God's command was not a condition, as he did not immediately leave his father's house, but had to wait until his father died in Haran. Nor did he immediately enter the land but had to wait until he was separated from Lot. This indicates that his "going forth" was a part of the divine plan, not the condition for its fulfillment.

Some point to Genesis 14:22-23, where Abram informs the king of Sodom that he (Abram) has raised his hand to the most high God and taken an oath, and therefore will accept nothing belonging to the king of Sodom. They conclude that such an oath appears to support a pattern of obedience and thus requires conditionality. But again, did this implied obedience precede or follow the divine gift unconditionally given to Abraham?

Still others insist that because the rite of circumcision was declared obligatory for Abraham and his descendants in Genesis 17:9-14 the Abrahamic covenant is conditional.[10] But the act of circumcision was not declared to be a condition for the validity of the Abrahamic covenant; rather, it was undertaken by the participants as a *sign* of the covenant. Yet again we see how the *provision* of the covenant must be held separate from the *participation* in the covenant.

An identical scenario arises in connection with the Davidic covenant. Many interpreters contend the "if" clause of loyalty and fidelity of David's sons (1 Kings 2:4; 8:25; 9:4-5; 2 Samuel 7:14-15; Psalm 89:31-33; and perhaps Psalm 132:11-12) are statements of conditionality. However, David himself reflected on the divine promise made to him and in 2 Samuel 23:5 called it an "everlasting covenant," "ordered in all things, and secured"— that is, guaranteed. He also rejoiced in Psalm 21:7 that Yahweh had made him "most blessed forever." In Psalm 89:30-37, God Himself declared that even if David's sons violated the covenant, He still guaranteed fulfillment because, as He said, "I have sworn by My holiness; I will not lie to

David" (verse 35). This is a strong statement of the unconditional nature of these covenants.

Statements of conditionality within a covenant only refer to *individual* and *personal* invalidation of the *benefits* of the covenant, and do not affect the certainty that God will fulfill His oath. This is why Hebrews 8:8, with reference to the first covenant, specifically states that God found fault "with *them*," but not with the covenant itself. The same disclaimer appears in Jeremiah 31:32—"My covenant which *they* broke." Clearly, the existence of conditions within a covenant does not mean the covenant is conditional, but that the dispersal of the blessings (for obedience) or discipline (for disobedience) is governed by human response in the relationship. Human failure is not permitted to abrogate or hinder the ultimate fulfillment of the covenant, which is based on God.

A Natural-Literal Versus a Reinterpreted Meaning of the Text

In his many writings, the popular author N.T. Wright employs a hermeneutic of reinterpretation that erases Israel's national and land promises and transfers them to the church. Wright says:

> He [Jesus] did not come to rehabilitate the symbol of the holy land, but to subsume it within a different fulfillment of the kingdom, which would embrace the whole creation...Jesus spent his whole ministry *redefining* what the kingdom meant...He powerfully subverted [the symbolic language of the kingdom from the] Jewish expectations.[11]
>
> Those who now belonged to Jesus' people were not identical with ethnic Israel, since Israel's history had reached its intended fulfillment; they [i.e., the Jesus' people] claimed to be a continuation of [a new] Israel in a new situation...to fulfill Israel's vocation on behalf of the world.[12]

Colin Chapman likewise adopts this method of spiritualizing and reinterpreting the Old Testament on the basis of what he believes is normative New Testament interpretation. As he complains about some Christians' literal use of the Old Testament to view current events, he writes,

Christians today do not have the liberty to interpret the Old
Testament in any way that appeals to them. Everything in the
Old Testament has to be read through the eyes of the apostles…Therefore, if Christians today find that certain details in
books like Ezekiel appear to fit certain situations in the Middle
East today, they should resist the temptation to draw direct connections with these contemporary events. The reason is that since
the apostle John has given us *the normative interpretation* of these
visions, and not only *one possible interpretation*.[13]

But what these scholars and many others like them fail to account for
is the strong tradition of literal interpretation that was dominant in the
first three centuries of the church. It was Augustine who, in the fourth
century, introduced the allegorical method of interpretation. While many
who espoused the Reformation continued in the Augustinian tradition
of excluding the Jewish people from the ancient promises that God had
made to the Patriarchs, other interpreters, such as the Puritans, did not
adopt replacement theology, but were committed to a straightforward
reading and understanding of Scripture.[14] A pro-Judaic stance was also
held by the Dutch Reformed theologian Wilhelmus à Brakel of Rotter-
dam, Holland (1635–1711), who took issue with the Augustinian view in
this matter. He refused to let the church be identified with the term *new
Israel* and said that the apostle Paul referred to true ethnic Israel in Romans
11:25. He taught that the Jews would return to their land, for God's promise was not about an eternal rest in heaven, but about the physical land
of Canaan.

Another Reformed leader sympathetic to the promises given to Israel
was Count Nicholas Ludwig von Zinzendorf (1700–1760). He started
the Moravian movement, which paralleled the Pietist movement. Other
names could also be added to the list, including Joseph A Seiss, David
Baron, Adolph Saphir, B.W. Newton, H. Grattan Guinness, J.C. Ryle,
Charles Haddon Spurgeon, George Peters, Nathaniel West, and Horatius
Bonar. Bonar (1808–1889), a beloved nineteenth-century hymn writer,
made a case for a literal interpretation of the Bible by taking 18 biblical prophecies about Christ's first coming that were fulfilled literally and

arguing that this demonstrated the proper method of handling the promises about Israel's future and the land. Only the literal method of interpreting the Old Testament preserves God's fulfillment of the land promise as
originally stated and affirmed in Scripture.

The Focus of God's Promises

God cannot lie, nor did He lie to Israel when He gave the promises about the seed (Psalm 89:3-4, 20-37), the land (Genesis 3:15; 17:7-8;
37:25), and the blessing to all the families of the earth (Genesis 12:2-3).
The Gentile church has always been invited to participate by faith in the
rich root of the olive tree (Romans 11:17-24), the Abrahamic covenant
(cf. Galatians 3:14). God did not make this covenant directly with the
church—and the biblical covenants, including the land covenant, must be
fulfilled by national ethnic Israel because God promised the land to them.

Unless Gentile believers within the church are anchored into the olive
tree of Israel, they are not tied into the promise, for the root is Israel alone.
As Paul said, "Remember that it is not you who supports the root, but the
root supports you" (Romans 11:18). For this reason, Israel today continues to have a right to the land promised to it, and we should thank God
for His promises made through Israel for all.

CHAPTER 4
READER RESPONSE

What Should We Think About Israel's Right to the Land?

WHAT DO *YOU* THINK?

I agree with the author on

I disagree with the author because

What was news to me?

How does this change the way I think about Israel's right to the land?

5

What Should We Think About Jerusalem as the Capital of Israel?

MITCH GLASER

Recently the United States moved its embassy to Jerusalem in recognition of its status as Israel's capital city, and Israel's Knesset passed the nation-state law establishing Jerusalem as the country's official capital. Israel's current prime minister, as well as all who preceded him, contends that Jerusalem has been the eternal and indivisible capital of Israel for more than 3,000 years. However, most of the nations of the world decline this recognition and oppose placing their embassies there. What is the biblical and historical basis for Jerusalem as the capital of Israel?

Before we can answer this question, we must ask yet another one: Does the Bible teach that Jerusalem is the capital of Israel? After all, the Bible should shape our understanding of all things—especially when a matter so important as the role of Jerusalem is so prevalent throughout its pages.

On May 14, 2018, the United States moved its Israeli embassy from Tel Aviv to Jerusalem. This was the first such action by a nation of superpower

status in the 70-plus years since Israel's establishment as a Jewish state, and
it called upon the church to more seriously consider its position on Jerusalem's place in God's plan for the ages.

This move was controversial and politically divisive—both Israel's enemies and supporters from around the globe vehemently disagreed with
this decision because they were hoping for a two-state solution that would
create a Palestinian capital in East Jerusalem for the Palestinian state and
another capital in West Jerusalem for the Jewish state. However, the two-
state solution is fraught with difficulties, and there is much disagreement
about how to implement it. This is just one of the many challenges to
bringing true and lasting peace to a complex and conflicted region.

The current situation in the Middle East is the result of centuries-old
tensions that are difficult for Westerners to fully understand. Moreover,
many Christians who read about the ancient Middle East in their Bibles
know little about the politics of the region. Yet they do recognize Jerusalem as the subject of many of God's promises and its significance in Scripture. In fact, the psalmist calls upon God's people to pray for the peace
of Jerusalem (122:6). We must ask ourselves, then: How should we pray?

A recent survey entitled "Evangelical Attitudes Toward Israel," initiated by LifeWay Research and supported by both Chosen People Ministries and author Joel C. Rosenberg, provides us with fresh insights as to
how evangelical Christians in the United States understand the role of
Israel in Scripture and today's world. The survey was commissioned in the
summer of 2017, and the results were released in two parts—the first on
December 4, 2017, at the National Press Club in Washington, DC, and
the second on February 28, 2018, at the National Religious Broadcast-
ers convention in Nashville, Tennessee. At the time the survey was taken,
the US government had not yet moved its embassy to Jerusalem, so there
were no questions relating to that. However, the survey does provide a
broad overview of evangelical attitudes about Israel. The survey suggests
that evangelicals would likely support Jerusalem as the capital for primarily biblical and not necessarily political reasons.

There were 2,002 survey participants, and 69 percent said they are
positive toward Israel. The survey also revealed that 80 percent of evangelicals agree that God's promise to Abraham and his descendants were

for all time. This promise included the land, of course, which would also mean Jerusalem.

The Bible speaks often about Jerusalem. According to general editor of this volume, Dr. Randall Price,

> Jerusalem is mentioned 800 times in the Bible and under one name or another in about two thirds of the books of the Old Testament and one half the books of the New Testament. Researchers have found 660 verses in the Old Testament and 142 in the New Testament that speak of Jerusalem.[1]

Price adds that 465 of the references to Jerusalem in the Old Testament and 24 in the New Testament appear in a prophetic context, implying a future status for the city. The survey reported that 67 percent of the survey respondents support the Jewish people's right to live in the sovereign state of Israel. This implies that evangelicals believe Israel has the right to determine the location of her own capital. Sixty-nine percent of the participants also said that Israel has a historic right to the land. This suggests that because Jerusalem is the historic capital of the land, they would likely say it should also be the modern capital. While this is a deduction because the survey had no direct questions about Jerusalem as the capital, it would seem to be a logical conclusion because evangelicals get most of their understanding of Israel and Jerusalem from the Bible.

What's more, 80 percent of the survey participants view the regathering of the Jewish people and the rebirth of Israel in 1948 as fulfillments of Bible prophecy that indicate we are getting closer to the return of Jesus Christ, whereas the other 20 percent say these were simply interesting geopolitical events.[2]

Sixty-six percent of evangelicals believe they should support Israel's existence, security, and prosperity. This indicates most of them understand that giving up half of Jerusalem would pose a security threat to the Jewish state. On the other hand, 23 percent of those surveyed say that Palestinians should be allowed to create their own sovereign state, while 31 percent disagree, and 46 percent are unsure. That is a significant amount of uncertainty for such a crucial question! In the court of those who view the modern state of Israel in a negative light is Gary Burge, a professor at

Wheaton College. Concerning the land question, including the site of Jerusalem, he writes,

> We do not promote what we call the "territorialism" of the Bible. We anchor our thinking not in the Old Testament's land-based promises, but in the Gospel, where the tribal or local theologies about Israel become global and universal, welcoming all people from every tribe and every land into a divine promise of blessing. Paul can refer to Gentiles as children of Abraham (Romans 4:11) because it's through faith, not ethnic lineage, that one gains access to the blessings of God. This shift in emphasis, which challenges the exclusivity of any one tribe and universalizes blessing, explains the world-mission of the ancient church and the inclusion of Gentiles in Jesus' Jewish messianic movement. From this vantage, arguments for ethnic land claims—such as disputes over Jerusalem—sound foreign.[3]

Burge views the Bible as a supersessionist, arguing that the land promises made to the Jewish people in the past should not be taken literally and therefore do not apply to Israel today. According to Burge, the earthly city of Jerusalem, like Israel itself, is irrelevant because the concern of the church is spiritual and its focus is global. The Jewish people no longer have a national covenant with God and therefore have no right to Israel as a land nor to Jerusalem as a capital. In contrast, those who hold to a literal interpretation of the land promises believe that Jerusalem was, is, and always will be the capital of the nation of Israel.

Jerusalem: Past, Present and Future

According to the Bible, Jerusalem has a great past, a challenging present, and a glorious future. How could those who read the Bible not understand that Jerusalem is the historic capital of Israel? The Bible presents Jerusalem as chosen by God (1 Kings 11:3; Psalm 132:13-14; Zechariah 1:16), the holy city where God dwells (Psalm 132:7; Joel 3:17; Zechariah 2:12) and that will be built up by Him (Psalm 147:2; Zechariah 8:7-8). The perspective that Jerusalem would remain the capital of Israel (Psalm

122:1-5) never changes, even though Scripture predicts that the city would know foreign occupation and domination until Jesus returns to it in the end times (Zechariah 14:4; Luke 21:24). After that, the Bible views Jerusalem as the center of the world, from where Jesus will rule over all the earth (1 Chronicles 17:14; Isaiah 24:23; Jeremiah 3:17; Micah 4:8; Zechariah 8:3; 14:9). The nations of the world will be commanded to come to Jerusalem to learn God's Word (Isaiah 2:3) and to worship the Lord (Isaiah 66:20; Zechariah 14:16-19).

Jerusalem in the Bible and in Jewish History

In order to determine what we should think about Jerusalem as the capital of Israel, let us examine what the Bible says and allow our understanding of Scripture to shape our politics. Our survey of the facts about Jerusalem's history begins with Abraham and Melchizedek.

Abraham, Melchizedek, and Jerusalem

Jerusalem, from the very start, was a city of destiny, set apart for a central role in God's plan for the ages. It is first referenced in Genesis 14:18, when Abraham was approached by Melchizedek, a mysterious priest (see Psalm 110:4-7) whose name means "the righteous king." We are told that he is from Salem, the earlier Canaanite name for Jerusalem. With regard to Melchizedek's significance, Randall Price writes,

> When Abraham later met a representative of the city he found that God was already there, for the representative was the Canaanite King, Melchizedek, who was a priest of God most high (Genesis 14:18). Think of the prophetic association here for Jerusalem's future role with the Messiah as in Hebrew, the name means king of righteousness and this historic King of Jerusalem came to present a gift to the father of all Israel.[4]

Clearly Jerusalem's importance was prefigured in this passage before the establishment of the Jewish people as a nation. The Abrahamic covenant shapes the biblical story and creates a pattern of significance for Jerusalem well before the city was populated with the physical descendants of Abraham, Isaac, and Jacob.

Moses and Jerusalem

Another passage key to understanding God's plan for Jerusalem is Exodus 15:17. There, Moses wrote, "You will bring them and plant them in the mountain of Your inheritance, the place, O LORD, which You have made for Your dwelling, the sanctuary, O Lord, which Your hands have established." This refers to Jerusalem, which King David made his capital (1 Chronicles 11:4-9) and where King Solomon built the Temple (2 Chronicles 3:1). In 2 Chronicles 6:6 we read, "I have chosen Jerusalem that My name might be there, and I have chosen David to be over My people Israel." There, a link is established between Jerusalem and the descendants of David, who would rule for God from the holy city. This is also true in a prophetic sense, for we are told that the greater Son of David, Jesus the messianic King, will reign in an eternal Davidic kingdom (Jeremiah 33:14-18; Ezekiel 37:25) and His throne will be established in Jerusalem at His second coming (Jeremiah 3:17; Ezekiel 43:7). All through the Bible, Jerusalem is predicted to be the national and spiritual capital of Israel, and ultimately, of the world.

King David and Jerusalem

David knew that the power of the nation rested with the presence and power of God, which was localized in the ark of the covenant (Exodus 25:21-22). Until David could bring the ark to Jerusalem, the capital city was not yet sacred. That's why David made it one of his first duties as king to bring the ark back to Jerusalem (2 Samuel 6:1-4). He also desired to build a more permanent home for the presence of God, the Temple (2 Samuel 7:1-3; Psalm 132:1).

The Temple and Jerusalem

David made the initial preparations for the building of the First Temple, which was erected during the reign of his son Solomon (1 Kings 6). David purchased the land for the Temple (2 Samuel 24:18-25), produced the plans, and raised the funds for the project (1 Chronicles 28:11-18; 29:1-9).

Jerusalem was a unique city not only because it's where the king's palace was located, but because it was home to the throne of God—the Temple. It was the Temple that made the city sacred. David clearly understood the vital link between Jerusalem and the king and the priest, which defined the national and spiritual life of the nation (1 Chronicles 29:10-20). This connection between political and priestly leadership elevated Jerusalem's spiritual significance, as God had called the Jewish people to be a light to the nations. It was at the Temple, and not the palace, where true authority resided. The throne needed to submit to the Temple in order to be successful. Whenever this principle was broken, the nation suffered. Ultimately, when the Jewish people disobeyed God, Jerusalem felt the most pain and experienced God's judgment centered on the Temple.

Divided Israel and Jerusalem

Israel split into two kingdoms in 935 BC, after the reign of Solomon. Jerusalem remained the capital in the southern kingdom of Judah, and Samaria became the capital of the northern kingdom. Jerusalem grew in prominence after the destruction of the northern kingdom in 722 BC, but that changed when the city was captured by the Babylonians in 606 BC.

The Babylonian Destruction of Jerusalem

The Babylonians destroyed the Temple and the holy city in 586 BC (Jeremiah 52:1-30) and took a large portion of the Jewish population into exile. During their captivity in Babylon, many of the Jewish people longed to return to the holy city. We are not exactly sure when Psalm 137 was written, but we do know that for centuries the Jewish people proclaimed this psalm as an expression of their mourning over the loss of Jerusalem and their belief that this sacred city was the biblical and historical capital of Israel. As the psalmist lamented so memorably, "If I forget you, O Jerusalem, may my right hand forget her skill" (verse 5).

The Rebuilding of Jerusalem

The return to Jerusalem and the rebuilding of the Temple is recorded in the book of Ezra (Ezra 1:1-4). We know that only a small remnant of Jewish people returned from their 70-year exile, and the rebuilding of the Second Temple was completed within five years, beginning in 521 BC and concluding in 516 BC. But the people were dismayed because this rebuilt Temple did not reach the level of splendor known by the First Temple. The elders who had worshipped at the First Temple wept because the rebuilt Temple was merely a shadow of what they had known previously (Ezra 3:12).

Jesus and Jerusalem

It is impossible to trace the story of Jesus or to maintain the integrity of the New Testament without Jerusalem. The story of redemption begins in Jerusalem with the death and resurrection and ascension of Jesus and ends with His rule in the capital of His kingdom, Jerusalem. The city is a major geographical setting for all four Gospels.

After His birth, Jesus was dedicated at the Temple in Jerusalem in accordance with Jewish law (Luke 2:22-24), and on the steps of the Temple prophetic statements were declared about Him (Luke 2:25-38). As an observant Jew, Jesus went to Jerusalem three times a year for the Jewish festivals (John 7:10,14)—He went to the city with His family for Passover, and on one occasion He stayed at the Temple to dialogue with the rabbis (Luke 2:41-51).

Jerusalem was also the venue for some of Jesus' greatest statements (Luke 22:19-20; John 7:37-39) and prayers (Matthew 26:36-45; John 17:20-21). Jesus wept over Jerusalem (Luke 19:41-44) as He walked toward His impending death in the holy city (Luke 9:51; 24:7). Jesus even declared, "It cannot be that a prophet would perish outside of Jerusalem" (Luke 13:33). Jerusalem became the epicenter of world redemption when Jesus died on the cross for sinners and was later resurrected from the dead, and it is there in Jerusalem that Jesus will one day return and rule (Matthew 16:21; Isaiah 9:7; Zechariah 14:4). Moreover, it is in Jerusalem that the great day of Jewish forgiveness will take place when the remnant of Israel turns to Jesus (Zechariah 12:10; Romans 11:25). Finally, the church—the body of Christ—was born in Jerusalem (Acts 2:41-47) and became the birthplace of Christianity. Jesus Himself had commanded that the proclamation of the gospel message was to start from Jerusalem (Acts 1:8-9).

For these reasons, it is impossible to separate the story of Jesus from the history and key role Jerusalem has played in God's plan for mankind through the ages.

UNESCO and Jerusalem

The United Nations Educational, Scientific, and Cultural Organization

(UNESCO) has recently denied any historical connection between the Jewish people and Jerusalem, and especially the Temple Mount. In doing this, UNESCO denies the historical accuracy of both the Old and New Testaments. This stance has offended religious Jews and Christians, both of whom believe the Bible to be true and link Jesus to the rich history of the sacred city. Chosen People Ministries brought forth a petition and gathered thousands of signatures from evangelical Christians who opposed this decision by UNESCO. The petition states,

> As concerned Americans we are disappointed by the recent resolution by the United Nations Educational, Scientific, and Cultural Organization (UNESCO) denying all biblical and historic links between the Jewish people and Jerusalem approved on October 13, 2016. The "Occupied Palestine" resolution undermines the sacred bond between Jews and Christians to holy sites in Jerusalem and throughout Israel.[5]

The UNESCO resolution may be challenged for a number of reasons:

- It falsely claims that Israel is as an occupying nation, implying that East Jerusalem, if not all of Jerusalem, belongs to the Palestinians.

- It falsely claims that Israelis are destroying sacred Palestinian sites through archaeological research, which is patently untrue, while conversely demanding the Dead Sea Scrolls and other archaeological discoveries made in the West Bank since 1967 be turned over to the Palestinian Authority.

- It falsely claims that the Temple Mount and areas surrounding the Western Wall and old city of Jerusalem are solely Palestinian sites. By rejecting the Hebrew term for the site—*Har HaBayit*—and its English equivalent, the Temple Mount, and using only by its Muslim/Arab names—Al-Aqsa Mosque and *Haram al-Sharif*—the resolution presents a skewed and biased representation of history.[6]

- It falsely claims that there is no Jewish connection to Hebron, which the Bible claims to be the burial site of Rachel, the wife of Isaac, and Bethlehem, the birthplace of Ruth, David, and Jesus.

The UNESCO mandate states that the UN's goal is to promote understanding "among nations and intercultural understanding by protecting heritage and supporting cultural diversity."[7] Yet this is not possible if UNESCO disrespects the view of the Bible, which is cherished by both Jews and Christians worldwide. In fact, the UN's actions will only further add to the tensions between Jews, Christians, and Muslims. The general director of UNESCO, Irina Boskova, rejected the resolution and wrote,

> Nowhere more than in Jerusalem do Jewish, Christian and Muslim heritage and traditions share space and interweave to the point that they support each other. These cultural and spiritual traditions build on texts and references, known by all, that are an intrinsic part of the identities and history of peoples. In the Torah, Jerusalem is the capital of King David, where Solomon built the Temple and placed the Ark of the Covenant. In the Bible, Jerusalem is the city of the passion and resurrection of Jesus Christ. In the Quran, Jerusalem is the third holiest site in Islam, where Muhammad arrived after his night journey from Al Haram Mosque (Mecca) to Al Aqsa.[8]

Both Jews and Christians have called upon UNESCO to retract the resolution and recognize the historic and sacred relationship between the Jewish people and all of Jerusalem, including the Temple Mount. Any attempt to change the historic connection of the Jewish people with Jerusalem or to deny that it has been the capital of Israel for more than 3,000 years is political in nature and should not be regarded as fact.

Both the United States and Israel have since retracted their membership in UNESCO.

The Nation-State Law and Jerusalem

In 2018, the Israeli Knesset enacted a new law declaring Israel as the historic Jewish homeland and Jerusalem as its official capital. The

European Union protested that this declaration would ruin the chances for bringing about a two-state solution—a Jewish state and capital existing alongside an Arab state and capital. However, the purpose of the law was to guarantee Israel's future as a Jewish country because up to the time the law was passed, Israel's identity as such was made clear only in its 1948 Declaration of Independence, which has no constitutional value.

In fact, the law is designed to ameliorate the problems that would be caused by a one-state solution that merges Israel, the West Bank, and the Gaza Strip into a country in which Arabs would outnumber Jews, a demographic goal that the Palestinians have long championed in order to displace the Jews in Israel. Palestinians have claimed that the new law was passed in an attempt to eradicate Palestine from history and have vowed that millions of martyrs will march on Jerusalem to redeem Palestine.[9] Yet the inclusion of Jerusalem in this law is simply a recognition of historical fact: For 3,000 years, Jerusalem was been the capital of Israel alone, and no Arab power, in the course of occupying Jerusalem, has ever made it their capital.

Letting the Bible Inform Our Minds

According to the Bible, Jerusalem is a Jewish city. How could those who are concerned about the facts not possibly understand that Jerusalem is the biblical and historic capital of Israel? Those who read the biblical text literally must allow Scripture to inform their minds and direct their actions as well as their political understandings with regard to the Middle East. The Bible does not differentiate between ancient Israel, the Israel that was formed in 1948, and the future messianic capital. It is clear from Scripture that Jerusalem is the capital of Israel and should remain the undivided capital of the modern Jewish state. Perhaps we should start there—with what we know. If someone asked me, "Was Jerusalem the capital of Israel, or will it be the capital of Israel?," my answer, based on the Bible, would be a resounding yes! Those who profess the Bible to be the guide for their lives should base their perspectives about Jerusalem upon biblical truth and not allow contemporary politics to influence their views about the city.

It is time for both Jewish people and Christians to delve into the inspired, inerrant text as literally as possible and take, at face value, what is said about Jerusalem at face value. We must view Israel's place in the world through a biblical lens. This will provide a helpful path for figuring out how we should think about the city of Jerusalem and the nation of Israel. May the present Jerusalem remind us each day of the glories awaiting all those who call upon the name of the Jewish Messiah, Jesus. Until then, we will continue to obey God and pray for the peace of Jerusalem, taking hold of the great promise attached to this prayer for the city: "May they prosper who love you" (Psalm 122:6).

CHAPTER 5
READER RESPONSE

What Should We Think About Jerusalem as the Capital of Israel?

WHAT DO *YOU* THINK?

I agree with the author on

I disagree with the author because

What was news to me?

How does this change the way I think about Jerusalem as the capital of Israel?

6

What Should We Think About the Temple Mount?

RANDALL PRICE

At the heart of the political controversy between the Israelis and the Palestinians (as well as between Judaism, Christianity, and Islam) lies the competing religious claims for Jerusalem and its sacred Temple Mount. Islamic authorities have denied the existence of the Jewish Temple and called it a political attempt to Judaize Jerusalem. Jewish authorities and the state of Israel have affirmed its historic existence and declared Jerusalem the holiest place in Judaism. What are the facts behind these claims?

The ownership of the holy sites in Jerusalem remains one of the most controversial and unresolvable obstacles to reconciliation in the ongoing Middle East peace process. The final-status negotiations in the Oslo Peace Accord were to address this issue, but only after a modicum of peace and mutual understanding had been obtained by the exchange of land for peace (by Israel) and the cessation of a state of belligerency (by the Palestinians). Unfortunately, because the first stage of negotiations failed to produce the results required to move on to the second and final stage, the disagreements over the holy sites have continued to escalate.

The Hashemite kingdom of Jordan (which was assigned protectorate status over the holy sites in Jerusalem per a 1994 peace treaty with

Israel) and the "State of Palestine" issued a joint-status report to UNESCO World Heritage Center alleging numerous Israeli violations against the holy sites since 1967.[1] Chief among the holy sites is the Temple Mount, located in the eastern part of the historic Old City. Even the mere reference to this site by its Hebrew name, *Har Habayit* ("the Temple Mount"), is controversial. The proponents of Islam, who have dominated the site for the past 1,381 years, call it *al-Haram al-Sharif* ("Noble Sanctuary") and deny that a Jewish Temple ever occupied this area.

In 2016, UNESCO caused controversy by recognizing Arab and Palestinian political claims to the Temple Mount over the claims of the Israeli nation and Jews worldwide, which are based upon longstanding published research done by historians and archaeologists.[2] As a result, Meron Benvenisti, the former deputy mayor of Jerusalem, has described the rival Jewish and Muslim claims to the Temple Mount as "a time bomb...of apocalyptic dimensions."[3]

In order to understand why this site is such a focal point in the Middle East conflict and so vital to the peace process, let us carefully examine the rival claims of Jews and Arabs and seek to separate historic fact from popular fiction.

The Jewish Claim to the Temple Mount

According to the Bible,[4] God directed the patriarch Abraham to take his son Isaac and go to an appointed mountain in the land of Moriah. At this place, historically known as Mount Moriah, Isaac was to be sacrificed as a burnt offering on a makeshift altar (Genesis 22:1-2,9). At the last moment, before Abraham was about to slay his son, God interceded and provided a ram as a substitute offering. Abraham therefore called the place *'Adonai Yireh* ("The LORD Will Provide") and dubbed it "the mount of the LORD" (Genesis 22:10-14).

Later, Moses was told by God to "bring them [Israel] and plant them in the mountain of your inheritance," which was then described as "the place, O LORD, which You have made for Your dwelling, the Sanctuary, O Lord, which Your hands have established" (Exodus 15:17).

This was understood by King David to be Mount Moriah in Jerusalem. It was there that David had asked God to allow him to build the First

Temple (2 Samuel 7:1-3), and there that he had purchased the threshing floor of Araunah (Ornan) the Jebusite and erected an altar in honor of God's merciful preservation of the city (2 Samuel 24:16-25). However, the honor of building the Temple went to David's son Solomon (1 Kings 7:51–8:10). The connection of the site from Solomon back to Abraham was recorded in 2 Chronicles 3:1: "Solomon began to build the house of the LORD in Jerusalem on Mount Moriah, where the LORD had appeared to his father David, at the place that David had prepared on the threshing floor of Ornan the Jebusite." Therefore, from a biblical and theological perspective, and on the basis of historical fact and a legal purchase, the Jewish people claimed a divine right to build a Temple on Mount Moriah, the Temple Mount.

The Bible further relates that the First Temple was destroyed by the Babylonians in 586 BC on *Tisha B'Av*, the ninth of the Hebrew month of Av (2 Kings 25:9). It was rebuilt 70 years later by the Jewish exiles who returned from the Babylonian captivity during the years 538–515 BC (Ezra 3:1-3; 6:15). According to Ezra 6:7, when a Jewish remnant returned to Jerusalem from Babylon under the edict of King Cyrus (2 Chronicles 36:22-23), they built the Second Temple in exactly the same place as the first: "Let the governor of the Jews and the elders of the Jews rebuild this house of God on its site." This fact is reinforced by the specific requirement that the Temple be rebuild it on its original "foundation" (Ezra 2:68; 3:3; cf. Haggai 1:8). The theological explanation for rebuilding on the same location is because there could be no other location for the Second Temple (or any future Temple) than that historically sanctified by the divine presence.

Around 20 BC, Herod the Great enlarged and refurbished this Second Temple, although improvements continued for another 46 years into the lifetime of Jesus (John 2:20). The Temple was later destroyed by the Romans in AD 70 during the First Jewish Revolt (AD 66–70). As happened with the First Temple, this took place on *Tisha B'Av*, convincing the Jewish people that this calamity was an act of divine discipline on their nation.

Despite the destruction, there is evidence that the Jewish population in Jerusalem continued to offer sacrifices at the ruined altar.[5] And during a brief three-year period of independence following the Second Jewish Revolt (AD 132–136), there was an attempt to rebuild the Temple.[6] This was unsuccessful, and after the Roman emperor Hadrian retook Jerusalem, he imposed harsh prohibitions against Jews entering Jerusalem. The only exception was that they could come on *Tisha B'Av* to the Mount of Olives and pray toward their ruined Temple Mount. Later, in AD 363, the Roman emperor Julian invited the Jewish community to rebuild the Temple, although this attempt was unsuccessful as well.[7]

Even after these failed attempts, the Jewish people continued to hope for a return to Jerusalem, a rebuilding of the Temple, and a restoration of their national life. Jewish prayers were turned toward Jerusalem and focused on the Temple Mount, a hope that is preserved in the Amidah, or Jewish daily prayer: "Restore the most holy service of Your house and accept in love the offerings and prayers of Israel. May it please You always to accept the service of Your people Israel. May our eyes see You return to Zion in mercy. Blessed are You, O Lord, who restores His Presence to Zion" (Benediction 17—*Avodah*).

Even though the Muslim conquest of AD 638 brought with it another foreign occupation of Jerusalem and the Temple Mount, religious Jews have been resolute in their conviction and intention to see the divine presence returned to the site with the rebuilding of the Temple.

When the Jewish state was declared in 1948, a war ensued with the surrounding Arab states. In the aftermath, Jerusalem was divided and the Temple Mount remained under Islamic control. During this time of foreign occupation (1948–1967), the Jordanian occupiers destroyed 58 synagogues in the historic Jewish Quarter of Jerusalem, cut off access to the Hebrew University on Mount Scopus, ransacked the Jewish cemeteries on the Mount of Olives, and prohibited Jews from having access to the Western Wall, that touchpoint with their most holy site, and the only place under Ottoman and British rule where religious Jews were allowed to pray. Therefore, an entire generation of Jews grew up viewing the Temple Mount from a distance.

In 1967, the Six-Day War broke the Jordanian hold on east Jerusalem and Israeli soldiers who had never visited the Western Wall wept upon regaining this historic site. While this victory offered the people of Israel the first opportunity in recent history to exercise Jewish sovereignty over the Temple Mount, they did not act on it. In popular culture, the Israelis are often depicted as those who conquered Jerusalem and usurped the Muslim's longstanding religious rights to the Temple Mount, but that is not what happened. When this chance to take possession of the Temple Mount was afforded the Jewish state, they did not seize the site, but returned control of it to Islamic authorities.

Immediately after the Six-Day War, Moshe Dayan, one of the Israeli commanders, sat down in the Al-Aqsa Mosque—respectfully with shoes removed according to Muslim practice—to meet with leaders of the Islamic waqf. To their surprise, he restored to them full rights to the Temple Mount, explaining later in his biography that this unexpected act of political generosity was based on a Jewish ethic forged in persecution and exile. He said that even though the Jews had suffered injustice and ill treatment by their conquerors, even to the point of genocide, they refused to treat others as they had been treated. He had acted as he did to demonstrate that Israel was willing to live together with the Arabs in peace.[8]

To be sure, the Israeli government extended sovereignty over all of Jerusalem and restored Jewish access to the Western Wall and demanded that access to it and the Temple Mount be available for all religions while requiring that the religious rights and practices of the Muslim sites not be violated (known as the Status Quo Agreement). This agreement, however, was violated by the Islamic authorities under Palestinian jurisdiction when they denied the Jewish history of the site and constructed a new mosque at the southern end of the Temple Mount (the site of Jewish entrance during the Second Temple period). During the construction of the mosque, the Palestinians ignored archaeological protocol by removing tons of ancient soil and tossing thousands of archaeological artifacts into garbage heaps, while Jewish access to the site was restricted from 1999–2003.[9]

Since 1987, when the first Intifada began, Jews have felt that the pressure from Palestinian protesters might influence the international community to force them from their access to Jerusalem and the Temple Mount. That prompted several Orthodox Jewish groups to form the Temple movement. Their goal is to prepare for the rebuilding of the Third Temple during this generation, for they believe that because they are the generation to whom God has returned the city and the site, they are therefore obligated to restore the sanctuary (see Exodus 25:8).[10] These ambitions in response to the Palestinian demonstrations have only increased the potential for violence at the site.

The Islamic Claim to the Temple Mount

As noted earlier, the Muslim term for this site is *al-Haram al-Sharif* ("Noble Sanctuary"), which refers to the entire 35-acre platform. According to the history of the Bedouin-Muslim conquest of Jerusalem that has come down to us,[11] Caliph 'Umar, upon arriving in the city in AD 638, sought the site made sacred by the prophet Solomon and was taken to an exposed outcropping of rock (known as the *Sakhra*) that had been almost completely covered by refuse dumped by inhabitants during the former Byzantine period. Wishing to resanctify the site, 'Umar forbade anyone to pray there until the area had experienced three rainfalls (a symbolic act of purification). 'Umar is believed to have offered prayers in the nearby Byzantine church of Saint Mary of Justinian, an act that transformed it into a mosque, the site of the present Al-Aqsa Mosque was built in 711.[12]

'Umar is said to have erected a wooden structure over the *Sakhra* as a shelter for pilgrims who wished to pray at the site. In 691, his successor, the Ummayyad caliph 'Abd al Malik, replaced it with an octagonal building in the Byzantine architectural style (known as *Qubbat as-Sakhra*, "Dome of the Rock"). This was a political move as the result of divisions within the Arab world between the Damascus-based Ummayyads and those centered in Mecca. The Ummayyads sought to damage the Meccan economy, which was based almost entirely on revenues from Muslim pilgrims, by diverting pilgrims to the Dome of the Rock in Jerusalem. This new structure, which now rivaled the Byzantine churches, also served a polemical purpose. It had been built using the same layout within the Church of the Holy Sepulcher and on the architectural model of local Byzantine Christian shrines of the time.[13] This prevented Muslims from being attracted to the splendor and theological focus of Byzantine Christendom, as is made evident by anti-Christian statements inscribed within the dome.[14] Moreover, according to the ninth-century Qur'anic historian and commentator Abu Jafar Muhammad al-Tabari, 'Umar wrote a letter to the Christian inhabitants of Jerusalem and declared that "no Jewish person shall be allowed to dwell with them in *Iliya* [the Roman name for Jerusalem since the second century AD]."[15]

Other writers reported this ban on the Jewish settlement in Jerusalem, yet 'Umar and his successors may have allowed a concession of sorts because Jews (along with Christians) were tasked to do menial labor within the buildings on the Temple Mount. For the next 1,300 years, with the exception of a break during the Crusader occupation of the city (1099–1187), Muslims have occupied *al-Haram al-Sharif* as one of their holy sites. Today, they declare that there was never a Jewish presence in Jerusalem until the late 1800s and that the Jewish historical claim of a Temple built on the Temple Mount is fiction. For example, Walid Awad, the Palestinian Authority minister of information, has stated, "Jerusalem is not a Jewish city, despite the biblical myth implanted in some minds…There is no tangible evidence of Jewish existence from the so-called 'Temple Mount Era.'…The location of the Temple Mount is in question…it might be in Jericho or somewhere else."[16]

This modern denial has been affirmed by the Jordanian and Palestinian muftis who have controlled the site, including Sheikh Ekrima Sa'id Sabri, who was appointed by the late Yasser Arafat: "There is not the smallest indication of the existence of a Jewish Temple on this place in the past; in the whole city there is not even a single stone indicating Jewish history."[17] Given this perspective, one can understand the Muslim intolerance toward Orthodox Jews who want to pray on the Temple Mount and to those who have announced they plan to rebuild the Temple sometime in the future.

What Do the Facts Show?

There is no question that the archaeological excavations that have taken place on and around the Temple Mount since the 1860s by Europeans and since 1967 by the Israelis have given incontestable evidence for the historical existence of both the First and Second Jewish Temples, which, in turn, verifies the 3,000-year connection of the Jewish people to Jerusalem and the Temple Mount.[18] Jodi Magness, Professor of Early Judaism at the University of North Carolina, Chapel Hill, has stated, "I know of no credible scholars who question the existence of the two temples or who deny that they stood somewhere on the Temple Mount."[19] Concerning the location of the Temple Mount as the site of the historic Temples of the Jewish people, historians Katharina Galor and Hanswulf Bloedhorn have concluded,

> Maintaining a sanctuary's location throughout changes of cultural and religious domination is a well-established custom in antiquity. In Jerusalem we can physically trace this continuity on the Haram al-Sharif, where the Dome of the Rock sits on top of the Temple Mount enclosure. Historical evidence suggests that Herod's Temple was built in place of Zerubbabel's Temple, which had been constructed soon after the return from the Babylonian exile and was meant to commemorate the exact spot of the First Temple. The monumental construction of the pre-Hellenistic (i.e., pre-Hasmonean and pre-Herodian) extension of the eastern enclosure wall has been identified as the original Temple Mount platform, which was designed to level off the natural topography and to support the earlier Temple.[20]

A century and more before the Muslim invasion of Jerusalem, Byzantine-era Christianity had discovered that Jerusalem had sanctity for them not just as an ideal of the heavenly Jerusalem, but as a physical city and especially as site of the sanctuary, which they revered as the "house of God."[21] At the beginning of the third century, Irenaeus of Lyon and two centuries later, Epiphanius of Cyprus wrote about the importance of Jerusalem respectively for the Ebionites and the Elkasaites. They reveal that these Byzantine-era Christian groups oriented their prayers toward Jerusalem and made pilgrimages to what they considered the holy city in the Holy Land.[22] This was in keeping with the Jewish community of the time, which preserved and continued the practice of reverence toward Jerusalem.

This evidence is conceded by Arab and Palestinian scholars, even though it runs contrary to the political position of the Palestinian Authority. For example, Sari Nusseibeh, president of Al-Quds University in Jerusalem, stated,

> If you [go] back a couple of hundred years, before the advent of
> the political form of Zionism, I think you will find that many
> Muslims would not have disputed the connection that Jews have
> toward [the Temple Mount]. The problem began arising with
> the advent of Zionism, when people started connecting a kind
> of feeling that Jews have toward the area with the political proj-
> ect of Zionism.[23]

In support of the scholarly view is the fact that during the early Islamic
period, Jerusalem was called *Bayt al-Maqdis*, an Arabic equivalent to the
Hebrew name for the Temple, *Bayt Ha-Miqdash* ("Holy House," "Sanctuary"). The Qur'anic historian al-Tabari, who chronicled the Muslim
conquest of Jerusalem, used this term when he recorded that when 'Umar
finished praying he went to the place where "the Romans buried the
Temple [*bayt al-maqdis*] at the time of the sons of Israel."[24] In the modern Muslim village of Nuva (near Hebron), the local mosque contains a
ninth-century Arabic inscription that mentions the *Sachrat Bayt al-Maqdis* ("Rock of the Holy Temple"). This accords with Islamic literature that
also calls the Dome of the Rock *Bayt al-Maqdis* ("Holy Temple").[25]

This view is upheld by historical sources. The Armenian historian and
pilgrim Sebeos, in AD 660, observed that the site of the ruined Temple
was the place the Jews revered and the Muslims usurped:

> I will relate a little more about the intentions of the rebellious
> Jews, who having earlier received help from the leaders of the
> children of Hagar, conceived a plan to rebuild the Temple of
> Solomon. Having discovered the place which is called the Holy
> of Holies, they then built on its foundations a place of prayer
> for themselves. However, the Ishmaelites, jealous of them, drove
> them from this place and called it their house of prayer.[26]

The Byzantine chronicler Theophanes the Confessor (d. 818), though
giving a Christian perspective of Caliph 'Umar's intentions when he came
into the newly conquered city, wrote, "'Umar donned the mask of hypoc-
risy. He wanted to see the Temple of the Jews that Solomon had built so he
could turn it into a place of worship for his infidels."[27] This location as the

site of the Temple was upheld by Islamic authorities into modern times. Beginning in the late 1920s the Muslim Supreme Council (Waqf) published a guide to the *Al-Haram Al-Sharif* that declared, "This site is one of the oldest in the world. Its sanctity dates from the earliest times. Its identity with the Temple of Solomon is beyond dispute."[28]

This view did not change until after Yasser Arafat stated, at the Camp David II peace negotiations, "I will not have it said of me that I acknowledged the existence the so-called Temple Mount." Today, this political view has become Islamic dogma and is one of the major impediments to achieving any level of dialogue in the negotiations over Jerusalem.

A Hope Based on God's Promises

The evidence of an ancient Jewish presence in Jerusalem, as revealed by historical documents (including the Bible) and archaeology, has been rejected by the Palestinian Authority and the majority of the Islamic world. However, for anyone to ignore the pre-Islamic history of the site only perpetuates the conflict over the city because this view excludes any basis for negotiations over one of the most controversial issues in the Middle East conflict.

Jews in Israel and around the world revere the Temple Mount as the holiest site in Judaism (Midrash *Tanhuma*, chapter 10), viewing it as the spiritual junction between heaven and Earth. Jews traditionally face the site of the Dome of the Rock when they pray because they believe that's where the Holy of Holies was located within the Temple. Even though Islam has dominated the site for 1,300 years, the Jewish people hope for a restoration of their land based on the promise of the biblical prophets, a promise that sets Jerusalem and the Temple Mount at the center of universal blessing (Isaiah 2:2-4). Until that restoration takes place, there will be conflict over the site of the Temple Mount and Jews will weep at the Western (or Wailing) Wall, especially on *Tisha B'Av*, the annual commemoration of the loss of the Temple.

On one occasion of *Tisha B'Av*, in the year 1799, when the French military leader (and later emperor) Napolean Bonaparte visited the port of Acre, he witnessed this traditional display of Jewish dedication to the Temple Mount. Seeing the Jewish community in mourning, he asked his officers about it. They replied, "It is for what happened 2,000 years ago when the Romans destroyed Jerusalem and their Temple." Napolean is said to have replied, "Any people that continues to mourn a building for 2,000 years will surely rebuild it someday!"

Religious Jews have experienced the *galut* ("exile") for two millennia, and believe the *geula* ("redemption") is coming. This will be the realization of the biblical prophet's promised restoration of Israel, inaugurated by the coming of the Messiah and crowned by the rebuilding of the Temple, which will serve as a means of establishing a permanent peace and mutual understanding between Jews and Gentiles.

Today there exists a revisionist history created in the wake of Israel's return to the Temple Mount in 1967 and the Palestinian nationalism that demands a capital in Jerusalem. This rewriting of the facts of history asserts there is no basis for a Jewish claim to Jerusalem or the Temple Mount. UNESCO, representing the view of the international community, has supported this claim. As a result, the Palestinian leadership opposes any claim of the Jewish state to Jerusalem. For the Palestinian authority, any concession on this point during the peace negotiations would be tantamount to sedition and punishable by death. For that reason, it is inconceivable that the Palestinians will ever compromise on their demand for total sovereignty over Jerusalem or retract their denial regarding the Jewish Temple. It remains for those of us who value facts to stand with the state of Israel in this great war of propaganda that is as pernicious and deadly as any weapon formed by man.

CHAPTER 6
READER RESPONSE

What Should We Think About the Temple Mount?

WHAT DO *YOU* THINK?

I agree with the author on

I disagree with the author because

What was news to me?

How does this change the way I think about the Temple Mount?

7

What Should We Think About Jewish and Arab Relations?

TIM M. SIGLER

The modern Middle East conflict is often framed as a struggle between Jews and Arabs. In recent decades, violence has escalated between these peoples, depicted famously by the wall separating the Jewish and Arab communities in Israel. Can relations ever be restored? And what hope is there today that points to such a future restoration?

After nearly 30 years of academic life that has permitted me to travel, study, and live in and around Israel and two of the surrounding countries, I wish I could say that I have found people to be of equal goodwill, increasing tolerance, desirous of improving conditions for all, proliferating a desire to put past hatreds and hurts behind them, and moving forward toward the formation of a peaceful future for themselves and their children after them. But this is not the case. I have intentionally sought out those who desire peace in the region, and occasionally I find them. But that is not the norm. One does not have to scour the pages of history or poke around online for long to find Islamists spewing "the blind hatred and ignorant prejudice of a fanatical populace."[1]

While a gentle cultural Islam that desires peaceful coexistence with non-Muslims exists, the purveyors who control cultures through media and education either promote religiously motivated violence directly or enable it through a helpless tolerance of fanatical elements within their societies. So for Jews (and for Arab Christians within the Muslim world, for that matter) relations are difficult, strained, and cautious. With the rise of Sunni Salafism and its goal of Islamizing the world under strict Sharia law, Christian Arabs are in danger and find themselves regularly targeted in Muslim-majority countries. They are often warned that "Saturday comes before Sunday"—a phrase that implies that after Islamists conquer the Jews, Christians will be next.

Palestinian Christians and Arab evangelical believers in the region often practice a self-censorship of their support for Israel or love for the Jewish people in order to avoid terrible repercussions in a culture where dissent can mean death. Thankfully, even in a culture of Islamic oppression, Arab evangelicals are thriving, and many are committed to a peaceful coexistence with Israel. Some Israeli Arab believers even serve in the Israeli Defense Forces. This chapter does not intend to impugn or overlook these quiet minorities, but to sympathize with their difficulty in the larger Arab world that chooses to define itself and its governments in terms of their commitment to Islam, which has given the Arab Christian communities a bad name that they do not deserve.

Forbidden Peace

Abdelsalam al-Majali, the Jordanian physician and politician who served twice as the nation's prime minister, defended the Hashemite kingdom's peace accord with Israel as follows:

> My mentality is a mentality of peace. I believe that peace is the
> best thing for our nation in its current…or rather, at the time of
> the peace process, as well as today. It is the best solution for us, as
> Arabs, and I still believe in it. As long as you do not have force of
> another kind, peace is your only option.[2]

He went on to clarify, "The Arabs do not have any power. If we ever have military power, will we let them keep Haifa? We'll take it. If tomorrow, we become stronger and can take Haifa by force."[3] Mind you, these are the words of Israel's closest friends in the region. Known enemies like

Hamas leader Yahya Sinwar are more straightforward when they speak about the goals of the terror organization's riots in Gaza: "We will tear down the border, and we will tear out their hearts from their bodies."[4]

These recent statements were made against the backdrop of a long history calling for the destruction of the state of Israel and for Arabs to liberate Palestine by driving the Jews into the sea.[5] Even in the very Westernized neighboring kingdom of Jordan, with which Israel enjoys a peace treaty, an American couple I know sent their son to an upscale modern Arab kindergarten in a nice neighborhood in Amman and were horrified by what took place during the year-end school celebration. Their son and his classmates walked out on stage in military fatigues, pointed toy machine guns at an effigy of an Israeli soldier, and together they sang about driving Jews "from the river to the sea."

The famous National Charter of the Palestine Liberation Organization (PLO) repeatedly calls for a similar destruction of Israel. Article 15 states, "The liberation of Palestine, from an Arab viewpoint, is a national duty and it attempts to repel the Zionist and imperialist aggression against the Arab homeland, and aims at the elimination of Zionism in Palestine."[6] Yasser Arafat assured President Clinton at the Oslo Accords that language in the PLO charter denying Israel's right to exist was now null and void. He said the charter would be changed to allow for peaceful coexistence with Israel. But despite ongoing requests from those promoting peace, the Palestine National Council (PNC) has never succeeded in ratifying these alterations with the required two-thirds majority vote. And calls for the elimination of Zionism and Israel continue to be commonplace.

Images of Yasser Arafat are emblazoned throughout the Palestinian territories as a symbol of nationalistic pride and continued resistance. During the first Intifada, he warned his followers, "Whoever thinks of stopping the uprising before it achieves its goals, I will give him ten bullets in the chest."[7] His historic calls for jihad against Israel should not be interpreted through the naïve Western lenses of political hyperbole, free speech, or the desire to liberate an oppressed people. He clarified his aims well: "We plan to eliminate the state of Israel and establish a purely Palestinian state. We will make life unbearable for Jews by psychological warfare and population explosion...We Palestinians will take over everything, including all of Jerusalem."[8]

Taking over everything should not be confused with a desire for self-determination, a fight for equality, or activism to promote human rights. The name chosen for the PLO is instructive. It is not the *Palestinian* Liberation Organization but the *Palestine* Liberation Organization, and it aims to recover all the land that was partitioned to form two separate homelands—one for Jews and one for Arabs. Israel is not recognized as having a legitimate right to exist, and maps from the Palestinian Authority and their sympathizers often show a single state of Palestine in the place of Israel.[9]

The United Nations Relief and Works Agency for Palestinian refugees in the Near East (UNRWA), which until recently was receiving $400 million a year from US taxpayers, supplies anti-Israel and anti-Semitic textbooks to Palestinian school children and promotes violence.[10] UNRWA schoolteachers and agency employees have been at the forefront of fomenting bad will by rejecting a future of tolerance, mutual respect, and peaceful coexistence—choosing rather to celebrate violence and glorify suicide bombers as martyrs. In 2007, then-senator Hillary Clinton said the following about UNRWA textbooks:

> These textbooks do not give Palestinian children an education; they give them an indoctrination. When we viewed this report in combination with other media that these children are exposed to, we see a larger picture that is disturbing. It is disturbing on a human level, it is disturbing to me as a mother, it is disturbing to me as a United States Senator, because it basically, profoundly poisons the minds of these children. Hate has no place in the curriculum of schools, and the glorification of violence has no place in the education of children.[11]

The Palestinian National Authority's news and information agency WAFA and their official daily paper *Al-Hayat Al-Jadida* released an official statement in July 2016 following a wave of Palestinian terror attacks in which 44 Israelis and others were murdered by 16 teenage Palestinian terrorists. On the day that these teenage terrorists should have been receiving the results from their high school matriculation exam, these news sources celebrated their deaths as follows:

> The families of the Martyrs and their relatives find themselves proud of the Martyrdom that their children achieved with the Creator...Sixteen [12-grade students] succeeded...for death as a Martyr is the path to excellence and greatness, and the path of those who know how to reach the great victory.[12]

Golda Meir, prime minister of Israel from 1969 to 1974, is often quoted as saying, "Peace will come when the Arabs will love their children more than they hate us." But the perceived injustice is so great that Palestinian media show parents promoting suicide bombers as heroes, weaponizing their children in the name of jihad, and sending them to summer camps to learn terror and martyrdom.[13] All this advocacy of violence is justified by the claim, "They took our land."

While other chapters of this book address the historical relationship of the Jewish people to the land of Israel and the charges of Israel being an illegal foreign occupier of native Palestinian lands, it is important to note here that the Jewish people acquired most of Israel's land through legal purchases made via the Jewish National Fund, through winning defensive wars, and through natural population growth requiring eminent domain where its government, like any other, expropriates private property for public use and pays the landowner a fair or better price for it. Often the so-called settlements are the results of urban sprawl as larger cities grow and expand to unpopulated areas. When land has been seized and there is proof of ownership, Israeli courts have ruled in favor of Palestinians even against the Israeli government.[14]

Rather than an Israeli genocidal land grab, the local Arab population was offered a state of their own in this land where there had never been an independently ruled state called Palestine. This offer was made three times before the establishment of the Jewish state (with the 1937 Peel Commission, the 1939 British White Paper, and the 1947 UN Partition Plan) and three times after the establishment of the state of Israel (under Yitzhak Rabin at the Oslo accords in the 1990s, under Ehud Barak at Camp David in 2000, and under Ehud Olmert in 2008). But Arab leaders rejected every one of these opportunities and promoted more violence instead of peace. Some Palestinian leaders spoke of peace to their Western counterparts in English but repeatedly assured their constituencies in Arabic that these concessions were merely part of "the plan of stages" that would eventually include reclaiming all of what is now Israel as Palestine.[15] They are not merely requesting an independent Palestinian state, self-determination, or human rights.

Rather, the oft-repeated goal is a world without Israel.[16]

Calls for peace or normalization of relations with Israel are difficult to find within Palestinian media. The Palestinian Broadcast Corporation (PBC) operates under President Abbas' office, and Al Aqsa TV is owned and operated by Hamas. Palestinians who would gladly live in peaceful coexistence with Israelis have learned to express their views discretely, and all are aware of the brutal executions carried out by Hamas against Palestinians who collaborate in any way with Israel.[17] Even seemingly innocent signs of a willingness to coexist are not permitted in the Islamic world. In 2017, the Miss Iraq contestant at the Miss Universe pageant, Sarah Idan, had to flee her home country after publicly befriending Miss Israel and posting a selfie on Instagram.[18]

Dennis Prager is correct when he states that the Middle East conflict "is probably the easiest conflict in the world to explain. It may be the hardest to solve, but it is the easiest to explain. In a nutshell, it's this: One side wants the other side dead."[19] Israeli prime minister Benjamin Netanyahu summarized it this way: "The truth is that if Israel were to put down its arms there would be no more Israel. If the Arabs were to put down their arms there would be no more war."[20] Yet many who believe they are helping alleviate the suffering of Palestinians end up promoting their version of justice by criticizing Israel. There is an enormous double standard when people evaluate the Israeli-Palestinian situation without reference to the fact that many Palestinian woes originate at the hands of their own leaders, who have enriched themselves on the backs of their own people.[21]

New York Times columnist Bret Stephens asks an important question: "Why is nothing expected of Palestinians, and everything forgiven, while everything is expected of Israelis, and nothing forgiven?"[22] Israel is not a utopian paradise, but it does have the structures and values that promote human rights (for example, freedom of speech, freedom of the press, freedom of religion, legal representation, due process, economic rights, separation of powers, etc.). All kinds of powerful people go to jail in Israel when they break the law: the politically connected, the wealthy, the famous, the religious, the secular, members of the Knesset, and members of the local school board. It's not the Wild West of the Middle East. Yes, there are always two sides to every story. But when one insists on *jihad* (struggle/fight) while the other asks for *shalom* (peace), it is very difficult to come to a middle ground.

Preludes of Peace

Divisions within Islamic factions, disillusionment with Islamic fundamentalism, and disciple-making among those who are drawn to the gospel is changing a world that was once shadowed under the veil and resistant to the gospel. Persecution has paved the path for peace.

Tom Doyle, in his book *Killing Christians*, reminds us of the pattern we have seen in the book of Acts and throughout church history:

> Oppressors over the centuries have never recognized that the persecution of Christians is always a failed initiative. It just doesn't work. To the contrary, killing believers routinely *accelerates* the spread of the gospel and the growth of the church…Jesus' message of love and reconciliation thrives in a climate where hostility, danger, and martyrdom are present.[23]

In recent decades we have seen war-torn Muslim countries with dictatorial strongman governments toppled by religious extremists who create even worse atrocities. Many Muslims are seeing the evils of their retaliatory systems and wanting out.[24] Increasing numbers of Muslims are testifying of coming to faith in Christ after having dreams and visions of Jesus, the Prince of Peace.[25]

David Garrison has documented how God is drawing Muslims from around the world to faith in Jesus the Messiah. His book *A Wind in the House of Islam* provides numerous case studies and statistical analyses showing the unprecedented response to the gospel in "nine geo-cultural clusters" or "Rooms within the House of Islam: (1) West Africa, (2) North Africa,

(3) East Africa, (4) The Arab World, (5) The Persian World, (6) Turkestan, (7) Western South Asia, (8) Eastern South Asia, and (9) Indo-Malaysia."[26] From each region, Garrison cites astonishing documented accounts of ongoing Muslim movements to Christ. The Muslim world is ripe for the gospel, and the harvest is being gathered. Violent Islam is causing many adherents to reconsider.

Iraqi Chaldean/Assyrian Christians have been targeted for killings, rape, torture, sexual violence, kidnapping, extortion, and much more. More than a million Christians have been killed or fled persecution in Iraq since 2003. ISIS forces gave their captives only three options: convert to Islam, pay a tax for being a Christian, or die. Mindy Belz tells the personal stories of the faithful in Iraq who suffered under the brutality of Islam but are also seeing the seeds of shalom sprout up in these places of persecution. Her book *They Say We Are Infidels: On the Run from ISIS with Persecuted Christians in the Middle East* documents personal accounts of enduring faith that are truly remarkable. The blood of these martyrs continues to be the seed of the church—the testimonies of those willing to sacrifice their lives for the truth of the gospel has led to the conversion of some of their Muslim torturers. In addition, believers in the West are beginning to see the need to extend political support for persecuted Christian refugees, prayer and hospitality toward refugee families, and hands-on help through their churches and aid organizations to show the love of Jesus to these refugees worldwide.

Even apart from the gospel, some Palestinians and Israeli Arabs are taking great risks to normalize relations with their Jewish neighbors. Many are simply tired of the status quo of perpetual conflict. Palestinian Muslim professor Mohammed Dajani brought his al-Quds University students to Auschwitz and taught them about Jewish suffering and the horrors of the Holocaust. As a result, he was removed from his academic position. There have been at least two assassination attempts on his life and one attempted abduction. But he persists as a Palestinian voice for cooperative coexistence.

Fellow Palestinian Nabil Basherat asks the question many Palestinians have asked quietly: "Why don't we, the Israeli side and the Palestinian side, try to live in peace for a while? Why not try two, three, four years of normalisation and of just living together? Fighting is always an option."[27] Thankfully, peaceful relations and sincere friendships between Jews and Arabs are possible even when negotiations over territorial rights are still forthcoming. Peace is possible because peace begins with people—brave people who will raise their children to love others and teach their communities the beauty of living in a world without hate. It is seldom admitted that despite the hatred promoted by the Palestinian Authority, this governing body regularly cooperates with Israel on matters of infrastructure, security, trade, economy, internet services, banking, and so on. But it is not permitted to celebrate these helpful initiatives.

Basherat was moved to adopt his peaceful views after both of his parents received medical care in Israeli hospitals on separate occasions. And the same is happening with others among Israel's war-torn neighbors to the northeast. It is now well known that medical help has been available for Syrians in Israeli hospitals. After reaching the limits of their medical technologies and treatments, Syrian doctors have attached notes with diagnoses and proposed treatments to the chests of their dying patients and had them smuggled to the Israeli border in the Golan Heights under cover of darkness. These dying patients are treated in Israeli hospitals without charge and secretly returned to the border. Hospitals throughout the Galilee are full of Syrians, but it is a quiet operation. They must return without being discovered lest they be punished for collaborating with the enemy, Israel.[28]

Israeli Jewish and Arab pastors have also been promoting peace by partnering together to help Syrian refugees at home and abroad. They visit the refugees in Israeli hospitals and they go abroad to meet refugees in Turkey and Greece, where Muslims feel more freedom to explore the gospel. Seeing Jewish and Arab believers in Jesus come to love their enemies, pray for them, and offer them help in their Messiah's name is a powerful witness that disorients the distrust and demonization they were taught in their homeland. It is hard to resist a peace that causes longtime enemies to embrace and turns cursing into blessing.

Judith Mendelsohn Rood, Professor of History and Middle Eastern Studies at Biola University, has studied the histories of these societies and cultures for decades, and her historical research provides a deep well of insight into the current political and spiritual realities. She suggests that the effects of ISIS and the Syrian civil war have resulted in the rise of an alliance between Israel and most of the Arab states against Iran. The genocide of Arab Christians by ISIS and the resulting spiritual awakening has dealt Arab nationalism and Muslim fundamentalism lethal blows. The flickering flame of the gospel has been growing brighter in Israel and the Muslim world. The growth of the messianic movement in Israel, as well as the emergence of the ancient Aramaic faith of the Maronite Arab allies of Israel (who fled Hezbollah's Lebanon to Israel), are signs of the reawakening of the ancient church. The old lies of Arab nationalism and Salafism are no longer believed; Hamas and the PLO are both epic failures. While the masses remain deceived, the Lord is turning untold numbers of Muslims toward Himself and His peace. We have reason to hope: The embers of the ancient faith can be reignited by the Holy Spirit. Are we ready to disciple the many new believers who have called on Jesus since 2011?[29]

Scripture reminds us that God loves Arabs, and so should we. God so loved the world that He gave His only Son to become people's Savior and Messiah. And we too should love our enemies. What is forbidden by men is commanded by God. Even if political peace is out of reach, personal peace through the Prince of Peace is not. And this personal peace found in Messiah Jesus is a prelude to the peace that will mark His benevolent rule and will shower His biblical shalom over all who worship Him.

Promised Peace

When Messiah returns, "there will be no end to the increase of His government or of peace" (Isaiah 9:7). Despite the fact Israelis and Palestinians are entrenched in their positions and there is a wall that separates them, Scripture holds out one hope for peace between the two sides—the covenant of peace God will make with Israel:

> I will make a covenant of peace with them; it will be an everlasting covenant with them. And I will place them and multiply them, and will set My sanctuary in their midst forever. My dwelling place also will be with them; and I will be their God, and they will be My people. And the nations will know that I

am the LORD who sanctifies Israel, when My sanctuary is in their midst forever (Ezekiel 37:26-28).

From this point forward, Israel will be in a perpetual state of peace, for this is "an everlasting covenant" that is described as lasting "forever" four times in the immediate context.

This biblical shalom refers to holistic well-being and implies reconciliation at all levels—politically, socially, emotionally, physically, and spiritually—between God and humanity as well as between formerly feuding parties.[30]

At Jesus' second coming, Israel will be restored to her Messiah. The people will look on Him "whom they have pierced; and they will mourn for Him" (Zechariah 12:10). "In that day a fountain will be opened for the house of David and for the inhabitants of Jerusalem, for sin and for impurity" to be cleansed (Zechariah 13:1). After the time of the great tribulation during which Israel as a nation will undergo a time of discipline and distress known as Jacob's trouble (Jeremiah 30:4-7), a period of writhing pain like that of childbirth (Isaiah 26:16-18), God will raise the Jewish people to participate in the great messianic banquet described in Isaiah 25:6-9. When He places Israel safely in the land He swore to them, *Israel will know* that He is the Lord (Ezekiel 37:11-14). And when He returns His Temple sanctuary to Jerusalem, *the nations will know* it as well (verse 28). At that point, the sovereignty of the Savior will be so undeniable as to unify all who see it in awe of Him. There will be no competing religious perspectives—instead, there will be a unified worship of Messiah: "The LORD will be king over all the earth; in that day the LORD will be the only one, and His name the only one" (Zechariah 14:9). Jews and Arabs and all the nations will recognize the One to whom all the Law and the Prophets point, Jesus the Messiah—the Prince of Peace through whom God will fulfill the covenant of peace mentioned above (Ezekiel 37:26).

What Should We Think About Jewish and Arab Relations?

What should we think of any relationship that is strained by a history of hatred and violence, cycles of death and revenge, preying on the weak, exploiting the poor? What should we think of any scenario in which cultural differences, racial tensions, and religious beliefs separate human beings who are created in the image of God?

We should think that the Prince of Peace is powerful enough to bring peace where it seems impossible (Isaiah 9:6). We should pray for the peace of Jerusalem and harmony for all its inhabitants (Psalm 122:6). Knowing God as the one who makes peace in the heavenly places (Job 25:2), we should pray that He will make peace for us today (Isaiah 26:12) and anticipate the time when He will be king over the whole earth (Zechariah 14:9).

While we wait, we should follow the Lord's divine example and seek the blessings He promises to all peacemakers (Matthew 5:9). We should also be biblically realistic about this peace. There will always be people who are enemies of peace, who profit from war, who refuse reconciliation. We should rather welcome every offer of kindness, every opportunity to be a light in the darkness, every opening to speak *shalom* and *salaam* (the Hebrew and Arabic words for *peace*). We should learn each other's greetings, languages, cultures, and histories—and appreciate one another as equally created in the image of God (Genesis 1:27; 9:6; 1 Corinthians 14:10-12). If possible, visit the Middle East for yourself. Many seminaries—like the one I teach at—are increasingly taking their students to the lands of the Bible and helping them gain firsthand knowledge of the struggles and hopes of the local believers while also learning the language, history, culture, and geography of the Scriptures.

The fact that the Bible warns us that the enemies of peace will increase in the last days and that perilous times will come (2 Timothy 3:1) does not diminish the hope for peace to follow these wars or the prayer for that day when nations will beat their swords into plowshares and no longer learn war (Isaiah 2:4). Because we know that these nations will one day cooperate under the command of Messiah Jesus and share a highway from Assyria to Egypt with Israel between them (Isaiah 19:23-25), we should also seek to build inroads of peace between our communities today.

Peace on the personal, congregational, and even community level is possible today even when we know that war is predicted for the future (Zechariah 14). True peace and loving friendships are available between Jews and Arabs even while we use discernment and reject the false messiahs who promise a false peace in order to wage a worse war (Matthew

24:3-5; 1 Thessalonians 5:3; Revelation 13). Jesus-believing Jews and Arabs have already had the enmity that existed between them remedied (Ephesians 2:15), and we can choose with God's divine enablement to extend that peace toward each other and love our neighbors (Leviticus 19:18; Matthew 22:39).

Resist the enemy (1 Peter 5:8-9)—the enemy of your soul, who comes to steal, kill, and destroy (John 10:10), and who forbids peace with Israel because he hates her even more than the most misguided *mujahideen* (jihadists). Satan knows that no amount of compensation and reparations paid by Israel will ever make Palestinians live in a harmonious society of mutual respect and goodwill under a bilaterally negotiated two-state solution.

By following their Savior's words and example to "love your enemies" (Matthew 5:44), Palestinian Christians can be a light to those trapped under the veil of Islam. Scripture calls for a new Palestinian—a Palestinian of power who defines himself biblically and who loves peace and will not allow the hatred of the past to define how he or she should respond to the challenges to peace in the present or the future. By following this same Savior, messianic Jewish Israelis demonstrate the hope (*hatikvah*) of Messiah to unbelieving Israelis who are still wondering whether peace will ever come. Spiritually renewed Israelis and Palestinians can lead the way for their fellow citizens to seek new paths of peace and goodwill by loving those who would otherwise be their enemies. In God's promises and in God's people, there is hope.

CHAPTER 7
READER RESPONSE

What Should We Think About Relations Between Jews and Arabs?

WHAT DO *YOU* THINK?

I agree with the author on

I disagree with the author because

What was news to me?

How does this change the way I think about relations between Jews and Arabs?

8

What Should We Think About Israel's "Occupation"?

PAUL WILKINSON

Much of the world believes that Israel has occupied land that was formerly Palestinian and that it continues the occupation by confiscating family farmland and destroying family homes. What are the facts of "occupation" and claims of modern political and ethnic oppression?

D uring the long, dark night of the Holocaust, the eminent German-born Jewish lawyer Ernst Frankenstein pleaded with humanity "to end the tragedy of the Jewish people."[1] His book, *Justice for My People: The Jewish Case* (1943), was "a cry from the heart of a very quiet man,"[2] a cry that evoked the age-old longing of his people for their homeland:

> For the Jews, Palestine is not just a land. It is the only land on earth which really matters. Given to them by divine promise, returned to them after the Babylonian captivity, liberated under the great Maccabean leaders, mourned for 18 centuries, goal of all their dreams and hopes, of prayers and songs, it cannot be separated from the life of the Jewish people. The people may exist in other countries, as it had to exist through the long centuries of dispersion. But it will live only in Palestine.[3]

Playing Games with Israel

In 2013, at the annual Greenbelt Festival in England, the well-established Christian humanitarian organization known as Embrace the Middle East launched its giant interactive floor game *Occupation—a Game of Life*. "Roll the dice, pass through a checkpoint, and see what it's like to live under Israeli occupation" was the invitation given to all ages. Greenbelt is renowned for its anti-Israel prejudice. According to the game's creators,

> There was no reference to the Jewish people or even to the Jewish state of Israel, which of course is the occupying power. We were simply bringing home to Greenbelt festival-goers the daily injustices and humiliations of occupation. There was nothing remotely anti-Semitic about the game.[4]

The same kind of reasoning and denial characterizes the World Council of Churches (WCC), the largest ecumenical body within Christendom. In 2002, it launched its campaign "End the Illegal Occupation of Palestine: Support a Just Peace in the Middle East" to mobilize members and coordinate a Christian response to the Israeli-Palestinian issue. In their endeavor to help end the alleged occupation, the WCC, along with mainstream Protestant denominations such as the United Methodist Church and the Presbyterian Church (USA), has since endorsed the global Boycott, Divestment, and Sanctions (BDS) movement, calling for a boycott of goods produced "in the illegal Israeli settlements in the occupied territories."[5] Evangelicals, usually recognized as Israel's friends, are spearheading the ecclesiastical front, aligning themselves with Israel's sworn enemies and broadcasting their own indictments against Israel via books, blogs, websites, interviews, petitions, conference papers, social media postings, campaign manifestos, NGOs, and denominational resolutions.[6] By exploiting words like *occupation, genocide, ethnic cleansing, land theft, war crimes,* and *apartheid,* they have singled out Israel for condemnation while remaining strangely silent about countries such as China, North Korea, Russia, Syria, Iran, Saudi Arabia, and Pakistan.

A case in point is British journalist Ben White, a frequent contributor to conferences that target Israel. In his latest book, *Cracks in the Wall: Beyond Apartheid in Palestine/Israel* (2018), White refers to what he calls

"Israel and the occupied Palestinian territory," describing it as "an area which, over the last five decades, has been incrementally but undeniably fashioned into a single, apartheid regime."[7] White is an advocate of BDS and other campaigns, such as Israeli Apartheid Week. In January 2014, then-Canadian prime minister Stephen Harper publicly denounced BDS and the apartheid allegation as "sickening," "outright malice," "the mutation of the old disease of anti-Semitism," and an attempt "to make the old bigotry acceptable to a new generation."[8]

In this chapter, we will focus on the charge of *occupation*. In the West, this word is generally applied to Israel's capture of the "West Bank"[9] and Gaza Strip during the Six-Day War of June 1967. However, as Israeli academic Efraim Karsh points out, the Arab world has consistently equated *occupation* with Israel's very existence. In 2001, during the infamous World Conference Against Racism held in Durban—a conference that demonized Israel—PLO official Hanan Ashrawi spoke about the flight of hundreds of thousands of Palestinians from their homes when the modern state of Israel was established: "In 1948, we became subject to a grave historical injustice...Those who remained were subjected to the systematic oppression and brutality of an inhuman occupation that robbed them of all their rights and liberties."[10]

San Remo, the Mandate, and International Law

In his seminal work on Jewish rights to the land, Jerusalem-based attorney Howard Grief (1940–2013) cited April 24, 1920 as the day when the Allied Supreme Council (Britain, France, Italy, and Japan) "converted"[11] the Balfour Declaration into "a binding act of international law."[12] The occasion was their conference at the Castello Devachan in San Remo, Italy.

The Balfour Declaration was a policy statement issued by the British government on November 2, 1917, during David Lloyd George's premiership; Arthur Balfour was the secretary of state for foreign affairs. The government committed itself to facilitating, in Palestine, the establishment of a national home for the Jewish people. The declaration was publicly endorsed by Britain's allies—notably the United States, France, and Italy. It is an inconvenient fact of history for Israel's implacable enemies that it was also endorsed by Emir Feisal bin Hussein, son of Hussein bin Ali, the sharif of Mecca and king of the Hedjaz (part of present-day Saudi Arabia).

In February 1919, during the Paris Peace Conference that settled terms of peace following World War I, Feisal led an Arab delegation that included British Colonel Thomas E. Lawrence ("Lawrence of Arabia"). When the delegation presented Arab territorial claims in relation to the defeated and dismembered Ottoman Empire, Palestine was *not* included![13] On the contrary, in a letter to Felix Frankfurter of the Zionist delegation dated March 3, 1919, Feisal expressed support for a Jewish national home in Palestine:

> We Arabs, especially the educated among us, look with the deepest sympathy on the Zionist movement. Our deputation here in Paris is fully acquainted with the proposals submitted yesterday by the Zionist Organization to the Peace Conference, and we regard them as moderate and proper. We will do our best, in so far as we are concerned, to help them through: we will wish the Jews a most hearty welcome home.[14]

Sadly, the Palestinian Arabs did not comply. Even so, at San Remo, the Allied Supreme Council finished the work they had started in Paris, allocating mandates to Britain for the administration of Palestine and Mesopotamia (Iraq), and mandates to France for Syria and Lebanon.

The wording of the preamble to the Palestine Mandate stated that Britain was to be held "responsible for putting into effect the declaration originally made on November 2nd, 1917,"[15] thus granting *political* rights to the Jews while safeguarding the *civil* and *religious* rights of Palestine's other inhabitants. The council further declared that "recognition has thereby been given to *the historical connection of the Jewish people with Palestine* and to the grounds for *reconstituting their national home* in that country."[16] No recognition was given to any historical *Arab* connection with Palestine; in fact, no special provisions were made for the Arabs *as a people*, even though they constituted the majority.

Furthermore, the political rights given to the Jews were not restricted to those inhabiting Palestine at the time; Jews worldwide were afforded the liberty of immigration. But the most remarkable aspect of the preamble was the phrase "reconstituting their national home"—wording almost identical to that which had been included in an early draft of the Balfour Declaration.[17] The council's intent was clear: They were not envisioning the creation of something new, but the restoration of what had once been! Chaim Weizmann, who led the Zionist delegation in Paris and was present at San Remo, described the development as "the most momentous political event in the whole history of our movement, and…in the whole history of our people since the Exile."[18]

Bible Maps and Boundaries

During the San Remo conference, David Lloyd George proposed that the boundaries of the Jewish national home should be based on the biblical formula "from Dan to Beersheba."[19] He submitted a map taken from George Adam Smith's *Atlas of the Historical Geography of the Holy Land* (1915, plate no. 34), which illustrated the boundaries of the land as they had been in the days of David and Solomon. The proposal was agreed to in principle by the council, having been approved by France during the conference at London two months earlier, and was ratified in December that year by the Franco-British Convention, which formally defined the boundaries between the mandated territories. The Palestine Mandate finally came into effect on September 29, 1923. On December 3, 1924, the Anglo-American Convention was signed in London, in which the United States—a nonmember of the Allied Supreme Council[20]—officially approved the mandate.

According to the mandate, the Arabs received "the lion's share" of the liberated Ottoman territories, "equal to twice the area of the USA."[21] The Jews, on the other hand, *never received* what was promised! Owing to volatile developments in Syria in 1921, the League of Nations granted Britain consent in September 1922 to exclude territory east of the Jordan River from mandated Palestine and create instead the new *Arab* emirate of Transjordan under the administration of Abdullah bin Hussein, the brother of Feisal. Transjordan comprised 77 percent of the territory originally allocated for the Jewish national home. What was left for the Jews was further diminished by Partition Resolution 181 (II), which was passed by the UN General Assembly on November 29, 1947—and even that was rejected by the Arabs, who then declared war on the Jews of Palestine.

Thus *any* protest by the Arab world against the Balfour Declaration and the Palestine Mandate is not only inconsistent and illogical, but also "an act of supreme ingratitude to their benefactors who suffered huge human and material losses"[22] during the war. This sentiment was echoed by the independent Palestine Royal Commission Report of 1937,[23] which declared that "in so far as the Balfour Declaration helped to bring about the Allies' victory, it helped to bring about the emancipation of all the Arab countries from Turkish rule."[24] According to Victor Cavendish, Winston Churchill's successor as British secretary of state for the colonies, "The Arabs as a whole…acquired a freedom undreamed of before the war."[25]

A Sacred Trust

Jacques Gauthier, an international human rights lawyer who has served as legal counsel to the Canadian, French, Spanish, and Mexican governments, insists that the question of sovereignty over Palestine was settled at San Remo once and for all.[26] The resolution reached by the Allies was in full compliance with Article 22 of the Covenant of the League of Nations, which had been signed at the Paris Peace Conference in June 1919. This article specified that by allocating mandates, the league was binding itself to a "sacred trust"[27] that would not be affected by the league's dissolution in 1946 or by Britain's relinquishing of the mandate in 1948. Therefore, when Egypt occupied Gaza, and Jordan occupied (and later annexed) Judea and Samaria during the 1948 War of Independence, they acquired no legal title or UN recognition of sovereignty over these territories.

Two further principles of international law come into play here: namely those of "acquired rights" and "estoppel." The principle of acquired rights, as codified by the Vienna Convention on the Law of Treaties (May 23, 1969), guarantees that all rights previously vested by treaty in any state are secured. The principle of estoppel then prevents these rights from being rescinded by nations that were originally involved in such treaties.[28] As Howard Grief clarified in his monumental work,

> Once international law in the form of the San Remo Resolution recognized that *de jure* [legally sanctioned] sovereignty over all regions of historical Palestine and the Land of Israel had been vested in the Jewish People, neither the Supreme Council of the Principal Allied Powers nor the Council of the League of Nations nor its successor, the United Nations, could thereafter revoke or alter Jewish sovereignty by a new decision. *Legal ownership or*

title to Palestine had been permanently transferred to the Jewish People...In the case of the League of Nations, it never had any right in its Covenant to deprive the Jewish People of its sovereignty over any part of Palestine...Nor does the United Nations possess this right in its Charter. If either of these bodies really had such a right in regard to Palestine and the Land of Israel, the sovereignty of every state in the world over its own territory would be put in jeopardy...The importance of the San Remo Resolution on Palestine cannot be overestimated...It is no less than the foundation document of the State of Israel.[29]

When we apply all this to the Six-Day War of 1967, we can conclude that Israel did not *illegally occupy* any territory. Instead, territories already belonging to the Jews by acquired right were *reoccupied* and *recovered* as part of their national home. From the standpoint of international law, then, it does not matter what "Green Line"[30] was drawn in 1949, what resolutions have been issued by the UN, or what politicians may pontificate from their Parliamentary podiums—the matter was settled on the Italian Riviera in April 1920. From a biblical standpoint, however, the matter had been settled long before!

The Divine Mandate

Prior to the Israelites' crossing of the Jordan into the Promised Land, God told Moses, "Send out for yourself men so that they may spy out the land of Canaan, which I am going to give to the sons of Israel" (Numbers 13:2). The land was thus given before it was taken, and given by one who had the supreme right to grant it. When the spies returned from their 40-day reconnaissance, Caleb declared, "We should by all means go up and take possession of it, for we will surely overcome it" (verse 30). Caleb's confidence rested not in the strength of Israel's armies but in the power and promise of Israel's God. Although Canaan was already occupied territory, the divine command was explicit:

> See, I have placed the land before you; go in and possess the land which the LORD swore to give to your fathers, to Abraham, to Isaac, and to Jacob, to them and their descendants after them (Deuteronomy 1:8; cf. 6:18; 8:1; 26:1).

Scripture tells us that God "made from one man every nation of mankind to live on all the face of the earth, having determined their appointed times and the boundaries of their habitation" (Acts 17:26). As God declared through the prophet Jeremiah, "I give it [the earth] to whomever it seems right to me" (Jeremiah 27:5-6 ESV; cf. Psalm 24:1). Of the land of Canaan, the Lord made a unique and specific pronouncement: "the land is mine" (Leviticus 25:23; cf. 2 Chronicles 7:20; Jeremiah 2:7; Ezekiel 38:16; Joel 3:2). In the book of Genesis, we learn that God established an everlasting covenant with Abraham and his descendants, and on the basis of that covenant determined where they were to settle: "I will give to you and to your offspring after you the land of your sojournings, all the land of Canaan, for an everlasting possession" (Genesis 17:7-8 ESV). In Deuteronomy we are further told that the Lord gave the land to the Israelites by dispossessing the Canaanites—this was God's initiative, not Israel's:

> When the LORD your God brings you into the land that you are entering to take possession of it, and clears away many nations before you…and when the LORD your God gives them over to you, and you defeat them, then you must devote them to complete destruction…The LORD your God himself will go over before you. He will destroy these nations before you, so that you shall dispossess them (Deuteronomy 7:1-2; 31:3 ESV).

Divine responsibility for Canaan's dispossession was hailed by the psalmist: "You with your own hand drove out the nations, but them you planted; you afflicted the peoples, but them you set free" (Psalm 44:2 ESV). In his devotional commentary on this psalm, Charles Spurgeon offered this insight: "Canaan was not conquered without the armies of Israel, but equally true is it that it was not conquered by them; the Lord was the conqueror, and the people were but instruments in his hands."[31] Furthermore, when the Israelites were themselves dispossessed through the agency of the Babylonians, the Lord was emphatic in assuring His exiled people that they would one day return:

> I will bring them out from the peoples and gather them from the countries [not just Babylon!], and will bring them into *their own*

land...Surely I have spoken in my hot jealousy against the rest of the nations and against all Edom, who *gave my land to themselves* as a possession...But you, O mountains of Israel, shall shoot forth your branches and yield your fruit to my people Israel, for they will soon *come home*...And *they shall possess you*, and you shall be *their inheritance*...I will take you from the nations and gather you from all the countries and bring you into *your own land*...You shall dwell *in the land that I gave* to your fathers...I will bring you *home* into *the land of Israel*...I will place you in *your own land*...I will take the people of Israel from the nations among which they have gone, and will gather them from all around, and bring them to *their own land*...They shall dwell *in the land that I gave* to my servant Jacob, where your fathers lived. They and their children and their children's children *shall dwell there forever*...I will leave none of them remaining among the nations [not just Babylon!] anymore (Ezekiel 34:13; 36:5,8,12,24; 37:12,14,21,25; 39:28 ESV).

Thus before there was international law there was God's law; and before there was a League of Nations mandate for Palestine, there was a mandate from God, which has never been rescinded and never can be rescinded. As the apostle Paul summed up, "I tell you that Christ became a servant to the circumcised to show God's truthfulness, in order to *confirm the promises* given to the patriarchs, and in order that the Gentiles might glorify God for his mercy" (Romans 15:8-9 ESV).

A Return and Not an Occupation

Israel is charged with many crimes by the Arabs, the United Nations, and a burgeoning movement within the church that imposes on the Bible a theological system that reinterprets and redefines Israel's land promises.[32] This chapter has focused on the charge of occupation and closes with an excerpt from a remarkable interview that was broadcast on Kuwaiti television in November 2017—an interview that ignited a firestorm of protest throughout the Arab world. To the amazement of his host and fellow studio guest, Kuwaiti writer Abdullah Al-Hadlaq declared Israel to be a legitimate state and quoted the Qur'an in support of his statement! The following excerpt is from a transcript provided by the Middle East Media Research Institute (MEMRI):

> Israel is an independent sovereign state. It exists, and it has a seat at the United Nations, and most peace-loving and democratic countries recognize it...Israel is a state and not a terror organization...It received its legitimacy from the United Nations...My colleague called Israel "a plundering entity," but this may be refuted both in terms of religion and politics...From the religious perspective, Quranic verse 5:21 proves that the Israelites have the right to the Holy Land. Allah says: "When Moses said to his people...Oh my people, enter the Holy Land which Allah has assigned to you." So Allah assigned that land to them, and they did not plunder it. The plundering entity is whoever was there before the arrival of the Israelites...The fact that I am an Arab should by no means prevent me from recognizing Israel. I recognize Israel as a state and as a fact of reality, without denying my Arab identity and affiliation...*There is no occupation. There is a people returning to its promised land*...Are you aware that the history of the Israelites is ancient, predating Islam? Therefore, we Muslims must acknowledge that the Israelites have a right to that land, and that they have not plundered it...When the State of Israel was established in 1948, there was no state called "Palestine." It didn't exist. There were various communities living in Arab countries. They were called "Canaanites," "Amalekites," or a whole host of other names. The Quranic verse even says: "in it are a people of great strength." Some people called them "Jabbareen." Therefore, there was no state called "Palestine." I insist on this...The Persian regime [Iran] boasts that it has occupied four Arab capitals, and that it will soon occupy the fifth. Has Israel ever said such a thing? Has it boasted about occupying anything? No, because it never occupied anything. Israel came to its own land.[33]

Israel's presence in the Holy Land, then, is a *return* and not an *occupation*. This is what the historical and biblical facts tell us. Are we willing to listen?

CHAPTER 8
READER RESPONSE

What Should We Think About Israel's "Occupation"?

WHAT DO *YOU* THINK?

I agree with the author on

I disagree with the author because

What was news to me?

How does this change the way I think about Israel's presence in the Holy Land?

What Should We Think About the Plight of the Palestinians?

JUSTIN KRON

The Palestinian people view their situation as oppression by an occupying force (Israel). There are widespread claims of suffering in the Palestinian territories, and publication of much of this plight has brought a sympathetic groundswell of response from the Christian and Islamic world. What are the facts behind the cause and continuation of the Palestinian plight?

I must begin my chapter with a confession. When I first started leading tours to the Holy Land for Christian young adults in the 1990s, I did not have much interest in or concern for the Arabs who lived there, particularly those who identified as Palestinians. It's not that I wasn't aware of their presence; rather, my focus was on the remarkable return of the Jewish people to their historic homeland and the fulfillment of God's redemptive promises to them. The Arabs did not play a significant role in that plan—or so I thought.

But I am at a different place today, which I will explain in a moment. I am now very aware and sensitive to the nearly four million Palestinians who live in the "disputed" or "occupied" territories (depending on who you ask)—more commonly known as the West Bank (controlled primarily by Fatah) and Gaza (controlled primarily by Hamas). These Arabs, who exclusively identify as Palestinians, live under the governance of the Palestinian Authority (PA), as well as under the watchful eye of the Israelis, who maintain a strong security presence.

In addition to the Arabs who live in the territories, nearly 1.7 million additional people, or approximately 20 percent of Israel's population, refer to themselves as Israeli Arabs, Israeli Palestinians, or the Palestinians of 1948. Many of the Arabs who live in the Holy Land can trace their lineage back multiple generations. Some of them migrated from surrounding regions in the early 1900s, when, at the same time, waves of Jews from Europe and the Middle East were fulfilling their longing to return to their ancestral homeland. Approximately 90 percent of these Arabs are Muslim. Most of the others identify as Christian. Regardless of their religious identities, they all have a strong emotional connection to this land—one that is comparable to that of the Jewish people.

My interest—and I would even say love—for the Arabs of this region was stirred to action in 2011 when I heard someone at my church speak about his own journey into learning about the challenges and complexities of the Israeli-Palestinian conflict. He said, "If your theology doesn't lead you to love your neighbors and your enemies, then something is wrong with your theology." He encouraged me to consider that God is not for one side over the other; rather, He is pro-people and pro-peace, pro-Israeli and pro-Palestinian.

I resonated with this, especially because I had been taught that all people matter to God, and therefore they should matter to us.

Learning the Palestinian Narrative

This speaker also shared about his experience on a trip to the Holy Land with a Christian organization—a trip that was designed to help evangelical leaders engage with the challenges and struggles of both Israelis and Palestinians so that we could learn how to be better advocates for peace between them. A couple years later, I had the opportunity to participate in one of these trips.

We met with a sheik from the Al-Aqsa Mosque, a retired Israeli general, Israeli and Palestinian parents whose children had been killed in crossfire, Jewish settlers who live in the West Bank (referred to by most Jews living there by its biblical designations, Judea and Samaria), Palestinian Christians, pastors, people who live in UNRWA[1] refugee camps, human rights activists, and recognized experts on challenges related to Jerusalem, Jewish settlements, refugees, borders, and security.

They all had stories to tell—some that resonated with me and others that didn't. The sheik we met with told us how significant Jerusalem was to the Muslims and explained their frustrations with not having unhindered access to the Dome of the Rock and the Al-Aqsa Mosque. He also told us that Palestinians trace their lineage back to the Canaanites and Philistines, and that the Jews were present in the land for a total of about a couple hundred years here or there. (I wanted to challenge the sheik on his revisionist history, but the trip organizers instructed us to just sit and listen cordially.)

Many of the Palestinians we met with told us they did not have regular access to running water, whereas Israelis—particularly those living in government-subsidized settlements in the West Bank—always did. One Palestinian who gave us a walking tour of the Old City of Jerusalem informed us there was no evidence a Jewish Temple had been present in Jerusalem. I politely challenged him on that assertion. He also referred to Jews living in Jerusalem as settlers. His inference was that the Jewish people were outsiders who were displacing the rightful inhabitants, the Palestinians. I have since come to learn that most Palestinians, when they refer to "settlers" and speak of "ending the occupation," they are talking about all Jews in all of Israel, not just those who live in the West Bank.

We also heard about the challenges of checkpoints and restricted movement, and how the security barrier—which most Palestinians call the apartheid wall (97 percent of which is a fence)—has made their lives incredibly difficult. I appreciated that a rabbi with whom we ate Shabbat dinner called the barrier "a necessary evil"—evil because of the hardships it brings for Palestinians. Necessary because it has significantly thwarted suicide attacks against Israeli civilians.

Another Palestinian Christian we met shared about how her family's olive groves had been cut down by the Israeli government and that the family members had been harassed on numerous occasions by Jewish settlers while the Israel Defense Forces (IDF) looked the other way. We heard about how they often felt humiliated and powerless and were misunderstood by the outside world, particularly evangelicals, who seem to care only about the Jews and little, if at all, about Palestinian believers (a point that I could not deny based on my own experience).

One Lutheran pastor whom we met in Bethlehem told us he felt that Christian Zionism—the belief that the reestablishment of Israel is the fulfillment of biblical prophecy—was the "software" that was blindly leading Christians to support the "hardware" of the Israeli occupation and the oppression of the Palestinian people. He also claimed that Palestinian Christians had lived in Palestine since the time of Jesus and that his great-great-great…grandmother may have babysat Jesus. The inference was that Jesus was a Palestinian who lived in a country called Palestine, despite the biblical narrative to the contrary.

The prevailing narrative that emerged from the Palestinians we met with could be summarized as follows:

> Relations between Arabs and Jews in Palestine prior to the early 1900s were pleasant. But then the Jews started emigrating from Europe and stealing our land. This followed with the UN giving away more than half of our land to the Jews, which led to the Naqba (Catastrophe) in 1948, when we were forcibly displaced from our homes and villages, leaving 800,000 of our people as refugees. Since then we have been subject to even further aggression and humiliation under the Israeli occupation.

Palestinian Christians also said that the Christian population was being decimated due to the harsh conditions of the Israeli occupation. However, factual studies reveal the Christian community in the territories has actually grown since 1967,[2] as well as within Israel itself, which can be evidenced by the growing number of Jewish Israelis who have embraced Jesus as their Messiah.[3] I could not help but notice that many of the stories we heard lacked key facts and the historical or situational contexts in which they occurred.

Digging Deeper into the Reasons for Palestinian Suffering

I returned from this trip very unsettled and agitated by a lot of what I heard—and especially by what I didn't hear. This provoked me to dig deeper into pursuing the truth and to what I believe is a more holistic perspective on what is going on within the Palestinian community and the reasons for their suffering. Since that trip I have taken several more of my own, and I have met and spoken with Palestinians who have shared a very different narrative with me than what is typically told, yet they had to do this discreetly and anonymously. Why? Because it can be a serious risk for them to say anything that does not support the popular narrative that Israel does not have the right to exist as a sovereign Jewish state. Those who live under the PA do not have free speech protections.

Oppression of Civil Rights

This danger was made very clear to me in 2014 during the height of Israel's military operation in Gaza, known as Operation Protective Edge, when I had the pleasure of speaking with a Palestinian Christian business owner in Bethlehem. I asked him about his take on the conflict. Being careful to make sure that no one was within earshot of our conversation, he informed me that he was not supportive of the actions that the Palestinian leaders had taken to provoke the conflict. I asked him what would happen if he spoke out against the policies and actions of the PA, and without hesitation (while making a horizontal slash across his neck with his hand) he said, "I'd be finished."

I wanted to make sure he wasn't just referring to his business being shut down, so I asked for clarification: "What do you mean by 'finished'?" With a stern look and a finger pointed to his head, he replied, "Finished as in a-bullet-in the-head finished." He added, "I just keep to myself, don't talk about politics with anyone, and try to live and let live."

I inquired further, wanting to know more about living under occupation in a society where he couldn't publicly express his thoughts without fear of retribution. I did not expect to hear what he said next. "If I had to choose between living under Israeli occupation or a sovereign Palestinian state—which would almost certainly become just as radical as Gaza or the Islamic State in Iraq—I would choose occupation." He continued, "The only reason we Christians aren't facing more persecution here [in the Palestinian territories] is because Israel is our buffer. Without Israel, there would be even fewer of us left." Aware that there were other Christians in his community who held a very different perspective than his, I asked him about the ones who say that the root of the conflict is the Israeli occupation. He made it clear that those Christians aren't telling the whole story about what it is like to live in a Muslim-dominated society where they must learn how to survive as a minority.

Another Palestinian Christian I met in a cafe located near the Church of the Nativity told me about how his wife would often get heckled by Palestinian men because she did not wear a hijab head covering. While I have been informed that relations between Muslims and Christians living under the PA are generally serene, I have been told by Christians living there that it is predicated upon maintaining the status quo that the right of Israel to exist—from the river to the sea—must be rejected. To help me understand what happens to Palestinians who (quite literally) give ground to Israel, another Palestinian Christian business owner told me about his father's friend who was shot in the face and later died of his wounds. He had been accused of selling land to a Jew, a "crime" long considered punishable by death according to the PA.[4]

This policy was reaffirmed in April 2018 by Sheikh Mohammed Hussein, who decreed in a fatwa,[5] "Palestine, which includes Jerusalem, is waqf (Islamic trust) land, and it is religiously forbidden to give it up or facilitate the transfer of its ownership to the enemy." Even mild criticism of the PA can land you in prison, which was the result for Mamdouh Hamamreh, a journalist for the al-Quds TV channel in Bethlehem. He was arrested and sentenced in March 2013 to a year in prison for a picture and comment on his Facebook page that was deemed to be offensive to PA president Mahmoud Abbas.[6] Far more disturbing was what happened in August 2014 when Hamas soldiers executed 18 people, including 2 women, in broad daylight for allegedly collaborating with Israel.[7] One report revealed that there were men and boys "cheering and clamoring" for a good spot to watch the executions.[8]

Resist Israel, No Matter the Cost

When the question arises as to the cause of Palestinian suffering, it appears that much of it is the result of their rejecting the right of Israel to exist no matter what the cost, even the well-being of their own people.

This is the conclusion of Professor Haim Gvirtzman, a member of the Israel Water Authority Council and a longtime advisor of the Israel-PA Joint Water Committee. In a report that addresses the water shortages experienced in the territories—shortages that Israel has been blamed for— he explains:

> Water shortages in the Palestinian Authority are the result of Palestinian policies that deliberately waste water and destroy the regional water ecology. The Palestinians refuse to develop their own significant underground water resources, build a seawater desalination plant, fix massive leakage from their municipal water pipes, build sewage treatment plants, irrigate land with treated sewage effluents or modern water-saving devices, or bill their own citizens for consumer water usage, leading to enormous waste…In short, the Palestinian Authority is using water as a weapon against the State of Israel. It is not interested in practical solutions to solve the Palestinian people's water shortages, but rather perpetuation of the shortages and the besmirching of Israel.[9]

Islamic Fundamentalism

Much of the antagonism directed at Israel is fueled by Islamic fundamentalist ideology and the anger that is stirred by religious and political leaders. This was made clear to me during a startling conversation I had with a self-described "non-religious Muslim" in Nablus,[10] a city that hailed more suicide bombers during the second Intifada than any other city in the West Bank. I was with a film crew for a documentary I was producing, *Hope in the Holy Land*, when a man approached me and asked what we were making a film about.

"The Israeli-Palestinian conflict," I said.

"What about the conflict?" he asked.

"Well…we want to help people get below the surface of what they see and read in the media," I replied

"That's good," he said. "But it goes much deeper than you think— much deeper."

"How so?" I asked.

He seemed a little hesitant to tell me, but obliged my curiosity. "Everyone knows that the Jews are coming here for their final destruction. I am not sad about getting all the Jews from all [over] the world here—because it's the start of the end of them. Honestly, it will be the end of them. It will be the end of them and the end of the world."

I recalled that something similar had been said in 2002 by Hassan Nasrallah, the Hezbollah leader in Lebanon:

> Among the signs…and signals which guide us in the Islamic prophecies…is that…the Jews will gather from all parts of the world into occupied Palestine…in order…that Allah the Glorified and Most High wants to save you from having to go to the ends of the world, for they…have gathered in one place—and there the final and decisive battle will take place.[11]

Wanting to know more of what this man would add to his end-times apocalyptic scenario, I probed.

"How does it end?"

"It's in our Holy Quran. In the end of the world—be sure about it—when all of the Jews come here in this land."

He then pointed to a tree. "You see this tree? This tree—look at it. When a Jewish person is hiding beside it, this tree will talk to me. It will tell me, 'My Muslim brother, there is a Jewish person behind me, come and finish him.' That is what it says in our religion, in our Holy Quran, what said our Prophet Mohammed—he told us that. Every tree, every rock, will talk to us. What our God says about it will happen…everyone knows this."

"Everyone?" I inquired.

No doubt every member of Hamas knows—and believes—this. Their original charter quotes this hadith[12] of Muhammad:

> The Day of Judgment will not come until Muslims fight the Jews, when the Jew will hide behind stones and trees. The stones and trees will say, "O Muslim, O servant of God, there is a Jew behind me, come and kill him."[13]

The conversation I had with this nonreligious Muslim reminded me of this warning from the apostle Paul: "We do not wrestle against flesh and blood, but against the rulers, against the authorities, against the cosmic powers over this present darkness, against the spiritual forces of evil in the heavenly places" (Ephesians 6:12 ESV).

Anti-Semitism

Coupled with the strong influence of Islamic fundamentalism within Palestinian society is the presence of anti-Semitism, which is well addressed by Olivier Melnick in chapter 11. But I want to share additional observations that are supported by a study conducted by the Anti-Defamation League in 2014. This study revealed that 93 percent of Palestinians hold anti-Semitic beliefs.[14] During multiple man-on-the-street interviews we conducted during the *Hope in the Holy Land* film project, we asked the following questions:

- Do you believe the Jews are trying to take over the whole world?
- Do you believe the Holocaust happened?
- Do you believe the Jews were the ones who attacked the US on 9/11?
- Do you think the Israeli government fabricated the numerous stabbing attacks that were perpetrated by Palestinians against Israeli civilians in 2015 and 2016?
- Do you believe the Jews are sons of apes and pigs?

To our dismay, every Palestinian we spoke to affirmed some or all of these ideas. Several rejected that the Holocaust ever happened. Some said that *if* it happened, probably fewer than six million people were killed. We even saw a street vendor in the heart of downtown Ramallah selling a copy of *Mein Kampf* ("My Struggle"), Adolf Hitler's diatribe against the Jewish people, long considered by many as one of the most harmful books ever published in the history of the world.

In the town of Turmis 'Ayya, a wealthy Palestinian village in the West Bank, two of our crew members found graffiti on a bus terminal stand that read "JEWS DID 9/11, TERRORIST ISRAEL DID 9/11," and "ISIS IS

JEWISH," along with a Star of David that was equated to a swastika. Sadly, there is no denying that anti-Semitic beliefs are commonplace within Palestinian society.

Israeli Hostility

To be fair, the Palestinians have also been the target of hateful graffiti and racially motivated violence stirred up by their Jewish neighbors. In 2018, in the month of April alone (in the same town our crew discovered the anti-Semitic graffiti), 14 apparent hate crimes were perpetrated. The graffiti (written in Hebrew) declared, "Wreak vengeance upon the nations," "We'll take our fate into our own hands," and "Let us take care of them" (that is, the Palestinians).[15]

When we asked some Israelis—including some who lived two miles away in Shiloh—about how Israel could improve in its conduct toward the Palestinians, not one felt compelled to cite these incidents, known as "price tagging," as a cause of hostility. But all honest indicators suggest the Jews we spoke with are the exception and not the rule within Israeli society. When Jewish-on-Arab violence occurs, it is almost always condemned by Israelis, especially if the act was perpetrated by a rogue IDF soldier.

Concerning the aforementioned "price-tagging" incidents, multiple articles from Israel-based media outlets reported and denounced them. In contrast, you would be hard-pressed to find any reports in the Palestinian media that condemn violence against Israelis, let alone the well-documented use of human shields by Hamas, the anti-Zionist indoctrination of their youth, the numerous images you can find along their streets that venerate the lives of those who died murdering Israeli civilians, or the financial incentives that are guaranteed to the families of Palestinian "martyrs."[16]

Political Corruption

There is rampant corruption and mismanagement of funds within the PA. According to calculations conducted by the Jerusalem Institute of Justice, the PA has received 25 times more money per capita than all the money given to Europe under the Marshall Plan.[17] In other words, we could have reconstructed the European economy at least 25 times over with all the money that has been given to the PA. This begs the question: Where has all the money gone?

A friend of mine who owns a business in Bethlehem thinks it's ending up in the pockets of the PA. He said, "When your government gives a million dollars to Israel, $900,000 gets to the people and $100,000 ends up in the pockets of the Israeli government. But when your government gives a million dollars to the PA, only $100,000 gets to the people and the other $900,000 ends up in the pockets of the PA." It has been reported that PA president Mahmoud Abbas is worth $100 million[18] and that Hamas political leader Khaled Meshaal is worth $2.6 billion dollars.[19] During the latter years of Yasser Arafat's reign as president of the PA, his net worth was estimated to be somewhere between $1 and $3 billion.[20] Given all this, there is no good reason why 25 percent of the Palestinian population is living below the poverty line.[21]

Accepting Israel's Rebirth

When all this data is taken into account—the risks Palestinians face for challenging the status quo, the rampant presence of Islamic fundamentalism and anti-Semitism, and the political corruption of leaders who are more interested in defaming Israel than the well-being of their own people—the reasons that the Palestinians are suffering becomes clear. They have been grossly misled and failed by their own leaders, all of whom consistently reject Israel's right to exist.

Those who purport to genuinely care about the Palestinians must acknowledge these realities and seek to identify and support the true people of peace within the Palestinian community. I've come to learn that it's not necessarily the people or the organizations that promote themselves as peacemakers, but the "Dietrich Bonhoeffers" and "Corrie ten Booms" within Palestinian society who are taking real risks to love their Jewish neighbors and bring about reform within their own community.

In closing, I appeal to the Palestinian Christian community to accept the rebirth of the state of Israel as a sovereign act of God and to practice biblical hospitality by welcoming the Jewish people back to their ancestral homeland. By doing so, you will participate in the apostle Paul's exhortation to provoke Jewish people to the gospel—a gospel that does not revoke God's gifts and call to the nation of Israel (Romans 11:13-15,29).

CHAPTER 9
READER RESPONSE

What Should We Think About the Plight of the Palestinians?

WHAT DO *YOU* THINK?

I agree with the author on

I disagree with the author because

What was news to me?

How does this change what I think about the plight of the Palestinians?

PART 2

What Should We Think
About Israel's Problems?

10

What Should We Think About the Holocaust?

MICHAEL L. BROWN

The most emotional topic in the Middle East debate concerns the attempted genocide of the Jews of Eastern Europe during the Holocaust. While Jews argue from this demonstration of universal anti-Semitism to justify the establishment of the safe-haven of their own State, opponents—such as the Iranians—claim the Holocaust never happened and that it has been used as a political tool to produce guilt and garner sympathy from the world for the continuance of the Jewish state.

It's common these days for people to casually throw around the word *Nazi*, using it as a common slur and insult. If someone doesn't like your opinion, you're called a Nazi. If your views are too conservative, you're a Nazi. If you are considered bigoted, you're a Nazi. But to use the word so indiscriminately is to cheapen it, for the Nazis were guilty of unspeakable evil. They committed indescribable crimes, some unparalleled in human history. During their reign of terror, nothing displayed the depth of the evil in their hearts more than the Holocaust, an event that truly defies description.

Consider that the Nazis slaughtered two-thirds of European Jews— and I mean slaughtered as in *killed in cold blood*. We're talking about babies and children, about the weak and the elderly. Jew after Jew was starved to death, tortured to death, worked to death, gassed to death, or shot to death. This was the fate of six million Jews in Europe.

Before the Holocaust, there were nine million European Jews. Afterward, the number was three million. The Jewish population of Poland alone was 3.3 million before the Holocaust. Afterward, only the .3 million remained. *Nine out of every ten Polish Jews were butchered.* Who can imagine a massacre on this scale?[1]

It's not as if they died in battle, rebelling against their rulers and fighting for their freedom. That was the fate of a precious few. Instead, the Jews were herded together into ghettos and from there they were shipped via cattle cars to concentration camps. Those who could work might survive a few months or more. Those who were too weak were murdered upon arrival.

Countless hundreds of thousands were forced to strip naked to take a shower (hygiene was important for new arrivals to the camps!). But instead of being drenched in water, the air was filled with poisonous gas. No one made it alive out of those showers.

Outside of the concentration camps, Jews were forced to dig long pits, after which they were lined up and shot to death, turning the pits into cavernous graves. Their bodies were then set on fire in giant pyres, which led to a new kind of madness: Babies were thrown alive into the fire, saving the Nazis from using their bullets. Who can conceive of such monstrous evil? On September 19, 1941,

> the German army took Kiev...and special SS squads prepared
> to carry out Nazi leader Adolf Hitler's orders to exterminate all
> Jews and Soviet officials found there. Beginning on September
> 29, more than 30,000 Jews were marched in small groups to the
> Babi Yar ravine to the north of the city, ordered to strip naked,
> and then machine-gunned into the ravine. The massacre ended
> on September 30, and the dead and wounded alike were covered
> over with dirt and rock.[2]

Can you wrap your mind around numbers like these? Thirty thousand Jews marched to death in a period of less than two weeks.

To say it again: This included children, toddlers, and nursing infants who were still in their mothers' arms. We're talking about teenagers and newlyweds and university students. Parents and grandparents and great-grandparents. Devoted rabbis and respected community leaders. Families and individuals. All of whom were slaughtered in cold blood for one reason only: They were Jews.

And what was life like for those who temporarily escaped death and were consigned to a concentration camp? What kind of living hell did the Nazis design for them? Those who were imprisoned during the winter could expect the following, according to one Holocaust survivor:

> It means that in the course of these months, from October to April, seven out of ten of us will die. Whoever does not die will suffer minute by minute, all day, every day: from the morning before dawn until the distribution of the evening soup we will have to keep our muscles continually tensed, dance from foot to foot, beat our arms under our shoulders against the cold. We will have to spend bread to acquire gloves, and lose hours of sleep to repair them when they become unstitched. As it will no longer be possible to eat in the open, we have to eat our meals in the hut, on our feet, everyone will be assigned an area of floor as large as a hand, as it is forbidden to rest against the bunks. Wounds will open on everyone's hands, and to be given a bandage will mean waiting every evening for hours on one's feet [wearing shoes that always cause pain] in the snow and wind.[3]

Such was the daily horror of those in the concentration camps.

And what was the experience of those who survived? What about those healthy enough to escape the "showers" where the weaker family members were sent? One man who lost his entire family to the Nazi butchers recounted their last seconds together: "It is impossible to describe the agony of those few moments before we parted. I will never forget the wise eyes of my father and the tears of my mother when we embraced for the last time. In my wildest dreams I would never have imagined that I was parting from my whole family forever, never to see them again."[4] Yet that was the stark reality not just for him but for millions of others.

It was not uncommon for someone to lose his or her spouse, children, parents, grandparents and siblings—every last one of them—to the systematic terror of the Nazis. Jews were parasites; they were vermin to be exterminated.

Before the Holocaust, these same Jews were your neighbors, your friends, and your fellow workers. Now they were the enemy, and it was your job to turn them in. Not one of them should escape! The Nazis went so far as to archive Jewish books, religious items, and other tangible aspects of Jewish life. Once this despised race was wiped out, only these artifacts would remain.

This was systemic evil. It was corporate wickedness—and it was all carried out with precise methodology and attention to detail. The Nazis turned murder into a science.[5]

Speaking of science, they had that too. They performed the cruelest, most unimaginable experiments and carefully documented the results. They performed surgery on their Jewish victims using no anesthesia, testing the limits of human pain. They infected Jews with typhus and other dreadful illnesses until they withered away and died. And they did horrific things to twins—things that literally cannot be spoken of—because twins were viewed as being able to provide unique medical data. (Did I mention that the madmen carrying out these experiments were trained medical doctors, some of whom had distinguished careers after the Holocaust?)

Again, the magnitude of this suffering is almost incomprehensible. This becomes clear when we compare the Holocaust to other terrible tragedies, such as the 9/11 terrorist attacks, which took the lives of 2,977 innocent victims, including my wife's brother. Almost 3,000 lives were snuffed out in a single day, and countless tens of thousands were directly affected by the loss.

Now, repeat that same massacre on September 12, 2001, then again the next day, then the next. Another 3,000 deaths and yet another 3,000 deaths. *Then repeat this daily for the next 2015 days*—yes, a 9/11 terrorist attack every day for more than five-and-a-half years. That's what it takes to get to six million deaths.

Even then, that doesn't paint an accurate picture because the Holocaust was perpetuated against a specific group of people, wiping out such large chunks of the populace in a few short years that only a minority remained. That is among the reasons this level of evil is unparalleled in human history.

That this actually took place is beyond dispute. Yes, there will continue to be irrational Holocaust deniers who stick their heads in the sand. But the reality of this monstrous horror cannot be denied by any human being who cares about the truth.

The question for us today is this: Why should we think about the Holocaust today? Why does this still matter to world Jewry? Isn't it time to move on?

On the one hand, the Jewish world *has* moved on, to the point that Israel and Germany have worked together closely for years, even sharing military and security technology. And to live in the past is to become embittered, captive, and stagnant. Jewish life worldwide, as well as in Israel, is anything but backward and stagnant.

Yet it is essential that we remember the Holocaust for at least three major reasons. First, anti-Semitism is alive and well today, which means that the demonic forces that fueled the fires of the Holocaust are still at work in our midst. In fact, for several years now, many experts believe that the level of anti-Semitism currently expressed in Europe has come to parallel the level of anti-Semitism that was present immediately before the Holocaust.[6] And where there is Jew hatred, there are violent acts against Jews. How can we not remember the Holocaust in a climate like this?

A July 22, 2018 headline in the British newspaper *The Telegraph* stated, "We no longer feel safe in Britain. Anti-Semitism is forcing us to leave our home."[7] According to a February 24, 2018 headline in the *New York Post*, "Anti-Semitism drove these Jews out of France."[8] More broadly, on April 26, 2018, the *Chicago Sun Times* reported that "70 years after Holocaust, Jews in Europe do not feel safe."[9] How can these Jews *not* think about the Holocaust when they do not feel safe in their own cities and homes? Yes, even in their own homes. As reported on August 30, 2018 on *World Israel News*, "Anti-Semitism in France has moved 'from the streets directly into the homes of Jewish people,' the head of the country's 465,000-strong Jewish community told *The Algemeiner* on Wednesday [August 29].

"'The Jews in France feel threatened in their own homes,' Francis Kalifat—president of CRIF, the French Jewish communal body—said during a discussion of the anti-Semitism that has resulted in several deaths and injuries among French Jews over the past decade."

Specifically, "In the last eighteen months, two elderly Jewish widows in Paris—Sarah Halimi in April 2017 and Mireille Knoll in March 2018—have been murdered in brutal anti-Semitic assaults, while several incidents of violent raids on Jewish homes involving gangs of mainly Muslim youths have also been reported."[10]

Both of these Jewish women were killed in their own apartments. The latter, Mireille Knoll, was an 85-year-old Holocaust survivor. She was stabbed at least 11 times, and then her body burned when her apartment was set on fire by her killer. What should French Jews be thinking?

As for Germany, BBC News reported on April 24, 2018 that "Josef Schuster, the president of the Central Council of Jews in Germany, told Berlin public radio that Jews should exercise caution in big cities." Specifically, Schuster stated, "I would advise individual people against openly wearing a kippah [the traditional Jewish head covering for men] in big German cities."[11]

This is absolutely chilling. Jews in Germany were urged not to identify publicly as Jews lest they be attacked. To repeat my question: How can these Jews *not* think about the Holocaust, especially as Europe becomes more Islamic by the day?

On December 10, 2017, about 2,500 demonstrators gathered in Germany to protest America's decision to move its embassy in Israel from Tel Aviv to Jerusalem. But the protests were not simply anti-American. They were anti-Israel and anti-Jew. This brought shock and shame to the German nation.

According to government spokesman Steffen Seibert, "At certain rallies over the weekend, slogans were chanted, Israeli flags were burned and slander against the state of Israel and Jews in general were spread which were shameful." Indeed, he said, "One has to be ashamed when hatred of Jews is put on display so openly on the streets of German cities."[12]

This is a common pattern worldwide when there are anti-Israel protests. Animus is expressed not only toward the nation of Israel, but to Jewish people as well. For example, one pro-Palestinian protester shouted at Jewish bystanders at an anti-Israel rally in January 2009 in Fort Lauderdale,

Florida, saying, "Go back to the oven! You need a big oven, that's what you need."[13] It would be an understatement to say that the local Jewish population, which is sizable, was shocked.

During the Holocaust, Jews who were killed in the concentration camps were then incinerated in massive ovens, with these crematoria running around the clock. That's why there were steady streams of smoke pouring from the camps. Jewish bodies were turned into ashes. Once again, the numbers involved are astonishing.

A PBS website notes that "by the early spring of 1943, four huge crematoria became fully operational at Auschwitz II (Birkenau). They housed eight gas chambers and forty-six ovens that could dispose of some 4,400 corpses per day. Trains would arrive at the camp and those most fit—approximately 10-30 percent of the arrivals—would be selected for a work detail. The remaining prisoners were sent to the gas chambers."[14]

Yes, 4,400 corpses could be incinerated each day in just one concentration camp, and a protester in America—in 2009—called for "a big oven." Similar taunts have been heard in Europe in recent years. Is it any wonder that it's hard for Jews to forget about the Holocaust?

In November 2008, a series of shocking terrorist attacks were carried out in Mumbai, India, by Pakistani Muslims. They carefully chose 12 different targets, killing 164 and wounding 308.[15] There was one target of special interest to these terrorists: a Jewish outreach center visited by many Israelis all year round.

Although the terrorists thought it was a center for Israeli intelligence (it wasn't), they were especially happy to kill Jews for any reason. As one of the terrorists explained, his organization "considers the Jewish people a number one target." Indeed, "Every person you kill there [in that Jewish outreach center] is worth fifty killed in the hotels."[16] For every Muslim terrorist, Jews are a primary target, and Europe is becoming increasingly Islamic.

This leads to the second reason we must still think about the Holocaust. The nation of Israel continues to face existential threats, as it is surrounded by mortal enemies sworn to its destruction. In fact, Israel's enemies are quite fond of the Holocaust—to the point of proudly displaying swastikas.[17] How is it conceivable, then, for the Jewish people to forget about the Holocaust? Not only are thousands of Holocaust survivors still alive, people who cannot possibly forget what they experienced, but Israel's staunch enemies, like Iran, regularly threaten the Jewish state with another Holocaust.

In early 2018, Hezbollah, an Iran-backed terrorist group based in Syria and Lebanon (both of which border northern Israel), claimed that there were 500,000 missiles pointed at Israel.[18] Israel lives with this reality 24/7. In the southern city of Sderot, which borders Gaza to the east, almost half of the children living there "suffer from symptoms of anxiety, fear and PTSD."[19] This is due to the frequent (and at times, incessant) bombardment of rockets from Gaza-based Hamas terrorists.

As for Hamas' goals, during the 2018 spring protests, one of their leaders proclaimed, "We will take down Israel's border and tear out Israeli hearts from their bodies."[20] There is no reason to doubt his intent.

Of course, the narrative that prevails in much of the media and on many college campuses throughout America paints a very different picture. Israel is the monster; it is the evil Goliath. The Palestinians are hapless victims, and the surrounding Muslim nations are no match at all for mighty Israel.

The reality is that the primary reason for Palestinian suffering is that they are the victims of the bad decisions made by their leaders, who have refused to recognize the Jewish right to a homeland for the last 80 years. Thus there is no resolution to the ongoing conflict.[21] And the reason Israel's military is so strong is because it has no choice. If the nation were to let down its guard for a moment, blood would flow in the streets.

In a book designed to reach out rather than repel, Israeli author Yossi Klein Halevi asks his Palestinian neighbors a pointed question:

> If Palestinians believe that Israel is the embodiment of evil and
> so must be destroyed—and there is no other reasonable conclu-
> sion to draw from the messages conveyed by Palestinian media
> and mosques and educational system—then genuine compro-
> mise becomes impossible...Your side denies my people's legiti-
> macy, my right to self-determination, and my side prevents your
> people from achieving national sovereignty.[22]

Compounding the problem is the threat from Iran, a nation of 80 million (compared to 6 million Jews who live in Israel), one of their senior leaders said in April 2018, "Iran has the capability to destroy Israel and given the excuse, Tel Aviv and Haifa will be razed to the ground."[23]

As for the radical Islamic theology that helps fan these flames of hatred, in a January 9, 2012 Palestinian Authority TV speech celebrating the forty-seventh anniversary of Fatah, Mufti Muhammad Hussein, the religious leader of the Palestinian Authority, cited a well-known hadith (an Islamic tradition attributed to Muhammad): "The Hour [of Resurrection] will not come until you fight the Jews. The Jew will hide behind stones or trees. Then the stones or trees will call: 'Oh Muslim, servant of Allah, there is a Jew behind me, come and kill him.'"[24] Shockingly, as reported by *Palwatch.org*, a July 2011 poll sponsored by the Israel Project indicated that a staggering 73 percent of Palestinians "believe" this hadith to be true.[25]

Unfortunately, reports and anecdotes and quotes like this exist in countless numbers. There is a massive amount of anti-Israel hostility in the Muslim world, and the more radical the expression of Islam, the more murderous the hatred. Against that backdrop, it is difficult not to think about the Holocaust.

This brings us to the third and final consideration. The Holocaust took place in civilized, cultured, and "Christian" Europe—not in a continent of savages. The people of Europe were educated. They appreciated the finer things of life. They had great universities, cultural centers, and religious centers. They had a Christian tradition dating back to the days of the apostles.

It was in Italy that the Vatican was (and is) based, making Rome the spiritual capital for hundreds of millions of Catholics. It was in Germany that the Protestant Reformation was birthed, from which it spread throughout Europe and the world. Plus, Europe was the home of a long line of great composers and artists and poets and intellectuals. Surely the most barbarous event in world history could not take place in such a place as this! And yet it did. Who is to say it could not take place again, even in America?

That's why it's important for Christians to stand with Israel as a nation, even though Israel is far from perfect. In doing so, we are saying to the Jewish people, "Never again!"

That's why it's important to expose anti-Semitism whenever it raises its ugly head. We need to defang the snake before it can spread its deadly venom.

That's why it's important to learn the devastating truth about the Holocaust. Having learned from history, we do our best not to repeat it.

CHAPTER 10
READER RESPONSE

What Should We Think About the Holocaust?

WHAT DO *YOU* THINK?

I agree with the author on

I disagree with the author because

What was news to me?

How does this change the way I think about the Holocaust?

11

What Should We Think About the New Anti-Semitism?

OLIVIER J. MELNICK

Older anti-Semitism was aimed at the Jew as a Jew, but contemporary anti-Semitism is aimed at the Jewish state. How dangerous is this new expression of anti-Semitism, and how can we recognize its presence in religious and academic institutions as well as governments?

The term *anti-Semitism* has been used broadly to describe racially motivated attitudes and hate crimes against the Jewish people. Some who are called anti-Semites object, claiming that they are simply responding to the problems in the Middle East that they blame on Israel and various Jewish groups. In order to understand what we should think about anti-Semitism, it is necessary to first understand the proper definition of the term because the word itself has evolved etymologically over the centuries.

Background of the Term

The word *Semite* describes any descendant of Noah's son Shem (Genesis 6:10). From the Semites descended both Jews and Arabs. Although the term *Semitic* can relate to both Jews and Arabs, the term *anti-Semitic* refers only to a person, event, or act that is directed against the Jewish people.

The word *anti-Semitism* was popularized in 1873 by German journalist Wilhelm Marr in the pamphlet *The Victory of the Jewish Spirit over the*

Germanic Spirit Observed from a Non-Religious Perspective.[1] From there the usage of the word continued to grow, and by the late 1880s, it had spread beyond Germany.[2]

Proper Definition

The US Department of State and the International Holocaust Remembrance Alliance jointly agreed in 2016 that "antisemitism is a certain perception of Jews, which may be expressed as hatred toward Jews. Rhetorical and physical manifestations of anti-Semitism are directed toward Jewish or non-Jewish individuals and/or their property, toward Jewish community institutions and religious facilities."[3]

Gavin I. Langmuir, in his volume *Toward a Definition of Antisemitism,* contends that it is much more than a racially motivated hatred of the Jews; "yet if we continue to use that literally most misleading term, we, as social scientists, should free 'antisemitism' from its racist, ethnocentric, or religious implications and use it only for what can be distinguished empirically as an unusual kind of human hostility directed at Jews."[4]

His definition draws us closer to a holistic approach to the word *anti-Semitism,* for which I would like to offer one more definition: "Antisemitism is an irrational hatred of the Jewish people, characterized by destructive thoughts, words and actions against them."[5]

When one surveys the history of the Jewish people through the ages, it is easy to discover that Jewish history has been punctuated by acts of anti-Semitism. Scholars speak of Jewish history pre- and post-Holocaust. Jakob Jocz wrote, "'After Auschwitz' marks the possibility of a new beginning for the Jewish people, for the Church, for the world."[6]

Historical Anti-Semitism

The new anti-Semitism didn't happen in a vacuum nor is it monolithic; it is a continuation of historical anti-Semitism, but different in many ways. Historical anti-Semitism spans thousands of years from the biblical record to the Holocaust—from the irrational hatred that Haman had for Jewish people in the book of Esther to Israel's archenemy, the Amalekites, all the way to the Holocaust. It is helpful to study it chronologically.

While a study of historical anti-Semitism is not within the scope of this chapter, a brief overview of the major events that led to the Holocaust is necessary to understand how the stage was set for the new anti-Semitism.

Anti-Semitism started as theological anti-Judaism borne out of differences between Jews and Christians. What started out as a thin fissure in the Judeo-Christian foundation continued to expand to become the chasm that it is today.

The church fathers[7] helped to formulate Christian doctrine and protect Christianity in its infancy. Some of them developed an interpretation of Scripture that led to replacement theology[8] centuries before this faulty approach to God's counsel ever got its modern name. The result was a changing perception of the Jewish people. Before long, educated church leaders and illiterate parishioners accused Jews of killing Christ. Origen, one of the church fathers, saw the Jews as damned by God and claimed that the church had replaced Israel in God's program. In *Contra Celsus* he wrote, "The city where Jesus suffered was necessarily destroyed, the Jewish nation was driven from its country, and another people was called by God to the blessed election."[9]

Laws were passed to further separate the Jewish communities from Christian ones. As the chasm progressively increased, Jewish people became further ostracized and demonized. The status and safety of the Jews worsened. As they were accused of usury and greed—a stigma that endures well into the twenty-first century—they slowly became the scapegoats of humanity.

The First Crusade, which began in 1096, convened to retake Jerusalem from Muslims and proved lethal to the Jews of Europe and the Holy Land. The crusaders went around parading the symbol of the cross and shouting at Jewish people, "Christ killers, embrace the Cross or die"[10] as they proclaimed the motto "God wills it!"[11] In addition, Jews were accused of killing Christian children and using their blood in the making of matzo (unleavened bread) for Passover. This is known as the *blood libel*,[12] and that accusation continues to this day, especially in those countries under Islamic influence.

The advent of the bubonic plague or "black death" brought a new round of accusations against the Jews. Because they suffered fewer casualties than other Europeans, they were accused of poisoning the wells of Europe and severely persecuted. That the Jewish people survived was, in great part, due to their communal isolation, liturgical washing of the hands, and kosher laws.[13]

Then came the Spanish Inquisition of the late 1400s[14] with forced conversions and baptisms, followed by the Eastern European pogroms.[15] Later, in 1903, the hoax known as *The Protocols of the Learned Elders of Zion* was published with the alarming message that the Jews intended to take over the world. Within a few decades of that came the Holocaust; the apex of historical anti-Semitism, and its six million innocent Jewish victims.[16]

Historical anti-Semitism had climaxed in a systematic ethnic cleansing of Europe, and from the ashes of the Holocaust the Jewish people came up with the motto "Never again!" By the late 1940s, it became taboo to defend racial anti-Semitism. Still in shock from the horrors perpetrated by Nazi Germany and affected by collective guilt, the world wanted to reject anti-Semitism. After the arrest and trial of Adolf Eichmann in 1961 and the convening of the Second Vatican Council of 1965, many believed that anti-Semitism was defunct.[17] In reality, it had been swept under the carpet of history for a short time, but within two decades it would resurface, having morphed into a different creature even more pervasive, destructive, and irrational than the previous one.

The New Anti-Semitism

The racial anti-Semitism of Nazi Germany, which painted Jewish people as vermin, germs, or a subrace, was no longer "politically correct."[18] It had to be repackaged to become more acceptable to the world.

One of the dangers posed by the new anti-Semitism is the very fact that it does not pretend to be racial. It covers itself with a false patina of social justice and tolerance that appeals greatly to our postmodern society. It also doesn't call itself anti-Semitism.

While historical/racial anti-Semitism was somewhat of a localized cancer affecting mostly Europe, the new anti-Semitism has spread and metastasized over the entire planet. It has new boundaries, a new methodology, and new players.

The New Boundaries

Outside of being a systematized attempt at destroying all European

Jewry, what made the Holocaust unique was that Hitler and his coperpetrators used Europe's railroad network to its fullest[19] to gather Jews from the four corners of the continent and ship them like cattle to death factories. Under the new anti-Semitism, the boundaries have extended to the whole planet. The goal is no longer—at least not openly—to annihilate the Jews, but rather to demonize and boycott them. Satellite communication, the internet, and social media networks have greatly contributed to the expansion of these new boundaries.

Manfred Gerstenfeld explains the extent and the spread of the new anti-Semitism[20] and its new grip through the internet and social media: "With its massive number of surfers, the internet has become a major instrument for dismantling antisemitic ideas and promoting the delegitimization of Israel...new internet media such as Facebook, Twitter and YouTube serve various originators of hate-promotion."[21] Along with pushed boundaries, the methodology has also changed, making Jewish existence even more of a challenge.

The New Methodology

1. A Role Reversal

Historical anti-Semitism went from early theological disagreements to cultural/communal ostracism, which in turn led to the belief in ethnic superiority based on the now-debunked science of eugenics.[22] The new anti-Semitism uses a different methodology whereby the victims (Jews) are painted as the perpetrators and the perpetrators (anti-Semites) are painted as the victims. We don't see this any clearer than in the Middle East conflict between Arabs and Jews.

An important change in the methodology of the new anti-Semitism is the inclusion of Israel. Whereas the Jewish people were the only ones in the crosshairs of historical anti-Semitism, Israel has now been added as a target. No longer are the Jews a subrace and no longer are modern anti-Semites racially motivated hatemongers. The anti-Semitism of yesteryear has become anti-Zionism or anti-Israelism. That new terminology is more acceptable to the social-justice hungry global community of today.

Gerstenfeld believes that the new anti-Semitism is just that—the old repackaged and repurposed for an easier and broader distribution: "From the perspective of contemporary anti-Semites, the transforming of ancient hate themes into contemporary versions has clear advantages. It is often the case that a proven motif that has succeeded in the past will work in the present if it is somewhat updated."[23]

Following that methodology, Israeli Jews are often painted as the new Nazis of the Middle East, a stigma emphasized in a myriad of anti-Semitic cartoons from that region and even other parts of the world.[24] In *A Lethal Obsession*, Robert Wistrich documents the source of these vitriolic drawings: "In Arab cartoons, Jews are portrayed as demons and murderers, as a hateful, loathsome people to be feared and avoided. They are invariably seen as the origin of all evil and corruption, authors of a dark, unrelenting conspiracy to infiltrate and destroy Muslim society in order to eventually take over the world."[25] The contemporary demonization of the Jews is often mixed with the accusation of a desired global takeover and the colonization of stolen "Palestinian" land. While the Palestinian plight will be covered in other chapters, its connection to the Boycott, Divestment, and Sanctions movement needs to be mentioned in the context of the new anti-Semitism.

2. The Boycott, Divestment, and Sanctions Movement (BDS)

BDS was cofounded in 2005 by Palestinian Authority leader Mahmoud Abbas and Omar Barghout—who openly seek the destruction of Israel.[26] On the premise that Israel is an "apartheid" country that deserves to be pressured through boycotts, as happened in South Africa, the BDS movement has spread like wildfire globally. The principle of economic, academic, or artistic boycott may have merit if the targeted entity is guilty and the boycotting entity is ethical and consistent. However, anti-Semites use BDS with malice and inconsistencies while uninformed followers join ranks with a clear conscience. Unfortunately, factual truth is no longer necessary to evaluate the validity of a claim, especially if it is made against Israel. Liberals, college students, politicians, entertainers, and even some Christian denominations justify ostracizing Israel in the name of tolerance and social justice.

BDS is not looking for reconciliation with Palestinians; it is aimed at destroying Israel. As'ad AbuKhalil, a California State University professor and BDS activist, said, "The real aim of BDS is to bring down the state of Israel…that should be stated as an unambiguous goal. There should not be any equivocation on the subject. Justice and freedom for the Palestinians are incompatible with the existence of the state of Israel."[27] Furthermore, as noted by French author Pierre-André Taguieff in *Israël et la Question Juive*, "BDS proponents expect uninformed or misinformed people to believe their pro-Palestinian message of anti-racism by accusing Israel of racism while being guilty of antisemitism."[28] The irony shouldn't be missed. Any way one looks at it, the BDS movement is anti-Semitic.[29] (For more on the BDS movement, see the next chapter.)

3. Campus Anti-Semitism

BDS uses many platforms to spread its message, but none more fertile than the American university campus, where students are indoctrinated to hate Israel and provided with a one-sided pro-Palestinian narrative. Ultimately this is more than just anti-Semitism; it is a deliberate attack on free speech in America. Many universities host lectures and invite speakers who not only deliver messages of hate and intolerance, but in some cases are linked to terrorist organizations.[30]

Numerous cases of campus anti-Jewish sentiment have been recorded in the past few years. Swastika graffiti in dorms, ethnic slurs and insults such as "Christ killers" have become more common.[31] When Jewish students file complaints they are almost always ignored, says Tammi Rossman-Benjamin in *Anti-Zionism on Campus*: "Unprecedented in their scope and aggressiveness, anti-Zionist student campaigns are successfully deflecting legitimate accusations of anti-Semitism."[32]

The organization Students for Justice in Palestine[33] and local chapters of the Muslim Student Association are very active on most American campuses, promoting anti-Semitism behind a thin veneer of social justice and tolerance. Both are connected to the Muslim Brotherhood,[34] which has been identified as having many terrorist ties. The days are gone when a university campus was a safe forum for learning and the civil exchange of ideas regardless of one's position on the ideological spectrum.

4. Christian Palestinianism

When some of the church fathers made a theological deviation from a literal hermeneutical approach and started to see no prophetic future for ethnic Israel, little did they know that down the road, many Christians would adhere to their faulty view and develop it further. With the advent of "Christian" organizations like Sabeel,[35] much damage has been done to the biblical record. The de-Judaizing of the Bible is happening in plain sight, and most evangelicals lack the discernment to distinguish how the interpretation of God's Word is being corrupted. Paul Wilkinson defines Christian Palestinianism in *For Zion's Sake,* where he claims that historical revisionism has inverted biblical truth.[36]

Christian Palestinianism aims at delegitimizing Israel and erasing any Jewish connection to the Holy Land. The accusations of occupation, colonization, and apartheid easily lead to the demonization of Israel and the disintegrating of the foundational rights to the Holy Land, including its historical and archeological sites. Christian Palestinianism is replacement theology on steroids and is part of the new anti-Semitism. It has infiltrated evangelicalism and continues to find new platforms to spread its poison. One such dangerous venue is Christ at the Checkpoint.

5. Christ at the Checkpoint Conference (CatC)

This biennial conference started at Bethlehem Bible College in 2010. Their mission is "to challenge Evangelicals to take responsibility to help resolve the conflicts in Israel/Palestine by engaging with the teaching of Jesus on the Kingdom of God."[37] Sadly, many unaware Christians attend and support this conference. They are convinced it is aimed at reconciliation in the Middle East when, in reality, it is a one-sided witch hunt against Israel. The Jewish state is accused of extremism and crimes against humanity (read: Palestinians), yet very little—if anything at all—is said about terrorism or Hamas. The bias is evident, even though CatC always invites participation by a prominent figure in the messianic Jewish movement. It appears that CatC does this to validate its claim of reconciliation through "dialogue." CatC's ethical challenge to Israel in the name of reconciliation and Christian peace-seeking could be fruitful, but in its current iteration, it only feeds into the new anti-Semitism.

The New Players

The players of this contemporary Judeophobia have changed because the "longest hatred" has to keep reinventing itself to attract the support of unsuspecting audiences. Because the racial anti-Semitism of the Holocaust era is no longer an option, the new anti-Semitism seeks to "subcontract" its hatred to other people. Historical anti-Semitism was black and white. Under the Nazi regime, Jews were said to be genetically inferior and deserving of extermination. Because the new anti-Semitism hides itself behind the cloak of anti-Zionism, people can easily adhere to it without guilt.

As a result, atheists, agnostics, liberals, evangelicals, Muslims, and even some Jews share in the ideology of the new anti-Semitism to one degree or another. The unifying factor is social justice in the name of tolerance and multiculturalism in a postmodern society. The irrationality of this new anti-Semitism shouldn't be missed. On what topic do liberals and atheists agree with radical Islam? Not one! They are on opposite sides of the ideological spectrum. Unless, of course, it has to do with the delegitimization and demonization of Israel. Then, amazingly, they are on the same page. From that perspective, we find partners in crime in academia, government, entertainment, the business world, and even within the evangelical church.

Behind the New Anti-Semitism

From antiquity to the modern jihad, it has always been the same personality behind anti-Semitism—Satan. From Genesis 3:15 on, he knew that he was in trouble and was determined to corrupt the messianic line or even destroy the very people Yeshua came through in His humanity—the Jews. Satan knows the Bible and is aware of God's end-times agenda. He knows that the Jewish people are a vital part of Yeshua's return. There is coming a day when they will look up to Yeshua corporately and cry out to Him, "Blessed is He who comes in the name of the Lord" (Psalm 118:26; cf. Matthew 22:39).

Scripture seems to indicate that this event will take place at the end of the seven-year tribulation, when all Jewish people will be in Israel and call upon the one "whom they have pierced" (Zechariah 12:10). Then, according to Romans 11:26, "all Israel will be saved" (referring to all the living Jewish people at the end of the tribulation). This also marks the end of Satan's "career," as seen in Revelation 20:10: "The devil that deceived them was thrown into the lake of fire and brimstone."

Satan wants to stop or postpone Yeshua's return (Revelation 12:13-17), but the very people who gave the world the Jewish Messiah will also be the ones calling on Him and initiating the second coming (Acts 3:19-21). All through history, Satan has worked overtime to stop the Jewish people from calling on Yeshua. Using anti-Semitism, he has driven a theological, cultural, political, and racial wedge between the Jewish people and the world.

What Can Christians Do to Fight Anti-Semitism?

In light of the new forms anti-Semitism has taken in our modern age, we have a responsibility to act so that the evils of the past are not perpetuated. If we fail to do anything, we will leave the wrong kind of legacy for those who record future history. Because we are at present experiencing anti-Semitism at an unprecedented level worldwide, it's vital that we act now—and here is how we can do so.

Educate Yourself

When we reach out to any ethnic group, we must take the time to know their history, culture, and any potential roadblocks to sharing the gospel with them. Anti-Semitism is baggage that all believers carry with them and cannot ignore as they start dialoguing with Jewish people. We must learn about anti-Semitism if we want to fight it.[38] By identifying the players, the agenda, and the ultimate goal of the new anti-Semitism, we will be able to educate ourselves, then others in our realm of influence.

Speak Up

After educating yourself and others, you should boldly speak up against all the lies that are being spread against the Jews, avoiding any form of personal character critique that could be construed as an ad hominen attack. Confront historical revisionism with the facts and with the Scriptures whenever possible.

Support Israel

When you hear of local acts of anti-Semitism against a Jewish person, synagogue, or Jewish community center, make a phone call and introduce yourself as a Christian who loves Israel and wants to help. You might receive a polite "No, thank you!" but your willingness to reach out will not go unnoticed. You might also consider attending Jewish and Israeli events in your community. In addition, when people advise you to boycott Israeli products, do the opposite. If you want to be proactive about this, you can visit a BDS site, look at their list of products to boycott, and buy them. BDS proponents have done all the research for us.[39]

Share the Gospel

The most important way to reach out is to share the gospel. Our efforts to help Israel and the Jewish people will fall short if we refrain from sharing the reason for the hope that is within us. The Jewish people gave the world the Hebrew Scriptures (Old Testament) and the Jewish Messiah. It is time we give back with the gift that never stops giving. The gospel is "the power of God for salvation to everyone who believes, to the Jew first and also to the Greek" (Romans 1:16).

Never Again

The new anti-Semitism is not so new. Much of it is historical anti-Semitism repackaged to appeal to a new audience without the stigma of racial supremacy. Under the new anti-Semitism, people can be an anti-Zionist or even anti-Israel without feeling like they are anti-Semitic. The new anti-Semitism is not going away, and it is predicted to intensify as we near the last chapter of God's program for the ages.

Many Christians were bystanders during the Holocaust. They felt powerless or lacked concern, and as a result, many Jews perished. A bystander who does nothing ends up facilitating the work of a perpetrator. May we not be found guilty of committing the same sin as those of previous generations.

CHAPTER 11
READER RESPONSE

What Should We Think About the New Anti-Semitism?

WHAT DO *YOU* THINK?

I agree with the author on

I disagree with the author because

What was news to me?

How does this change the way I think about the New Anti-Semitism?

What Should We Think About the Boycott, Divestment, and Sanctions Movement?

TUVYA ZARETSKY

The Boycott, Divest, and Sanctions movement has a wide following from faculty and students on university campuses to pastors and parishioners in mainline denominational churches. It is endorsed in online social media and championed by celebrity figures. What is its purpose, and why is it so popular? Is its public presentation an accurate picture of its political agenda and the aims of those who established and direct the movement? What are the actual social and political effects of the movement?

The Boycott, Divestment, and Sanctions (BDS) movement is an ideology working as a political ploy to harm Jewish people and replace the Jewish state of Israel. Sadly, some Christians have been influenced by and embraced the false narratives of BDS lies. In this chapter, you will see how the BDS movement originated, the harm it does, and why it should be viewed as anti-Zionist, anti-Semitic, and immoral.

Perhaps you have taken a guided tour of the Holy Land by a BDS-affiliated agency like the Telos Group. Or you have heard podcasts or webinars in which Christian speakers who are sympathetic to the BDS cause make false allegations, saying that Israel has imposed an unlawful "military occupation" upon the Palestinian people and is a fascist, racist, or apartheid state. These proponents might even have embraced the goals stated in the Kairos Palestine document. In this chapter we will learn truth about the claims of the BDS movement and whether they stand up to scrutiny. This will enable you to think for yourself about how to respond to the movement.

The Roots of the BDS Movement

Boycotts against Jews are nothing new. Through the centuries, Jews have been segregated, forced to live in ghettos, and stigmatized. When the Nazi regime came to power in 1933, it immediately called for a boycott of Jewish culture and academic works. At the end of World War II, the Arab League—a group of 21 Middle Eastern and African nations—agreed to boycott Israeli companies and Israeli-made goods. They claimed to do this for political reasons, but they are effectively engaging in anti-Semitic human rights violations.[1]

In 1974, the Palestine Liberation Organization (PLO), chaired by terrorist leader Yasser Arafat, was granted observer status in the United Nations (UN). Subsequent Palestinian leaders used that concession to request and receive nonmember observer-state status. That is similar to the standing granted to the Vatican.[2] In fact, up to this point, no independent state of Palestine has ever been declared or received international recognition.

In 1975, the nonmember observer "state of Palestine" used its new status to influence the Organization of African Unity (along with South Africa) to issue a condemnation of Israel as a "racist and colonial regime" before the UN Human Rights Commission. In November of that year, the Soviet Union partnered with the PLO to draft a UN resolution condemning Zionism as racism. Nobel Peace laureate Andrei Sakharov warned that such a UN action would give the abominations of anti-Semitism and anti-Zionism historic and global sanction. The resolution passed, giving roots to a BDS ideology and a temporary aura of legitimacy to an idea that was supposedly a human-rights concern.[3] In 1991, the "Zionism as racism" resolution was repealed in the UN, but the damage had already been done.

History and Aims of the Movement

The Boycott, Divestment, and Sanctions movement gained its founding platform and momentum from the 2001 UN World Conference Against Racism (WCAR) in Durban, South Africa. A preconference meeting of nongovernmental organizations (NGOs) and political activists, held in Tehran earlier in that year, set the agenda and framed a "Declaration and Plan of Action" for the Durban conference later in the year. The program and language for the declaration were orchestrated by the Organization of Islamic Cooperation (OIC). Within the declaration, a section on Palestine was to serve as a propaganda weapon attacking Israel, reading, in part, "Israel engages in ethnic cleansing of the Arab population of historic Palestine" and is guilty of "apartheid, a crime against humanity." That fall, the WCAR in Durban followed the OIC plan and produced a declaration that included the false and inflammatory allegations against Israel. US Congressman Tom Lantos provided an eyewitness report and stated the implications of the event, which justified the walkout by US and Israeli delegates.[4]

In its 2005 call for action, BDS activists took key sections from the UNWCAR declaration to condemn Israel. Based on those fabricated claims, these activists have called on the international community to force Israel to accept a Palestinian "right of return" and an end to the "colonial military occupation" of the West Bank and Gaza Strip. At the heart of the BDS plot is the aim of ending Israel's existence as a Jewish state. In other words, Israel must go away.

Omar Barghouti, born 1964 in Qatar to a Palestinian family, earned an MA degree in electrical engineering from Columbia University and an MA in philosophy from Tel Aviv University. In 1993, he moved to Israel after marrying an Arab-Israeli woman. Barghouti is a founding committee member of the Palestinian Campaign for the Academic and Cultural Boycott of Israel (PACBI) and cofounder of the BDS movement. In fact, he wrote *the* book on the BDS movement.[5] As he did so, he parroted language from the Durban NGO Forum Declaration section on Palestinians and Palestine and inserted it into his BDS-ideological attack on the Jewish state.[6]

Section 419 alone advocates the following:

- ...the United Nations should compel "withdrawal of the Israeli colonial military occupation" of the Gaza Strip and the West Bank. No mention is made of the Arab attacks on the Israeli State at its declaration of independence in 1948 and the 1967 defensive actions repeated in response to unprovoked joint Arab country attacks in 1967 and 1973.

- ..."the right of return for refugees"—not the approximately 700,000 refugees from 1948, but their 5 million descendants. That number, combined with the 1.3 million Arabs in the West Bank and Gaza, plus 1.7 million Israeli Arabs would overwhelm an Israeli Jewish population of just over 6.5 million.

- ..."reinstitution of UN resolution 3379 determining the practices of Zionism as racist..."

- ..."to obliterate their national identity and...the exclusive nature of the State of Israel as a Jewish state..."

In light of this information about the history and aims of the BDS movement, let's now shine a light on the harm it is doing.

What Harm Is Caused by the BDS Movement?

As'ad AbuKhalil, professor of political science at California State University, Stanislaus, has stated,

> The real aim of BDS is to bring down the State of Israel...that should be stated as an unambiguous goal. There should not be any equivocation on the subject. Justice and freedom for the Palestinians are incompatible with the existence of the State of Israel.[7]

John Spritzler of the Harvard University School of Public Health and a pro-BDS activist, says,

> BDS's stated goals (ending the Occupation, equality for non-Jews and Jews, and the right of return of the Palestinian refugees)

logically imply the end of Israel as a Jewish state…The "state of
the Jews" is actually an instrument by which a Jewish elite ruling class of billionaires and generals and politicians secures its
oppressive grip on ordinary Jews in Israel…This is why there
should not be a Jewish state.[8]

Jonathan Kuttab, lawyer and board member of The Sabeel Ecumenical Liberation Theology Center in Jerusalem and Bethlehem Bible College, writes,

> Armed struggle is never an end in and of itself. It is only a method
> for achieving political ends, which seem to be illusive now. Thus,
> "armed struggle" against Israel is moral and legitimate, but "for
> now" he advises Palestinians not to use violent means only
> because it will be *ineffective* and "counterproductive" in the face
> of potent Israeli defenses.[9]

Omar Barghouti, the cofounder of BDS, declares,

> Israel will never accept our rights unless it is forced to. Our 60
> years of experience with Zionist colonial oppression and apart-
> heid has shown us that unless we resist by all means—particu-
> larly through civil resistance—to force Israel into a pariah status
> in the world, like South Africa was turned in the 1980s, there is
> no chance of advancing the prospects for a just peace…we are
> saying that this [boycott] can mobilize universal support from
> around the world—except from those who are keen to maintain
> Israel as a racist, ethnocentric state.[10]

Let there be no doubt: The BDS movement seeks an end of the Jewish state and supports whatever harm that may cause its citizenry, especially the 78 percent who are Jewish. Yet the population of Israel today also
includes secular Jews and Arabs, adherents of all forms of Judaism, messianic Jews, Muslim and Christian Arabs, Jews intermarried with Arabs,
and other non-Jewish ethnic citizens.

A community of self-described Palestinian Christians in the West
Bank supports the aims of the BDS movement. They include activists

from the Jerusalem-based Sabeel Ecumenical Liberation Theology Center, Holy Land Trust, Musalaha ("Reconciliation"), and Bethlehem Bible College. Some espouse the fundamentals of Palestinian Liberation Theology, which interprets Scripture through the plight of the poor and works to bring about social and political change for what they view as a more just society. Not surprisingly, conversations between those Palestinian Christians and Israeli messianic Jews have become increasingly complicated due to the socio-political aims of BDS.

American Christians who support the BDS movement, even for the most earnest sociological and seemingly Christlike reasons, must take responsibility for identifying with intended BDS harm to the Jewish state, which affects Israel's multifaceted population as well as messianic Jewish brothers and sisters in the body of Christ. Christians must also recognize that identifying with BDS efforts will negate their testimony to Israelis as witnesses to gospel forgiveness and the transforming love of Jesus.

Thinking About BDS Propaganda and Actions

Boycott of Israeli Academia and Intellectual Institutions

The Boycott, Divestment, and Sanctions movement seeks to isolate and condemn Israeli intellectual, technological, and Jewish cultural voices. Historically, that was the same intent of a newly empowered Nazi party in Germany when, in May of 1933, Jewish academia and intellectuals were attacked. Nazi Germany lit the skies with bonfires to purge their land of Jewish writings. That propaganda machine sought to isolate and condemn Jews from international academia and conversation. The Nazi aim was to wipe out world Jewry. As already shown, BDS ultimately wants to de-Zionize Israel, bringing an end to the Jewish state.

The 47,000-member American Association of University Professors has rejected the academic boycott.[11] However, in December 2013, the much smaller American Studies Association voted to support the BDS movement. That resolution was passed by less than the 23 percent of its membership that cared to vote. Activist Omar Barghouti recognized that act as a BDS infiltration of American academia.[12]

In apartheid South Africa, education was not a right of black Africans.

Interestingly, Omar Barghouti is reluctant to mention the freedom given him in Israel to pursue and receive a master's degree from Tel Aviv University. And the 2014 valedictorian at Technion University Medical School was a Muslim Arab from near Nazareth named Mais Ali-Saleh. She stated, "An academic boycott of Israel is a passive move and it doesn't achieve any of its purported objectives." Further, BDS "perpetrates falsehoods." In fact, she asserted that as an Arab woman in Israel she has more freedom, academic opportunities, and liberty than women find in any other country of the Middle East. It was her opinion that those Arab countries should emulate Israel's academic freedom and democracy.[13]

Divestment and Sanctions

Omar Barghouti used outrageous, inflammatory language in his 2011 justification for the Boycott, Divestment, and Sanctions movement—language similar to that which appears in the anti-Semitic hoax of the early twentieth century known as *The Protocols of the Elders of Zion*.[14] That propaganda piece claimed that Jews were conspiring to dominate the world by manipulating the economy, controlling the media, and fostering religious conflict. The conspiracy and its alleged leaders, the so-called elders of Zion, never existed. The BDS tactics utilize a similar fabrication of lies, disinformation, and efforts to negatively judge the Jewish state. Barghouti's aim is not merely to call for sanctions in protest of Israeli policies, but to permanently end Jewish sovereignty over the land by calling for a Palestinian state that would replace—not coexist with—the current Jewish one. It is his one-state solution.[15]

American universities and liberal American Christian denominations appear no different than the Arab League when they embrace the Boycott, Divestment, and Sanctions effort. There is no positive contribution toward finding peace in Israel by divesting from Israeli banks or imposing sanctions against Israeli companies or government-sponsored contracts. The Christian denominations that have embraced BDS (including the Presbyterian Church [USA], the Episcopal Church in America, and the United Methodist Church) have accomplished nothing more than calling into question their own testimony to the uniqueness of salvation in Christ. Israel's people and government leaders will not cower to pressure by the world community. The anti-Semitic acts committed by the Arab League over the past 70 years have done nothing to achieve the aim of eliminating the Jewish state.

How Should We Think About the Issues Raised by the Boycott, Divestment, and Sanctions Movement?

Now that you know BDS is founded on ideology that is anti-Zionist and anti-Semitic, and that it seeks the demise of the Jewish state, how can anyone continue to support it? Following are examples of the kinds of charges BDS makes against Israel and the issues that need to be understood to withstand the inflammatory propaganda that is deceptively couched in terms of social and humanitarian justice.

Apartheid

The 2001 Durban Conference Declaration calls Israel an apartheid state. The sole purpose of this political tactic is to stigmatize Jewry. However, it is a baseless accusation that serves no humanitarian purpose. On November 10, 1975, when UN Resolution 3379 passed, equating "Zionism with racism," US Ambassador to the UN Daniel Patrick Moynihan spoke on behalf of the United States. He declared, "The lie is that Zionism is a form of racism. The overwhelmingly clear truth is that it is not."[16] South African judge Richard Goldstone, who reported to the UN Human Rights Commission in October 2011, concluded, "In Israel there is no apartheid." To say otherwise is a lie and does an incredible dishonor to those courageous South Africans who fought and won against the dehumanizing sin of a real apartheid regime.

War Crimes and Genocide

The Palestinian charge that Israel committed war crimes and genocide began in 2006. Hezbollah terrorists from Lebanon, supported by Iran, captured two Israeli soldiers on a raid across the northern Israeli border. Israel took military action in Lebanon against terrorists to retrieve their soldiers. Once again, the Palestinian Authority went to the UN and accused Israel of committing war crimes when, in reality, it was defending its people against terrorists.

According to Omar Barghouti's strange ethics, Israel's so-called "genocide" against Palestinians will be stopped only when Israel's economy is destroyed. In 2014, the fizzy-water company SodaStream closed its factory in the West Bank after it was targeted by international protests that were urged on by the BDS movement, which claimed the company was complicit in discrimination against Palestinians. After the closure, BDS advocates said its pressure was behind SodaStream's economic decision to close.[17] But the BDS pressure actually had no effect on the Israeli economy nor upon the SodaStream company. Rather, SodaStream relocated inside of Israel and continues to operate. Ultimately, the only people who suffered loss were 500 innocent West Bank Palestinian workers who are now unemployed.

Christians have been accomplishing wonderful social connections and humanitarian kindness in the name of Christ; that isn't part of the BDS scheme.

Christian Endorsement of BDS

The BDS movement is a political ideology that is anti-Semitic at its root and aims to end the Jewish state of Israel. How should lovers of Jesus respond to Palestinian Christians who are unashamedly anti-Zionist and wholeheartedly in support of the BDS movement? The late Arthur Glasser, an esteemed missiology professor, said, "Nationalism is the last sin of which the church confesses." National self-determination is one motivation of Palestinian Christians who, for various reasons, stand by and support the BDS movement. We should not judge their Christian faith, nor do we need to attempt to discern what their views say about confidence in the Scriptures. The BDS movement is clearly not a Christian effort. As a campaign that works for the demise of Jewish people, Christians must question having any part in it.

Some Christians will disagree over eschatological positions, specifically whether the modern state of Israel is a fulfillment of biblical prophecy.[18] BDS advocate and New Testament professor Gary Burge claims that modern Israel is illegitimate. In his view, the Jewish people have no right to the land of Israel because they are not living up to the demands of their Scriptures.[19] However, God's covenant promises to Abraham and his descendants were meant to display the Lord's faithful character to all nations and the permanent truthfulness of His Word. That is why His covenant to Abram in Genesis 15 is unilateral and unconditional. Fulfillment of the contract is dependent solely on the Lord's integrity and not Israel's moral fiber. Deny the historical-grammatical reliability of the Bible and its inspiration from God's mouth, or dismiss His covenant promises, and you are left with a serious spiritual attack. The secular BDS movement is a war machine in that battle.

Christian supporters of BDS must recognize what they are promoting in this brand of nationalism. Anglican priest Naim Ateek advocates Christian Palestinianism through the Jerusalem-based Sabeel Ecumenical Liberation Theology Center. He envisions the eventual removal of Israel and its replacement with a "binational country" ruled by Palestinians. That message is repeated to Christians abroad by Friends of Sabeel networks in North America and Europe. Bethlehem Bible College is another Palestinian Christian supporter of these views and of BDS. The college was founded in 1979 by Arab pastors under the leadership of Bishara Awad and actively supports BDS nationalism and the end of the Jewish state. The college also hosts conferences in Israel (such as Christ at the Checkpoint) and the US to actively promote the BDS message among Christians.

Kairos Palestine is a coalition of Palestinian Christians who produced the Kairos Palestine document in 2009.[20] That document unequivocally supports the aims of BDS, restating the anti-Zionist propaganda in spiritualized terms. For example, it speaks of "the Israeli occupation of Palestinian land as a sin against God..." [2.5]. It pits Palestinian Christians and Muslims against Jewish "occupiers" without recognizing the historic or geopolitical background of the current Israeli state. The document is intended to persuade Christian denominations internationally to support and act on the BDS proposals against Israel.[21]

What Should Christians Do in Response to BDS?

First, recognize that BDS ideology is immoral because it does not accept Israel's right to exist as a nation-state of the Jewish people. The state of Israel is a fact based on international law. It is recognized as such by the international community and has been defended by its citizenry against multiple attacks by hostile enemies from without and terrorists from within.

Second, BDS disinformation is immoral because it promotes false views of Israel and Jews. It distorts and inflates Israel's flaws while promoting lies to legitimize anti-Semitic views. German Christians were too slow to speak up when Nazi propaganda justified the "final solution" against European Jewry. Let's not make the same mistake today; the BDS movement is no less a threat. In order to get a balanced and responsible view of the BDS movement and how to properly respond to it, please consult the following publications:

Babbin, Jed with Herbert London. *The BDS War Against Israel: The Orwellian Campaign to Destroy Israel Through the Boycott, Divestment and Sanctions Movement* (New York: The London Center for Policy Research, 2014).

Dershowitz, Alan. *The Case Against BDS: Why Singling Out Israel for Boycott Is Anti-Semitic and Anti-Peace* (New York: Post Hill Press, 2018).

Shavit, Ari. *My Promised Land: The Triumph and Tragedy of Israel* (New York: Penguin Random House Company, 2013).

Swindell, Daniel. "How Palestinian Activists Manipulate Western Christians," *The Times of Israel* (May 30, 2018); https://blogs.timesofisrael.com/how-palestinian-activists-manipulate-western-christians/.

Third, agreeing with BDS tactics is wrong because doing so enables the Palestinians to reject reasonable compromise solutions. Bolstering their hopes of achieving change by punishing Israel and isolating it intellectually or damaging her economically is absolutely fruitless. What Israel needs are reasonable Palestinian leaders in the West Bank and Gaza who will work to find political compromises with mutually satisfying goals. Supporting BDS is a distraction to the hard work necessary for real solutions.

Fourth, BDS is doomed to failure. The Israeli people will never bend to the kind of pressure and guilt that is aimed at them by the BDS movement. Israel is prospering economically and is capable of defending itself. No one should underestimate the *survival instinct* of the Jewish people. Whatever you may think about God's covenant with Israel and the state of Israel, you should know that after the horrors of the Holocaust, Israeli Jewry will resolutely look after its national security and the safety of its people.

Finally, to love Jews does not mean you have to hate Arabs. Likewise, God forbid anyone should work against Jews out of love for Arabs. All of us ought to pray for the salvation of Jews and Arabs in Messiah Jesus. We should pray for the shalom (peace) of Christ to guard the hearts of messianic Jews and Palestinian Christians who live in the state of Israel. May their hearts be one.

CHAPTER 12
READER RESPONSE

What Should We Think About the Boycott, Divestment, and Sanctions Movement?

WHAT DO *YOU* THINK?

I agree with the author on

I disagree with the author because

What was news to me?

How does this change the way I think about the Boycott, Divestment, and Sanctions Movement?

What Should We Think About Replacement Theology?

MICHAEL J. VLACH

Behind much of the opposition to the existence of the State of Israel is a form of theology that maintains the Jewish people were rejected by God and replaced by others (usually the church or Islam), and therefore no longer have a biblical/theological claim to promises formerly made to Israel by God, including the right to the land. What is the basis for this theological view, and how is it manifested in the current religious and political arenas?

A straightforward reading of the Bible reveals that the nation and people of Israel are a strategic part of God's purposes. Genesis 12 through the book of Revelation reveals this truth. In fact, we cannot rightly understand the Bible's storyline if we do not properly comprehend the identity and role of Israel in Scripture. Historically, one of the greatest threats to grasping God's plans is the false doctrine of replacement theology—the view that Israel as an ethnic, national, and territorial entity has been permanently replaced or superseded as the people of God.

According to this view, Israel is no longer the people of God and no more possesses a strategic place in God's historical purposes. Allegedly, the special role and identity of Israel have been transferred to another—the church in Jesus. While not all who assert this view explicitly call it replacement theology, the replacement view is a well-documented position. And the result has been much the same—Israel is said to have been replaced or superseded as the people of God.[1]

Not only does this view distort the Bible's storyline, it also impugns the integrity of God because it asserts that God does not fulfill His promises just as He said. In addition, replacement theology has often been the soil that spurs the growth of anti-Semitism and opposition to the modern state of Israel. It has also been the basis for condemning Christian support for Israel. The purpose of this chapter is to offer an introductory understanding of replacement theology so that this harmful perspective can be detected and exposed.

Historical Backdrop

Through history, most replacement theology has been in the form of the Christian church seeing itself as replacing, superseding, or fulfilling Israel in God's purposes. In reality there is no such thing as "Christian replacement theology" because such a view is not really Christian. The biblical view is that Israel remains important to God's plans and will experience a national salvation and restoration (see Matthew 23:39; Acts 1:6; Romans 11:26-27). But with replacement theology, the church is perceived as the "new" or "true" Israel that has taken over the identity and purpose of Israel. Most adherents of this view do not identify themselves with the title replacement theology, but the position remains nonetheless.

There is also a form of replacement theology called Islamic replacement theology. Because Muslims view Islam as the true and final form of religion, adherents of Islam believe their religion has superseded both Judaism and Christianity. When Islam becomes dominant in a geographical region, it is not uncommon for mosques to be placed over churches and religious sites. Perhaps the greatest examples of this are the presence of the Dome of the Rock on the site where the Jewish Temple once resided on the Temple Mount in Jerusalem and the Hagia Sophia Mosque in Istanbul, which replaced the Hagia Sophia Church (in former Constantinople) that was a center of early Byzantine Christianity. Muslims perceive Islam as superseding both Israel and the church.

Replacement theology is problematic because it does not hold that God will keep His promises as stated to the people to whom His promises were made. That God made eternal and unconditional promises to ethnic/national Israel is plainly evident in passages such as Genesis 12; 15; 17; 22; 2 Samuel 7; Jeremiah 30–33; and Ezekiel 40–48, to name a few. Yet replacement theology claims that those promises will not be fulfilled with Israel in mind, as God predicted. This assumption is based on a *spiritualization* or *reinterpretation* of God's Old Testament promises. For example, the influential theologian George Ladd declared belief in a reinterpretation of God's promises to Israel when he stated,

> The Old Testament must be interpreted by the New Testament. In principle it is quite possible that the prophecies addressed originally to literal Israel describing physical blessings have their fulfillment exclusively in the spiritual blessings enjoyed by the church. It is also possible that the Old Testament expectation of a kingdom on earth could be *reinterpreted* by the New Testament altogether of blessings in the spiritual realm.[2]

Also, replacement theology has often been linked with anti-Semitism in history. Not all who hold to a replacement view are anti-Semitic, but history is littered with atrocities committed against the Jewish people when the church overwhelmingly adopts replacement theology and has an influence on society. Roman Catholic replacement theology influenced the Inquisitions of the Middle Ages. Jews in Europe "lived in constant terror of the Inquisition fires."[3]

Sadly, the leader of the Protestant Reformation, Martin Luther, contributed significantly to the anti-Semitism that arose in Nazi Germany in the 1930s and 1940s. In his later years, Luther held to a strong punitive replacement theology in which he believed the Jewish people were permanently punished and rejected by God for their unbelief in Jesus.[4] His 1543 work *The Jews and Their Lies* was a vicious attack on Jewish people. In it he called for the burning of Jewish schools, homes, and synagogues, as well as the confiscation of money and property and the forbidding of rabbinic activity. Even some of the Protestant clergy in Germany used Luther's words against the Jews to support Nazi Germany.[5] As David L. Larsen observes, "The Holocaust was conceived and carried out in the heart of Christendom. Germany since the Reformation had been at the very center of professing Christianity."[6]

These examples are only a sampling of the horrible acts committed against the Jews by professing Christians who affirmed replacement theology.[7] As stated earlier, replacement theology has been the soil from which anti-Semitism grows and flourishes. This historical lesson should not be forgotten today, although that may be happening. The number of anti-Semitic incidents reported in the United States surged 57 percent in 2017 from 2016, according to an annual report by the Anti-Defamation League.[8]

The Rise of Replacement Theology

Many Bible passages affirm the continuing significance of Israel in God's plans. Yet while many in the early church affirmed the importance of Israel, it was not long before replacement theology took root. Paul dealt with an early form of replacement theology in Romans 9–11. Concerning unbelieving Israel, Paul exclaimed, "God has not rejected His people, has He?" (Romans 11:1). He then emphatically answered his own question by stating, "God has not rejected His people whom He foreknew" (verse 2). In reference to Paul's words in Romans 11, Douglas Moo notes, "These Gentile believers were apparently convinced that they belonged to a new people of God that had simply replaced Israel."[9] Paul also linked replacement theology with arrogance later in Romans 11: "Do not be arrogant toward the branches [Israel]" (verse 18). For Paul, replacement theology was a major problem.

In the middle of the second century AD, Justin Martyr became the first person to explicitly identify the church as "the true spiritual Israel."[10] Robert L. Saucy observed that Justin represented "a developing tendency in the church to appropriate to itself the attributes and prerogatives that formerly belonged to historical Israel."[11] This would open the floodgates for others in the church to make similar declarations. Clement of Alexandria (c. 195) claimed that Israel "denied the Lord" and thus "forfeited the place of the true Israel."[12] Tertullian (c. 197) declared, "Israel has been divorced."[13]

But with Scripture so clear on the significance of Israel in God's plans, why did so many in the church adopt a replacement theology view? Three factors come into play.

The first is *the increasing Gentile composition of the early church.* The church, in its early stages, was composed primarily of believing Israelites. But as the church grew and spread it became increasingly Gentile in number, particularly after the failed second Jewish revolt of AD 132–135. Increasing Gentile salvation was a good thing, but the tendency of Christian Gentiles to believe they had permanently replaced Israel was not healthy. According to Jeffrey Siker, Jewish Christians "were eventually absorbed into an overwhelmingly Gentile Christianity."[14] As a result, the church increasingly became the *Ecclesia ex gentibus* ("Church of the Gentiles"). This growing Gentile presence led to "theological questions regarding the status of the Jews before God."[15]

Second, *the disastrous destructions of Jerusalem in AD 70 and 135 led many Christians to view these events as God's permanent rejection of Israel.* As Wayne House observes, "After A.D. 70, and especially after A.D. 135, the Jewish religion increasingly became the enemy of the gospel of Christ and the followers of Christ."[16] Origen said, "A sign that she [Israel] has received the bill of divorce is this, that Jerusalem was destroyed along with what they called the sanctuary of the things in it which were believed to be holy."[17]

Third, *the acceptance of allegorical hermeneutics concerning Israel and Bible prophecy also contributed to widespread acceptance of replacement theology.* Jaroslav Pelikan pointed out that "spiritual exegesis" was applied to the Old Testament Scriptures by the early church.[18] As a result, "There was no early Christian who simultaneously acknowledged the doctrinal authority of the Old Testament and interpreted it literally."[19] Tertullian, for example, allegorically interpreted Genesis 25:21-23 and its statement that "the older will serve the younger." For him, this was evidence that national Israel would become subservient to the church:

> Accordingly, since the people or nation of the Jews is anterior in time, and "greater" through the grace of primary favor in the Law, whereas ours is understood to be "less" in the age of times, as having in the last era of the world attained the knowledge of divine

mercy: beyond doubt, through the edict of divine utterance, the prior and "greater" people—that is, the Jewish—must necessarily serve the "less" and the "less" people—that is, the Christian—overcome the "greater."[20]

It's important to note that the reasons the church adopted replacement theology were not good. Replacement theology did not arise as a result of good Bible interpretation principles or the solid exegesis of Scripture.

Modern Promoters of Replacement Theology

Ever since the first century, some in the church have espoused some form of replacement theology. Fortunately, in the aftermath of the Reformation, many rejected this and returned to the biblical view of Israel's significance in God's purposes. This was true for many English Puritan and Dutch Reformed theologians.[21] The rise of dispensationalism thinking in the nineteenth century (although tenets of dispensationalism went back centuries before[22]) convinced many that the church had not replaced Israel. Also, two twentieth-century events—the Holocaust and the establishment of the modern state of Israel—caused many Christians to rethink and reject the validity of replacement theology. In reference to these two historical events Kendall Soulen observes, "Under the new conditions created by these events, Christian churches have begun to consider anew their relation to the God of Israel and the Israel of God in the light of the Scriptures and the gospel about Jesus."[23] This includes a "revisiting [of] the teaching of supersessionism after nearly two thousand years."[24]

While much progress has been made, replacement theology/supersessionism is still popular today and taught in many churches and seminaries. In fact, the replacement view appears to be growing these days. In his defense of a covenant theology approach to the church, Robert L. Reymond refers to "our Lord's 'replacement theology.'"[25] Theologian Bruce K. Waltke says the New Testament teaches the "hard fact that national Israel and its law have been permanently replaced by the church and the New Covenant."[26]

Even more concerning is the recent promotion of replacement theology to criticize evangelical support for the state of Israel and Israel's right to the land of promise. Evangelicals traditionally have been supportive of the modern state of Israel, affirming the Jewish people's right to exist and live peacefully in their land. A LifeWay Research study in 2017 found that "eighty percent [of evangelicals] say God promised the land of Israel to Abraham and his descendants for all time."[27] And "eighty percent say the rebirth of Israel in 1948 was a fulfillment of biblical prophecy."[28] Also, "sixty-nine percent say the Jewish people have a historic right to the land of Israel."[29] These findings do not mean evangelicals affirm everything the state of Israel does. Nor does it downplay the fact that Israel as a whole remains in unbelief and in need of salvation. Evangelicals also want fair treatment for other peoples in the region. But overall, they have been supportive of Israel. The same LifeWay Research study found that only 1 percent of evangelicals "do not support the existence, security, and prosperity of the State of Israel."[30]

But some danger signs are starting to surface. Younger evangelicals today (58 percent) have a less positive perception of Israel than older evangelicals (76 percent). They are also less sure that Israel's rebirth as a nation in 1948 was a good thing.[31] This trend away from the support of Israel seems to coincide with the growing popularity of replacement theology.

Also concerning is the fact some evangelical scholars use replacement theology to oppose Christian support of Israel. One example is Stephen Sizer, former vicar of the Anglican parish of Christ Church in England. Sizer's dissertation and published works have strongly opposed Christian Zion and have chastised Christians for supporting the modern state of Israel. Sizer rejects the term *replacement theology* but says there is "biblical basis for a kind of supersessionism."[32] For Sizer there is no future for ethnic/national/territorial Israel because God has already fulfilled the promises originally made to Israel.[33]

To avoid taking Old Testament promises of a restoration of national Israel literally, Sizer believes that "Jesus and the apostles *reinterpreted* the Old Testament."[34] Sizer claims that the disciples were "still confused" when they asked Jesus, "Lord, is it at this time that You are restoring the kingdom to Israel?" (Acts 1:6).[35] With a supersessionist view as his foundation, Sizer has been very strong in condemning the modern state of Israel as an oppressive "apartheid state" involved with ethnic cleansing.[36]

Gary Burge, Professor of New Testament at Calvin Theological

Seminary, also has spoken out against Christian support for the state of Israel. He endorsed Sizer's book and joins Sizer in calling for a reinterpretation of God's promises to Israel in the Bible:

> For as we shall see (and as commentators regularly show) while the land itself had a concrete application for most in Judaism, Jesus and his followers *reinterpreted* the promises that came to those in his kingdom.[37]

Perhaps one of the more influential and popular Bible scholars of our era is the English New Testament scholar and retired Anglican bishop N.T. Wright. Wright has promoted a strong replacement theology position that accompanies his sharp criticism for Christians who support Israel. Significantly, Wright introduces a radical discontinuity in the Bible's storyline by using several "re-" words to argue that God redefined His own purposes. For example, although the Bible strongly links the kingdom with Israel (see Matthew 19:28; Acts 1:6), Wright believes Jesus redefined the kingdom of God:

> Jesus spent His whole ministry *redefining* what the kingdom meant. He refused to give up the symbolic language of the kingdom, but filled it with such a new content that, as we have seen, He powerfully subverted Jewish expectations.[38]

There are other notable examples where Wright introduces change to the Bible storyline. He says Jesus was "*reconstituting* Israel around himself,"[39] and "*reinterpreting* Israel's eschatological hope,"[40] and "*reusing* Israel's prophetic heritage and *retelling* its story."[41] Such "re-" language offers radical discontinuity to God's plans. This is a far cry from Paul's message in Romans 15:8 that "Christ has become a servant to the circumcision on behalf of the truth of God to confirm the promises given to the fathers." Jesus did not come to *redefine* Israel's promises, but to *confirm* and bring them to fruition.

Wright also uses his replacement view to argue against Christian support for Israel that is linked with Bible prophecy: "To suggest, therefore, that as Christians we should support the state of Israel because it is the fulfilment of prophecy is, in a quite radical way, to cut off the branch on which we are sitting."[42]

In the same paragraph, Wright challenges the Christianity of those who support the current state of Israel because of the Bible. He says, "Say that if you like, but don't claim to be Christian in doing so."[43] Wright even refers to Christian Zionism as "the geographical equivalent of a *soi-disant* [self-proclaimed] 'Christian' apartheid, and ought to be rejected as such."[44] Wright's negative views of Israel contrast with the more biblical approach of another English Anglican bishop from the nineteenth century, J.C. Ryle (1816–1900). Ryle said that national Israel's return to Palestine and conversion "appear as clearly and plainly revealed as any prophecy in God's Word":

> Time would fail me, if I attempted to quote all the passages of Scripture in which the future history of Israel is revealed. Isaiah, Jeremiah, Ezekiel, Hosea, Joel, Amos, Obadiah, Micah, Zephaniah, Zechariah all declare the same thing. All predict, with more or less particularity, that in the end of this dispensation the Jews are to be restored to their own land and to the favor of God. I lay no claim to infallibility in the interpretation of Scripture in this matter. I am well aware that many excellent Christians cannot see the subject as I do. I can only say, that to my eyes, the future *salvation* of Israel as a people, their *return* to Palestine and their national conversion to God, appear as clearly and plainly revealed as any prophecy in God's Word.[45]

God Has Not Rejected Israel

What should we think about replacement theology? We should understand that it is an unbiblical doctrine with bad results. It distorts the Bible's storyline, ignores significant biblical evidence concerning national Israel's significance, and often leads to anti-Semitism. Fortunately, many have rejected this view, but some still affirm and use it as a theological basis for hostile views toward Israel and negative critiques of Christians who affirm God's promises for Israel. Instead, we should affirm what Paul stated: "God has not rejected His people, has He? May it never be!" (Romans 11:1).

CHAPTER 13
READER RESPONSE

What Should We Think About Replacement Theology?

WHAT DO *YOU* THINK?

I agree with the author on

I disagree with the author because

What was news to me?

How does this change the way I think about replacement theology?

PART 3

What Should We Think About Israel's Prospects?

14

What Should We Think About the Role of the Jews in World History?

JIM MELNICK

In a review of what people have achieved over the course of world history, the Jews and their accomplishments top the list. The historical record shows that Jewish medical, scientific, and technological discoveries and inventions have changed the world and improved life for millions. There are perhaps more startup companies in Israel today than anywhere else in the world. What does this say concerning the role of the Jewish people in the history of mankind?

Let's start with this proposition: In very many respects, world history *is* the history of the Jews! That sounds like a bold assertion, but I believe it is true. The history of the Jewish people represents the trajectory of world history. In his book *A History of the Jews,* historian Paul Johnson asked, "Is history merely a series of events whose sum is meaningless?...No people has ever insisted more firmly than the Jews that history has a purpose and humanity a destiny."[1]

Russian philosopher Nikolai Berdyaev (1874–1948) declared, "To Jewry has belonged...an intense sense of historical destiny...The Jewish people are, predominantly, a people of history, and in the historical destiny of this people is felt the inscrutability of God's destinies." In his youth Berdyaev was a materialist, but when he tried to make sense of his materialism in light of examining the history of the Jews, everything broke down. He could not explain "the case of the Jews, where destiny seemed absolutely inexplicable from the materialistic standpoint..."[2]

As a whole, the Jewish people (Hebrew, *Kol Yisrael*) represent what we call a singularity. Regarding their connection to history, we could paraphrase Theodosius Dobzhansky's famed comment "Nothing in biology makes sense except in the light of evolution" and say, "Nothing in history makes sense except in light of the role of the Jewish people"!

There is not now among the peoples of the world, nor has there ever been, another people like the Jewish people. But wherever they have been scattered across the globe throughout the centuries, there has always been one place on planet Earth toward which their hearts have been turned—the city of Jerusalem in the land of Israel. This yearning in Jewish souls for Jerusalem is matched by the heart of God (2 Chronicles 7:16; Isaiah 49:6). It is also the only city that we know Jesus wept over (Luke 19:41-42). In this age of globalist thinking, secular elite opinion wishes that Jerusalem and the Israel "problem" would just go away. Do the Jewish people continue to have special meaning today in God's eyes? I believe they do, although secular globalists (the spirit of "Babel," Genesis 11)—combined with Islamists—seek to demolish the very idea of a special place for the Jewish people in God's plan for the world.

That idea is tied to the notion that the Jewish people are a witness for God to the world.[3] It is in this light that we must understand both the role of the Jewish people throughout history and their contributions today.

The Story of the Jews: History Is Going Somewhere

The continued existence of the Jewish people shows that world history is going somewhere, that it has a God-ordained purpose and a destiny.[4] I believe that Jewish giftedness also is a phenomenon connected to God's hand of blessing (as well as judgment) upon the Jewish people as a "nation of witness to the world." Many Christians saw the establishment of the state of Israel in 1948 as related to that purpose and destiny, but it actually goes deeper than that. It goes to the heart of God's covenant with the Jewish people. There's a reason Jesus said to the Samaritan woman, "Salvation is from the Jews" (John 4:22). Nevertheless, the church has become so "Gentilized" in its interpretation of the gospel that it has often either forgotten or tried to ignore its Jewish roots.

Meanwhile, in today's hypersensitive politically correct culture, even asserting that one group of people is special (as in "God's Chosen People") is interpreted by many globalists, radical progressives, and even some evangelicals as parochial, narrow-minded, even racist, regardless of what God says about the matter. One well-known evangelical told a leader in Jewish missions that "God has cast away ethnic Israel" and that "the Jews are no longer God's people and there is no future hope for them." Another said the very idea that the Jews are God's chosen people is "total rubbish," claiming that this is not taught in Scripture.[5]

But these allegations are false. The idea that the Jews are God's chosen people *is* taught—all through Scripture! How things have changed from the time of Algernon J. Pollock, who in the 1930s wrote *The Amazing Jew*, which went through multiple editions. Pollock wrote that the story of the Jews "is a story that is inexplicable apart from the Scriptures and the power of God." He added, "The history of the Jew is the finger of God."[6] More recently, Kelvin Crombie noted that the Gentile nations "soon forgot that God had made an everlasting covenant with Israel, and that despite her present national reluctance to accept Jesus as King Messiah, God [has] not broken covenant with them."[7]

Saying that the Jewish people are special or gifted does *not* mean they are better than others. All men and women are equal in God's sight, but Scripture does delineate two types of people: Jews and Gentiles. The Bible also speaks clearly of God's irrevocable covenant with the Jewish people (Romans 11:28-29) and His blessing upon them, with "glory and honor and peace to everyone who does good, to the Jew first and also to the Greek" (Romans 2:10b) as well as being first in line for judgment: "There will be tribulation and distress for every soul of man who does evil, to the Jew first and also to the Greek" (Romans 2:9-10a).

Another Aspect of Chosen-ness

That is the spiritual side of things, but this "chosen-ness" also has a more earthly dimension—one that we see played out not only in the continued miracle of Jewish existence in such a hostile world, but also in the *thriving* of the Jewish people against all odds. This has intrigued and astounded many people throughout the centuries, including author Mark Twain (at the same time, it has infuriated anti-Semites). In 1899, Twain wrote that the Jews' "contributions to the world's list of great names in literature, science, art, music, finance, medicine, and abstruse learning are…way out of proportion to the weakness of [their] numbers." They have done this "with [their] hands tied behind" them. He wrote,

> The Egyptian, the Babylonian, and the Persian rose, filled the planet with sound and splendor, then faded to dream-stuff and passed away; the Greek and Roman followed, and made a vast noise, and they are gone…The Jew saw them all, beat them all, and is now what he always was…All things are mortal but the Jew; all other forces pass, but he remains. What is the secret of his immortality?[8]

This is an extraordinary passage, written even before all the tumult, triumph, and tragedy of the Jewish people in the twentieth century. During the last hundred-plus years since Mark Twain penned his words, their significance has become even more relevant. But beyond Jewish existence, in our day Jewish contributions to the world have soared. Is this also evidence of God's hand of blessing upon the Jewish people?

Jewish Contributions

The late Shimon Peres (former prime minister of Israel) said, "The greatest contribution of the Jewish people in history is dissatisfaction."[9] Many Jewish people have a deep personal quest for excellence and a strong drivenness to attain it.[10] In his 1998 book *The Gifts of the Jews,* author Thomas Cahill concluded that the Jewish people were "the progenitors of the Western world."[11] In physics alone, as I discuss in *Jewish Giftedness and World Redemption: The Calling of Israel* (Messianic Jewish Publishers, 2017), "original and unique contributions to physics by Jewish scientists, theorists and scholars exceed every other nationality on earth by a huge margin."[12] Various secular theories have been floated to explain this phenomenon, but they all fall short.

A few Jewish scholars have written about Jewish contributions to world civilization, but generally there is a strong reluctance among Jews to discuss this topic (although Jewish parents are happy to *kvell*—the Yiddish word for "burst with pride" over their children's achievements!). Joseph Jacobs noted this reticence even back in 1920 in *Jewish Contributions to Civilization* when he wrote that "the Jewish origin of many professional, scientific, and artistic celebrities is often unknown and sometimes concealed even by themselves."[13] As a result, most general-audience books and articles about historic and current Jewish contributions to civilization have usually been written by Gentiles. Examples include Thorstein Veblen, George Gilder, Charles Murray, Steven Pease, and myself.[14]

A "Colossal" Phenomenon

Even very *public* achievements—such as the highly disproportionate number of Jews (relative to other people groups) who have won Nobel Prizes—is rarely mentioned, but when it *is* pointed out, the reactions are interesting. You know that you're onto something when the world's most famous atheist, Richard Dawkins, acknowledges that this is a "colossal" phenomenon. Dawkins notes that the percentage of Jews who have received Nobel Prizes for scientific work "is exceedingly high...I don't have the answer to it. I am intrigued by it," he adds. "I didn't even know this extraordinary effect until it was pointed out to me by the [former] chief rabbi of Britain, Jonathan Sacks...He shared it with due modesty, but I thought it was astounding, and I am puzzled about it."[15]

This is indeed an extraordinary phenomenon—one I have chronicled at length in *Jewish Giftedness.* I don't have the space here to reproduce all of the data in that book, but let me encapsulate just a few key facts: Jews today make up far less than one percent of the world's total population, yet they "have won more than 20 per cent of all Nobel Prizes."[16] The greatest violinists, pianists, technology wizards (think of Google, Facebook, WhatsApp, Waze), philanthropists, physicists, mathematicians, chess masters, and on and on are either Jewish or else Jews make up a very highly disproportionate percentage of the leaders in those fields.[17] Collectively, these constitute what author George Gilder has termed the "globally enriching gifts of spirit and intellect."[18]

Not Just Limited to Ashkenazi Jewry

World Jewry is divided into three large groupings: the Ashkenazim, the Sephardim, and the Mizrahim (Oriental Jews).[19] Some observers claim that the phenomenon of Jewish giftedness and genius is almost exclusively limited to Ashkenazi Jews (primarily Central and East European Jews and their descendants) and does not extend to the Jewish people as a whole.[20] I believe that notion is flawed.

Well-known sociologist and political scientist Charles Murray would agree. He "suspects that elevated Jewish intelligence was (a) not confined to Ashkenazim and (b) antedates the Middle Ages" and that a strong case can be made "that Jews everywhere had unusually high intellectual resources that manifested themselves outside of Ashkenaz and well before the period when non-rabbinic Ashkenazi accomplishment manifested itself."[21] When the Sephardim had some degree of freedom and security, they blossomed—while their Ashkenazi brethren were just surviving.[22] In later centuries under other historical conditions, those roles were reversed. This is consistent with what Steven Pease observed in *The Golden Age of Jewish Achievement*: "In any meritocracy, Jews [have] prevailed."[23]

Are you beginning to see a pattern here? When the Jewish people are treated well (or at least given some level of freedom and security), they flourish. Gilder has noted, "In any free society, Jews will tend to be represented disproportionately in the highest ranks of both its culture and its commerce."[24] At the same time, when Jews are persecuted, they sometimes *still* excel and prevail—*if they survive*, but for different reasons. A Hebrew/Yiddish word—*davka*—tries to capture this sense: "The more they try to put us down, the more we will show them."[25]

"A light to the nations"; *Tikkun Olam* for a Broken World

God called Israel (as the Jewish people) to be "a light to the nations" (Isaiah 42:6). They have "a divine mission to accomplish…to be a witness to the true God in the presence of the other peoples" of the world.[26] Adolph Saphir, a Jewish believer in Jesus in the nineteenth century, proclaimed that "no other nation was taught from the very commencement of its existence that its object was to benefit all the world, that its mission was to be a lightbearer to all people that on earth do dwell."[27] One Jewish writer has amended this idea to refer to Judaism itself (wrongly, in my view): "…Judaism's survival is a phenomenon of such magnitude that it is a near-unassailable validation of God's intent to guarantee the continuing ability of the Jewish nation to fulfill its unique role as a 'light unto the nations' in the unfolding of world history."[28] Close but not quite right—it is missing the main ingredient!

When a 2016 issue of the magazine *Israel Today* proclaimed on its cover, "It's not easy being 'a light to the nations,'"[29] it was closer to the mark. The reality is, it's not only difficult but actually *impossible* to truly be "a light to the nations" without the One who is the true source of that light—Yeshua the Messiah.

Parallel to trying to bring "light to the nations" (without relying on the true Light) is the effort by many Jewish people to try to "restore" this broken world, even if those efforts often take worldly, radical, and other unbiblical paths. Ever since the *Haskalah* (the "Jewish Enlightenment") during the late eighteenth and early nineteenth centuries, that concept has been related to *tikkun olam* ("repairing the world"). Today it pervades nearly all of Judaism, from the most secular-minded to the most religious.[30] One Jewish observer said that "being Jewish means striving for *tikkun olam*."[31]

In a way in which many Jewish people probably have never thought about it, the notion of *tikkun olam* is also a driving force behind the desire to make an important contribution to the world, to leave something of value behind, to excel, to be the best (if possible) at what one does. Jewish rabbi Juan Marcos Bejarano Gutierrez says that the phrase *tikkun olam* "is seldom found explicitly in Jewish sources. Nevertheless, one could argue that it remains the heart of classical Judaism" and "includes the idea of a godly partnership with humanity to make the world a better place."[32]

In the ancient world, being "a light to the nations" centered on the Jewish Temple in Jerusalem, as well as Jewish synagogues scattered throughout the then-known world. This is why those Gentiles in the Hellenistic world who were repelled by paganism were attracted to Jewish synagogues and the God of Israel. When Paul preached in the synagogue in Thessalonica, for example, some of the Jews "were persuaded and joined Paul and Silas, along with a large number of the God-fearing Greeks" (Acts 17:4).

What was this "large number" of God-fearing Gentiles doing in or near the Jewish synagogue in the first place?! There was no flash-mob social media notice telling everyone to gather to hear this man Paul. Rather, the synagogues were where devout, God-fearing Gentiles already went to learn something about the one true God (Acts 15:21). The synagogues were the initial means God used to bring the message of salvation that Jesus is the Messiah to the Gentiles (through the apostle Paul—Acts 17:1-2). Gentiles in the first century would have thought that the new Christian faith had *everything* to do with the Jews (Acts 10:1-2; 15:22-31). It wasn't until later that Christianity came to be stripped of its Jewish roots and the church's shameful history of persecuting the Jews began.[33] Historically, the Jewish people were the vessels through whom the message of the gospel was first brought (John 4:22), and it will be the Jewish people through whom it is last brought (Romans 11:15; Revelation 7:1-8).

"Start-up Nation"; The "Israel Test"

Charles Murray's magisterial work *Human Accomplishment: The Pursuit of Excellence in the Arts and Sciences, 800 B.C. to 1950* asks why there were not more Jewish contributions prior to the nineteenth century, as well as more "significant [Jewish] figures" earlier on in world history. The answer is straightforward. It is because of the "Jews' near-total exclusion from the arts and sciences" before the modern era.[34]

What about today? Economic metrics show that Israel has developed "the greatest concentration of innovation and entrepreneurship in the world today." It has "the highest density of start-ups in the world."[35] And this process keeps building upon itself. As the authors of *Start-Up Nation* have observed, "a thread runs through the founders' time of draining swamps and growing oranges to today's era of start-ups and chip designers."[36]

Many Israeli high-tech entrepreneurs got their start in elite military units in the Israel Defense Forces (IDF), where they forged friendships and developed problem-solving skills that would last a lifetime. These elite units are Israel's "equivalent of Harvard, Princeton, and Yale," and also serve "as incubators for thousands of Israeli high-tech start-ups."[37]

Famed investor, economist, and author George Gilder has written a remarkable book titled *The Israel Test*. In it, he notes that "the leading entrepreneurial talent of the world is disproportionately Jewish."[38] He adds that "Israel today concentrates the genius of the Jews." And that "genius has lifted the culture and economy of the world."[39] Elsewhere Gilder has written that "Western civilization, in part, originated in Israel...Israel is a crucial source of invention, military intelligence, and entrepreneurial creativity that may yet save the West."[40] The "Israel test" is whether the world will recognize this or will instead try to tear Israel down.

The Russian Jews and a Great Move of God

Immigration has been key to Israel's "economic miracle." The country is "home to more than seventy different nationalities and cultures." Jews from the former Soviet Union have figured extensively in that miracle: "Walk into an Israeli technology start-up or a big R&D center in Israel today and you'll likely overhear workers speaking Russian." For Soviet Jewish dissident and former prisoner Natan Sharansky, who rose to become deputy prime minister of Israel, being a Jew in the former Soviet Union "had no positive meaning for us then, only that we were victims of anti-Semitism." As a result, "you had to be exceptional in your profession, whether it was chess, music, mathematics, medicine, or ballet...That was the only way to build some kind of protection for yourself, because you would always be starting from behind."[41]

What's astonishing to consider is this: The Jewishness of Soviet Jews had almost been extinguished by the 1970s under atheistic Soviet Communism.[42] And yet it wasn't *because of anti-Semitism!* It was anti-Semitism that let Soviet Jews know there was something different about them. God turned that terrible hatred around not only to preserve His people but also to bring many of them to the land of Israel, where they are making enormous contributions to science and technology.[43] Who could have imagined this beforehand? Not only that, but this generation of former Soviet Jews has been more open to the gospel than any Jewish group in memory. Russian Messianic Jewish believers have transformed the body of believers in Israel.[44] They have also remade "the landscape of the modern Messianic movement."[45]

Per Capita Statistics

Israel "leads the world in the percentage of its GDP that goes to research and development."[46] Because it has so many start-ups, Israel is often referred to as Silicon Wadi. The city of Be'ersheva, once the site of Abraham's well (Genesis 21:25-33), now hosts one of the most important cybersecurity hubs on the planet.[47] Be'ersheva itself has "more chess grand-masters per capita than any other city in the world."[48] For that matter, Israel "has more engineers and scientists per capita than any other country and produces more scientific papers per capita than any other nation."[49] It also "dwarfs other nations" when it comes to per capita innovation.[50]

Investment, not Divestment

I believe in investment, not divestment. Billions of dollars in venture capital are now pouring into Israel's R&D and high-tech sectors in support of cutting-edge technologies, providing a glimpse of possible break-throughs in the future: artificial intelligence, agri-tech, autonomous vehicles, bioengineering, cybersecurity, nanotechnology, robotics, drone search and rescue, industrial applications, and on and on.[51] I believe that God will continue to bless Israel in many different ways. For example, I think that some of the next great medical breakthroughs in the world will come out of Israel.

You may say, "This is all well and good, but what about the Pales-tinians?" Well, we need to help them (and they too benefit from Jewish giftedness)! The church could and should play an important role in the Middle East instead of largely sitting on the sidelines or being an arm-chair critic. Even as I write this, rockets from Gaza are raining down on cities across Israel, including the town of Sderot, where I have friends who minister the gospel to Russian Jews. But not everyone in Gaza is a jihad-ist. There are many ordinary people there whose daily lives are a living hell. What can we do? Can we not help both suffering Palestinians and Israe-lis? The answer is *yes*. There are constructive ways we can at least help our brethren in the faith among the Palestinians, including a tiny group of per-haps a thousand or so in Gaza who still name the name of Christ among some two million Muslims. If you are interested, I invite you to contact me at info@frji.org for more information about what you or your church or other organization can do.

All peoples of the Middle East desperately need to hear the gospel. Whether or not I have persuaded you to support Israel—and to do so in a biblical way—I urge you not to *oppose* Israel. Yes, critique Israel when it's appropriate, but do not oppose. Do you really want to be on the wrong side of God's flow of history?[52] From Haman to Hitler to Saddam Hussein, those who have opposed the Jews or attacked Israel have ended up on the ash heap of history.

God will have His way with Israel and the Jewish people according to *His* timing. We as Christians need to proclaim the gospel and to stand for truth and righteousness, trying to draw more and more peoples of the region to know our Jewish Messiah, awaiting His return and that great day when "all Israel will be saved" (Romans 11:26) and "the earth will be full of the knowledge of the LORD as the waters cover the sea" (Isaiah 11:9).

CHAPTER 14
READER RESPONSE

What Should We Think About the Role of the Jews in World History?

WHAT DO *YOU* THINK?

I agree with the author on

I disagree with the author because

What was news to me?

How does this change the way I think about the role of the Jews in world history?

15

What Should We Think About Israel's Future?

ANDY WOODS

The Old Testament and Jewish religious sources predicted that Israel, as a people, would return to the land and restore it as they awaited the coming of their Messiah, who would elevate them to a position over the nations of the world and establish their rule from Jerusalem. However, over the course of history, others have had different views about Israel's future, including those within the Christian church. What are these dissenting views? Are they biblical? And what difference does it make what Israel and others believe about the nation's future?

Scripture is about the Jews. The Bible reveals an abundance of information concerning Israel's past, present, and future. Yet many people who accept the Bible marginalize and even dismiss what Scripture reveals about Israel's future. This chapter offers a corrective by explaining what Scripture teaches. We will begin by highlighting why Israel will one day reign supreme over the nations. Then we will examine why belief in a future for Israel matters. And last, we will expose the inadequacy of the scriptural arguments employed by those who argue that Israel has no future.

Why a Future for Israel?

To arrive at a conviction concerning Israel's future, it is necessary to examine the nature and scope of God's past commitments to the Jewish people.

Israel's Origin

God personally created Israel (Isaiah 43:1). Why? After the fall of man (Genesis 3), God announced that His redemptive program will be accomplished through a coming one, the seed of the woman Eve, who would inflict a fatal wound upon the serpent, or Satan (Revelation 12:9; 20:2), by crushing his head (Genesis 3:15; Romans 16:20). Through which nation would this Messiah come?

A crisis soon developed, for none of the then-existing nations were seeking God (Romans 3:11). Rather, all had a tainted origin; each had gone its own way (Genesis 11:1-9). With the call of Abram (Genesis 5:1-32; 9:26; 11:10-26) out of Ur of the Chaldeans, God set about to create a new nation from Abram's physical descendants. The promises of a coming Messiah were later narrowed not just to Abram's seed (Genesis 12:3) but to the descendants of Isaac (Genesis 17:18-19) and Jacob (Numbers 24:17). Through this lineage, otherwise known as the Hebrews or Israel, God's chosen one would come to redeem the world.

Israel's Promises

Because of her significance, God articulated numerous promises to Israel (Genesis 12:1-3). Three core promises are identifiable: first, a stipulation of *land* (Genesis 12:7; 15:7) extending from modern-day Egypt to Iraq (15:18-21). The promises also included *seed* or descendants (15:2-6) as well as personal *blessing* to Abram (15:1). These divine promises of land, seed, and blessing were eventually ratified into covenantal form (15:18) in the Abrahamic covenant. Before we can arrive at a proper perspective about Israel's future, it's essential to understand the key features of this covenant.

First, the terms of the covenant are to be construed in their ordinary sense. That this covenant was terrestrial in nature became evident when God told Abram to walk about the land that his descendants would come to possess (Genesis 13:17).

Second, the terms were made to a specific group of people, Abram's physical descendants (15:4-5).

Third, because the terms emanate from God, they are entirely trustworthy (Numbers 23:19; Titus 1:2; Hebrews 6:18).

Fourth, these terms furnish the foundation of God's later subcovenants with Israel. He made additional covenants with the nation that clarified His initial obligations. Just as the Hebrew word *berith*, or "covenant," is used to describe God's commitments to Israel in the Abrahamic covenant (Genesis 15:18), it is also used in each of the subcovenants (Deuteronomy 29:1; Psalm 89:3-4; Jeremiah 31:31). The *land* provision is amplified in the land covenant (Deuteronomy 29–30). The *seed* aspect is clarified in the Davidic covenant (2 Samuel 7:12-16). The *blessing* component is elaborated upon in the new covenant (Jeremiah 31:31-34).

These subcovenants are to be fulfilled literally. For example, the land covenant includes predictions of both Israel's scattering and regathering. Deuteronomy 30:3 says, "God will…*gather* you…from all the peoples where the LORD your God has *scattered* you." If Israel's scattering in the diaspora beginning in AD 70 was literal, then the predicted regathering must be literal as well.

Fifth, as of today, the covenantal promises remain unfulfilled. Although some elements of them have been fulfilled, the promises themselves remain largely unrealized. For example, the nation has gained, both historically and presently, a mere fraction of all that God initially promised (Genesis 15:18-21).[1] Moreover, the Abrahamic covenant predicts that the nation will possess the land as an "everlasting possession" (Genesis 17:8). Because Israel has been thrice evicted from her land, this eternal land possession has not yet materialized.

Sixth, God's covenants with Israel are unilateral or unconditional. Thus they rest upon God alone for their ultimate fulfillment.[2] According to the commonly practiced ancient Near Eastern covenant ratification ceremony, both parties to a covenant were to pass between two rows of severed animal parts, thereby signifying that they too were to be severed should they fail to meet their covenantal obligations. However, in this case, God put Abram to sleep while He alone, as represented by the oven and the torch, passed between the animal parts (Genesis 15:9-17). This signified that God alone would be responsible for the fulfillment of the covenant's terms. Furthermore, there are no conditions stated in the Abrahamic covenant for Abraham's descendants to fulfill. Surely such human conditions would be conspicuous if God had intended for the covenant to be bilateral rather than unilateral.

Moreover, the Abrahamic covenant is called both eternal (Genesis 17:7,13,19; 1 Chronicles 16:17; Psalm 105:10) and immutable (Hebrews 6:13-18), meaning it must rest upon an eternal (Psalm 90:2; Romans 16:26) and immutable (Malachi 3:6) God for its fulfillment. Finally, the fact that the covenant was unconditional becomes apparent upon noting it was continually reaffirmed regardless of Israel's repeated disobedience. For example, the covenant was reiterated to Abraham (Genesis 15) despite his lie that Sarah was his sister (Genesis 12:10-20), to Jacob (Genesis 28:10-22) after he cheated Esau out of his birthright (Genesis 27), to Israel (Jeremiah 31:35-37) despite her disobedience that led to the divine discipline of the Babylonian captivity (2 Chronicles 36:15-16), and to Israel (Romans 11:25) despite her national rejection of her own Messiah (Acts 2:23).

Seventh, the covenant will be fulfilled in phases. Israel will be brought back into her land following worldwide dispersion in unbelief in preparation for the discipline to take place during the tribulation period. Then she will be restored to her own land in preparation for millennial blessing (Isaiah 11:11).[3] Ezekiel predicted the nation would be regathered to her land, and then the Spirit would be poured out upon her (Ezekiel 36:24-28). Similarly, Ezekiel predicted the nation will form like a human body without breath, and then breath (the Holy Spirit) will enter her (37:1-11).

That Israel has a prophetic program to fulfill not only in belief but also initially in unbelief seems apparent through predictions concerning Jerusalem's role in the tribulation as analogized to the spiritual forces of Sodom and Egypt (Revelation 11:8). Also, Israel will enter a covenant with the Antichrist (Isaiah 28:18; Daniel 9:27) while she is in unbelief. The fulfillment of these prophecies is impossible unless Israel is first regathered to her ancient homeland in unbelief, and this process is taking place today. In sum, when we consider Israel's unique purpose and promises, it becomes apparent that God has a future for Israel.

Israel's Importance?

Why is God's commitment to Israel important? Why can't these promises be abrogated or changed in the future, especially if Israel rebels against God and violates the covenants?

First, God works in history according to His prior covenantal obligations. For example, the exodus, one of the greatest redemptive events in history, happened because of God's remembrance of His promises in the Abrahamic covenant (Exodus 2:24).[4] If God indeed moves His hand in history on the basis of His covenantal promises, and His covenantal promises remain unconditional and unfulfilled, then we can expect God to work once again to fulfill His end-time program with Israel (Ezekiel 36:22). This understanding of the nature of God's Old Testament promises furnishes the basis for believing Israel has a future place in God's plans.

Second, to say God doesn't have future plans for Israel is to question God's reliability with regard to keeping His other promises. If God can break the covenants He made to Israel, then how can He be trusted to keep the promises He has made to today's believers?

The apostle Paul, when he wrote Romans, made a rather significant digression when it came to Romans 9–11. Paul ended Romans 8 on a crescendo by proclaiming God's inviolable promises to the Christian (Romans 8:31-39). Can we trust those promises? Paul's response was a resounding yes in Romans 9–11, where he affirms that God has not broken His covenant obligations to Israel. In fact, God has a plan in place through which He will keep His commitments.

Paul explained that Israel was elected by God in the *past* (Romans 9), rejected Him in the *present* (Romans 10), and will accept Him in the *future* (Romans 11). Because God is vindicated as a covenant-keeping God who will fulfill His promises to Israel, He can be trusted to keep the promises He has made to church-age believers. Believers can be so confident in God's trustworthiness that they can, in worshipful response, offer their body to Him as a living sacrifice (Romans 12:1).

Not only do God's promises to Israel serve as a basis for believing in a future for Israel, but they also serve as the foundation for believing that God can be trusted to faithfully execute all of His other commitments, especially as they relate to the New Testament believer.

Answering the Arguments Used to Dismiss Israel

Despite the evidence in support of God's continued commitment to Israel, many evangelicals marginalize Israel's future. What are some of the scriptural arguments they use, and how can they be answered?

The Land Promises Already Fulfilled?

It is common for proponents of replacement theology[5] to contend that because the prophecies regarding Israel's land promises have already been fulfilled, either in the days of Joshua (Joshua 11:23; 21:43-45) or Solomon (1 Kings 4:21; 2 Chronicles 9:26),[6] there remains no future expectation for their realization. Yet how can Joshua's conquest be considered a fulfillment of the Abrahamic covenant when the context of these same passages demonstrate that the Joshua generation gained only a fraction of what God initially promised to Abraham (Joshua 13:1-7; Judges 1:19,21,27,29-36)?[7] In addition, there were key territories that did not fall into Israeli hands during the days of Joshua. Not until centuries later did they come under Israel's control. Examples include Jerusalem (Joshua 15:63; Judges 1:21), which would not become an Israeli city until four centuries later during the reign of David (2 Samuel 5:6-9), and Gezer (Joshua 16:10), which did not come under Jewish control until the days of Solomon (1 Kings 9:16-17).

Moreover, the Solomonic era hardly constitutes a complete fulfillment of Israel's land promises because Israel's territory extended only to the *border* of Egypt (1 Kings 4:21), while the Abrahamic covenant promised territory to the *river* of Egypt (Genesis 15:18).[8] Also, because the nations surrounding Israel during the Solomonic empire were merely tributary vassals, they were never formally annexed into Israeli borders. That's why they quickly defected once Solomon left the throne. Phoenicia, or Lebanon, retained its independence during Solomon's reign.[9] And why would the prophet Amos predict the realization of the land promises as late as 755 BC (Amos 9:11-15) if they were already fulfilled during the conquest (1400 BC) and Solomonic eras (971–931 BC)?[10] Finally, in light of the fact that Israel was twice evicted from her land following the demise of the united kingdom (722–586 BC, AD 70), how could the "everlasting" requirement of the Abrahamic covenant (Genesis 17:8) have been satisfied during that time?

The Church a Kingdom of Priests?

Replacement theology contends that because 1 Peter 2:9 applies Israel's description as "a kingdom of priests" (Exodus 19:5-6) to the church, the church has superseded Israel.[11] However, similarity does not mean equality. Although I own two cars that look similar, they are separate entities. Just because the church, like Israel, is also called a kingdom of priests (Revelation 1:6) does not automatically mean that the church equals Israel. Rather, this can be taken to mean that Israel is like the church in some limited respects.

In addition, replacement theology reads too much into the scope of 1 Peter, which could be construed as addressing only a believing Hebrew remnant within the church rather than the church as a whole.[12] Because Peter was an apostle to the Jews (Galatians 2:7-8), his target audience was likely also Jewish. While the word *church* or *churches* does not appear in Peter's opening salutation, he does address the letter to those who were "scattered" or in the diaspora (1 Peter 1:1), a word used *only* of Jews. All other uses of the word *diaspora* refer to Hebrews, whether these uses appear in the biblical text (John 7:35; James 1:1), the Septuagint (Deuteronomy 28:25; 30:4; Isaiah 49:6; Jeremiah 41:17; Psalm 147:2; 2 Maccabees 1:27; Judith 5:19), or the pseudepigraphical literature (Psalms of Solomon 8:28; T. Asher 7:2). While the universal church is comprised of individuals from all races, nations, and peoples, the singular nouns "race," "people," and "nation" are used to describe Peter's audience (1 Peter 2:9). In fact, Paul rejected the designation of the church as a "nation" (Romans 10:19). Thus, Peter's designation "kingdom of priests" was aimed only at the believing Jewish remnant within the church. Peter's point was this: While the nation of Israel had failed in the past to live up to her calling to be a kingdom of priests, the believing Jewish remnant within the church would presently fulfill this calling.

The Church the Seed of Abraham?

Some argue that the church has replaced Israel because the church is referred to as "Abraham's seed" (Galatians 3:29 NKJV). However, the noun "promise" in this same verse is singular. Thus, rather than the church taking over Israel's multiple "promises" (Romans 9:4), the point Paul was making is that Christians are to imitate the faith of Abraham (Romans 9:6-8).

Just as he was justified by faith alone (Genesis 15:6), so also is the church-age believer. In this limited sense, Christians became spiritual children of Abraham, just as those who imitate the character of Satan likewise become his spiritual lineage (John 8:44).

Also, the designation "Abraham's seed" does not make something Israel, for that designation belongs only to those who are not only descendants of Abraham, but also of Isaac and Jacob. Those who were Abraham's seed through his son Ishmael (Genesis 17) certainly were never considered Jewish! Thus Galatians 3:29 is yet another biblical text that replacement theology has stretched beyond its legitimate meaning.[13]

The Church the Israel of God?

Proponents of replacement theology also point to Galatians 6:16 as a proof text—they believe this passage equates the church with the "Israel of God."[14] In actuality, the verse has a more limited meaning. Rather than calling the entire church the "Israel of God," the nomenclature applies only to the smaller believing Jewish remnant within the church.[15] Although replacement theologians rely on the translation of *kai* as "even," thereby equating Israel and the church, this translation represents a rare use of the conjunction. The normal translation of *kai* is "and," which instead communicates that the "them," or the Gentile Christians, are a different entity than believing "Israel" within the church. Furthermore, throughout Scripture, "Israel" *always* means the physical descendants of Abraham, Isaac, and Jacob.[16] Why would Galatians 6:16 represent the single exception to this rule and instead refer to the predominately Gentile church? Beyond this, the repetition of "upon" or *epi* indicates that two groups are in view. Thus, it appears Paul was addressing a narrower believing Hebrew group within the church rather than the church at large when he used the phrase "Israel of God."

Other questions related to the replacement theology's use of Galatians 6:16 remain. If it is so clear that Paul here is teaching that the church is the new Israel, why did it take more than a century after Galatians was written for any church father to use Israel as a synonym for the church? Justin Martyr was the first to do so in AD 160—long after the Galatians letter had been composed in AD 49.[17] Also, why would Paul wait to introduce such a sweeping notion—that the church has replaced Israel—in the conclusion of a letter? It would seem more appropriate to introduce such a major point in the book's doctrinal section (Galatians 3–4). Rather than interpreting "Israel of God" to mean that the church has become the new Israel, it seems more accurate to interpret Paul's statement as an affectionate reference to the smaller group of Jewish believers within the church. He may have done this to counteract any potential charge of anti-Semitism due to alleged anti-Judaistic statements he made earlier in Galatians (1:8-9).[18]

No Mention of Israel's Restoration in the New Testament?

Replacement theologians also claim that Israel's restoration is not spoken of in the New Testament, and consequently, God's Old Testament promises to Israel have been cancelled.[19] Assuming, for the sake of argument, this premise, the New Testament never expressly cancels Israel's program. Silence should not be equated with cancellation. Beyond this, it stands to reason that Israel's program would not find as much development in the New Testament because the divine commitments to her were already articulated in the Old Testament. If we expect the New Testament to validate Israel's promises by restating what the Old Testament already says, then we are asking the New Testament to be redundant. Besides, we would expect the case for Israel to be less comprehensive in the New Testament because at this point, the church, rather than Israel, has become the center of salvation history.[20]

However, the replacement theologian errs in asserting that the New Testament fails to mention Israel's end-time program. Although this program is not dealt with in as much detail as is found in the Old Testament, it is still presented in the New Testament. We find God's commitments to Israel reiterated by Christ in the Gospels (Matthew 19:28; 20:20-23; 23:38-39; 24:31; 25:31,34; Luke 21:24), by Paul in Acts (Acts 1:6-7; 3:19-21; 5:31; 13:23; 15:16-18; 26:6; 28:20), in the epistles (Romans 11:25-27), and by John in the Apocalypse (Revelation 7:1-8; 11:3-13; 12:6-17; 14:15; 20:9; 21:2).[21]

Israel Cursed by the Mosaic Covenant?

Replacement theology states that Israel's national disobedience has placed it under the curses of the Mosaic covenant (Deuteronomy 28:64), and thus God has cast off His commitments to Israel.[22] However, this approach confuses the purposes behind each of God's covenants with Israel. As mentioned earlier, Israel's foundational covenant, the Abrahamic covenant, granted to Israel unconditional and perpetual ownership of her three blessings: land, seed, and blessing.

The Mosaic covenant then came alongside the Abrahamic covenant and stated to subsequent generations of Israelis the conditions necessary for her to enjoy or possess what she already owned based upon obedience (Exodus 19:5-6). Despite the fact that the curses for disobedience are severe (Deuteronomy 28:15-68), they do not represent a cancellation of Israel's program. Rather, while disobedience may deprive any given generation of Israelis the opportunity to enjoy what God promised to them, it does not cancel the initial promise of ownership. Such an abrupt cancellation would unnecessarily pit the subsequently given Mosaic covenant against the foundational Abrahamic covenant.

The Kingdom Taken from Israel and Given to the Church?

In Matthew 21:43, Jesus said, "I say to you, the kingdom of God will be taken away from you and given to a people, producing the fruit of it." Replacement theologians interpret this verse as teaching that the kingdom would be taken away from national Israel and then given to the church. Both assertions are invalid.[23] Matthew 21:45 reveals to us the audience that Christ was addressing: "When the chief priests and the Pharisees heard His parables, they understood that He was speaking about them." Christ was not addressing national Israel at large; rather, He was addressing the discipline that only first-century unbelieving Israel would experience.

Also, according to Matthew 21:43, the kingdom would be given "to a people." The word translated "people" is the noun *ethnos*, which means "nation." This word could not apply to the international church, which is not a singular nation (Romans 10:19), but rather consists of believers from all nations (Galatians 3:28). Although a poor description of the church, in the New Testament, the word "nation" or *ethnos* is frequently used to describe Israel (John 11:51; Acts 24:17). So rather than communicating that the kingdom would be taken away from Israel and given to the church, Matthew 21:43 merely indicates that the kingdom would be taken away from unbelieving first-century Israel and given to a distant believing generation from Israel during the future tribulation period.

This limited interpretation fits well with the subsequent context of Matthew's Gospel, which predicts a future national conversion of Israel (Matthew 23:38-39; 24:31; 25:31). This view also harmonizes well with Matthew's Hebrew-Christian audience,[24] who knew well from their own Scriptures how unbelief could cause God to remove His hand of blessing from one Israeli generation and instead place it upon a subsequent believing Hebrew generation (Numbers 13–14). Replacement theology, then, has distorted the limited meaning of Matthew 21:43.

God Will Keep His Promises

To accept the Bible is to accept Israel, the central character in the divine drama. In the Bible, the same Israel that has a past also has a future. The expectation of a future for Israel is confirmed by God's unconditional and unfulfilled commitments to His elect nation, which are repeated all through Scripture. None of the arguments used by replacement theologians convincingly shows any cancellation of these divine commitments. That Israel still has a place in God's future plans is a matter of practical concern because it affirms that God keeps His covenants. He can be trusted to keep His promises—to both Israel and church-age believers.

CHAPTER 15
READER RESPONSE

What Should We Think About Israel's Future?

WHAT DO *YOU* THINK?

I agree with the author on

I disagree with the author because

What was news to me?

How does this change the way I think about Israel's future?

16

What Should We Think About the Jews as a Chosen People?

ARNOLD G. FRUCHTENBAUM

In modern society, the claim that one race is above another is called racism. What is the origin of the Jewish people's belief that they are the chosen people, and how is it presented in the Bible? Furthermore, what affect has this belief had on the Jewish people collectively, on Israeli policies toward others, and on the response of other groups toward Israel?

There are few concepts in religion that are more emotionally loaded and misunderstood than the claim that the Jewish people are God's "chosen people."[1] In an era during which equality is such a major issue, such a claim seems obsolete and offensive. As Jon Levenson observes, "Few religious doctrines have attracted more virulent criticism than the idea of the chosen people. Over the past several centuries alone, both Jews and non-Jews have judged this key tenet of classical Judaism to be undemocratic, chauvinistic, superstitious—in short, retrograde in every way that matters to the progressive mind."[2]

Indeed, this idea of "chosenness" has been said to be the root of anti-Semitism and to have spawned *The Protocols of the Elders of Zion*, a notorious forgery that originated in czarist Russia and alleges a Jewish plot to achieve global domination. Furthermore, those who are calling for peace in the Middle East view this concept of chosenness as being inherently divisive and detrimental to attempts at reconciling the opposing factions in the conflict. For many religions this is an outdated concept, referring now only to a broken covenant relationship with God that has been superseded by more recent revelations. How then are we to understand the Jewish claim to chosenness in the twenty-first century?

As stated in the preface, the contributors to this book are united in their approach to presenting the facts about Israel from a biblical worldview. Because God's Word is everlasting and does not change, it is the only sure standard upon which we can gain an understanding of Israel, the Jewish people, and the Middle East conflict—no matter what the latest cultural opinion polls say.

According to divine revelation, Israel did not choose for itself the burden of being a chosen people. Nor was the application of the term intended to stir enmity or to imply that the unchosen are the enemies of God. Rather, God's intent was to produce humility and generate a servant people who would represent Him before the world and ultimately be the means to blessing all nations who come to the God of Israel through the Messiah of Israel (Genesis 12:3; Galatians 3:8).

Israel as the Chosen People in the Past

The Old Testament explains the concept of chosenness and affirms national (or ethnic) Israel as a chosen people. It provides the basis for Israel being afforded this special status as well as the purposes for Israel's chosenness. As we consider what the Old Testament says, we can gain a better understanding of Israel's special relationship with God and its unique role in the world.

The Understanding of Israel's Chosenness

As we seek to understand Israel's status as a chosen people, we must first consider the biblical teaching of election. In doing so, we must make a theological distinction between individual election and national election. Individual election extends to any person and results in the salvation of that individual.[3] By contrast, national election concerns only Israel and does not result in spiritual salvation (which only individual election can do) nor the physical deliverance of every member of the nation. Its purpose is to guarantee that God's purpose(s) for choosing the nation will be accomplished and that the elect nation will always survive as a distinct entity. These purposes include an elect remnant of Israel obtaining national salvation (Romans 11:25-27), experiencing physical restoration in its promised land (Ezekiel 37:25-26), and realizing its role as a blessing to the nations (Zechariah 8:23). This national election of Israel is the basis for its status as the chosen people.

The Unconditional Basis of Israel's Chosenness

It is a common misconception that the Jewish people's chosenness was based on some virtue they possessed or status they had achieved. In fact, they were chosen by God *before* they existed as a people or a nation. Scripture reveals that Israel was chosen as a nation in the time of Abraham (see Genesis 12:2; 18:19)—before the birth of his sons Isaac and Jacob (whose name was changed to Israel). It was God's choosing of the *seed* of the Patriarchs that made them the chosen people before this people or nation existed.

The unconditional nature of Israel's election is emphasized in Deuteronomy 4:37: "because He loved your fathers, therefore He chose their descendants [seed] after them; and He brought you out of Egypt with His Presence, with His mighty power" (NKJV). In this verse, Moses stated that the basis of Israel's election was God's love for Abraham, Isaac, and Jacob, with whom He had made a covenant, and He chose their descendants on the basis of that covenant relationship.

In Deuteronomy 7:6–8:1, Israel is declared to be "a holy people," not because of any innate righteousness on their own part, but because "YHWH your God has chosen you" (7:6). God's choosing Israel to be a holy people set her apart from other nations. She was God's "own possession out of all the peoples who are on the face of the earth" (7:6; cf. 26:18). Moreover, in Deuteronomy 7:7-8, Moses said that the basis for Israel's election was not due to its size (verse 7), for it was smaller than other nations, but because God loved Israel and established a covenant relationship with her founding fathers (verse 8). Because of this covenant relationship, God delivered Israel from Egypt (Exodus 3:6-10) and set her above the other nations (Deuteronomy 10:15). As a result, the people of Israel were obligated to obey God's commandments (Exodus 19:6) and to "circumcise their heart" (Deuteronomy 10:16), which was a spiritual sign of personal faith and individual salvation.[4]

The Unique Purpose of Israel's Chosenness

While Israel was chosen on the basis of God's love, there were multiple purposes for God's election of Israel. We find the primary purpose stated at the outset of God's revelation at Mount Sinai in Exodus 19:6: "You shall be to Me a kingdom of priests, and a holy nation." While Israel's status as "a holy nation" was based on her election, the purpose for her election was to be "a kingdom of priests." Even though Israel had a priestly tribe (Levi), the nation collectively was to serve as a priesthood. The historical function of a priest was to represent man to God. Therefore, just as the tribe of Levi represented Israel before God, Israel was to represent the Gentile nations before God.

Another purpose for Israel's chosen status was so that she could be the recipient and recorder of God's revelation. It was for this reason Israel received the Mosaic Law (Deuteronomy 4:5-8; 6:6-9; Romans 3:1-2). Yet another purpose for her chosenness was so she could serve as a witness for the one true God. In Isaiah 43:10-12, we read,

> You are My witnesses, said YHWH, and My servant whom I have chosen; that you may know and believe Me, and understand that I AM He: before Me there was no God formed, neither shall there be after Me. I, even I, am YHWH; and besides Me there is no savior. I have declared, and saved and proclaimed; and there was no strange god among you: therefore, you are My witnesses, said YHWH, and I AM God.[5]

In this passage, Israel was chosen to proclaim to the Gentile nations that YHWH, the God of Israel, is the one and only true God and Savior, and therefore all who seek salvation must find it exclusively in Him.

A final purpose for Israel's chosenness was to produce a lineage for the Messiah (Romans 9:5; Hebrews 2:16-17; 7:13-14). He would be born of the seed of Abraham and of the lineage of David (Matthew 1:1), bringing salvation first to Israel (Acts 3:26; Romans 1:16) and then to the nations (Acts 13:47; Titus 2:11).

The Unconditional Program of Israel's Chosenness

Just as national Israel's chosenness had a *purpose*, there was also a divinely designed *program* that would support and perpetuate the promises made to her as a chosen people. This program consists of the four biblical covenants made by God to Abraham and his descendants after him. These covenants begin with the Abrahamic covenant, the wellspring of the other three covenants and the basis on which the Messiah came to bring redemption to Israel (Luke 1:54-55,68-73). The three promises in this covenant of a land, a seed, and a blessing (Genesis 12:1-3; 22:17) became the basis for three separate covenants: the land covenant (Deuteronomy 30), the Davidic covenant (2 Samuel 7), and the new covenant (Jeremiah 31–33).

These covenants were unconditional ("I [God] will…") and unending ("forever") and form the basis for God's preservation of the Jewish people through time, their return to the land of Israel, the future rule of Messiah, and Israel's future physical restoration and spiritual blessings in the kingdom of God. Due to the chosen people's national sin (idolatry and defection from God—see Isaiah 30:1; 9-14; 31:6-7), they did not experience the fulfillment of all the provisions promised in these covenants—and those that they did experience were temporary. This lack of fulfillment has made some people wonder whether Israel's past rejection of God and His Messiah has cancelled their chosen status and replaced them with another chosen people (the church).

Israel as the Chosen People in the Present

Proponents of covenant theology teach that to a lesser or greater degree God's biblical covenants to Israel are now being fulfilled in, by, or through the church.[6] Their view of God's covenants controls how they interpret the nature, extent, and application of the biblical covenants made with national Israel. Some covenant theologians argue that these covenants were made with the church from the very beginning (elect Israel = the church in the Old Testament). Others concede that the covenants were originally made with national Israel but contend they have now been transferred to the church. As for national Israel, all that was promised either has already been fulfilled or has been forfeited through Jewish unbelief. Even covenant premillennialists, who see a future for ethnic Israel, believe that Israel will ultimately be amalgamated into the church.

This view, popularly stated, asserts that Israel *was* a chosen people in the past but was disinherited by God due to the people's rejection of their Messiah. Therefore, the church has replaced Israel under the new covenant and has become the new chosen people. Replacement theology maintains that because the church is the new Israel and has spiritually inherited Israel's covenants, modern Israel and the Jewish community have no special relationship with God that constitutes chosenness.

Is this, in fact, what the New Testament teaches? Should we make a theological distinction between Israel in the past and Israel in the present? What are the practical and political consequences of such a theological position? To answer these questions, we must look more closely at the four unconditional covenants God made with Israel in the past and determine if their legal language could allow for God's promises to be cancelled and transferred to a different entity.

An Overview of the Biblical Covenants in the Present

In the New Testament, the term *Israel* is used a total of 73 times, with the vast majority of instances referring only to national ethnic Israel. The three exceptions are Romans 9:6, 11:26, and Galatians 6:16; however, a strong case can be made for these also referring exclusively to ethnic Israel.[7] Based on the New Testament usage of *Israel*, we can conclude that the church is never called a "spiritual Israel" or "new Israel." The term *Israel* is either used of the nation or the people as a whole, or of the believing remnant within it, but is never used of the church in general or of Gentile believers in particular.

For that reason, we can know that national Israel continues to be God's chosen people. Whether or not the people are functioning within the purpose of their chosenness, if they exist as a distinct ethnic people, the covenants that were unconditionally promised to them must in some sense continue to operate in the present time. An overview of this present function of the covenants will help us realize this fact.

First, the biblical covenants were made exclusively with the Jewish people designated as Israel. This is stated in Romans 9:4-5: "...who are Israelites, to whom belongs the adoption as sons, and the glory and the covenants and the giving of the Law and the temple service and the promises, whose are the fathers, and from whom is the Christ according to the flesh." In that passage, not only is the emphasis on their ethnic identity ("fathers…flesh"), but on their *present* possession of these covenantal promises as well. If the writer, the apostle Paul, had understood that the rejection of Messiah by national Israel (as represented by its leaders), which had occurred 20-plus years earlier, had caused it to forfeit these promises, he would not have used the present tense in that statement. This demonstrates that the New Testament understood Old Testament "elect Israel" as ethnic (no Gentiles included), distinguishing it from the church, which is inclusive of both Jews and Gentiles.

Second, the content of these covenants, which are legal contracts, must be interpreted literally if they are to be fulfilled as originally given in the context of a particular people (the Jewish people) and a particular place (the land of Israel). Since, as stated above, these covenants were made exclusively with Israel as an ethnic and national people, they must be fulfilled with them alone. This is not to say another entity (the church) could not *participate* in them (under the new covenant, cf. Ephesians 2:11-22; Romans 11:17-24), but that their fulfillment must take place as originally intended. In contract law, both parties must unambiguously understand the terms of the contract before agreeing to them. This is called "a meeting of the minds." Israel could not have understood God to have promised her something that would be fulfilled by another people (the church). God could not have intended something different than what He promised without stating it or letting the people continue in their misunderstanding. This would constitute deception, rendering the contract null and void, and God has told Israel that He cannot lie but will always do what He has promised (Numbers 23:19).

Third, the covenants God made with Israel are eternal and are not conditioned by time. The eternality of the covenants is stated variously as "forever" (Genesis 13:15; Exodus 32:13; 2 Samuel 23:5) or "forever and ever" (Jeremiah 7:7; 25:5; cf. Psalm 48:14) or "everlasting" (Genesis 17:7-8,19). While the basic Hebrew term used here (*'olam*) may have the sense of undefined time, the one defining it in context is God, who is called "God the Eternal" (*El 'olam*—Genesis 21:33) and has an unlimited view of time with respect to the fulfillment of His legal obligations (Exodus 15:18; Deuteronomy 32:40; Psalm 90:2).

While, as stated above, nothing over time can change the terms of the covenants (literal fulfillment with Israel), fulfillment *can* be delayed or postponed. The fact that a covenant is made at a specific point of time does not mean that all the provisions of the covenant must go into effect immediately. Some can, but others may not—even for centuries. For example, Abraham was promised a son through Sarah but had to wait 25 years before that promise was fulfilled. Other provisions were not fulfilled until later in Jewish history, such as the deliverance from Egypt, which was also part of the covenant (Genesis 15:13-16). Finally, other provisions are still future and have not yet been fulfilled, such as Israel's ownership of and settlement in all of the Promised Land (Genesis 15:18; Exodus 23:31; Deuteronomy 11:24; Joshua 1:4; 13:1). Under the present condition of Israel's discipline for disobedience, fulfillment must wait until that time in the future when Israel repents as a nation at the coming of the Messiah (Zechariah 12:10–14:11; Matthew 24:30-31; Acts 3:19-26; Romans 11:25-27).

Fourth, God's covenants to Israel are unconditional, which means their fulfillment is totally dependent upon God. Even though these covenants include conditional aspects, these aspects are not the basis by which the covenants will be fulfilled. While Israel's failure to meet the conditions within these covenants has resulted in divine discipline, the covenant promises cannot be abrogated (Jeremiah 30:11; Romans 11:11-15). This fact was clearly stated in Scripture to assure Israel that even when it was exiled to foreign lands on account of divine judgment, God would still fulfill His promises by regathering Israel to the land and restoring her relationship to Him (Jeremiah 29:14; cf. Deuteronomy 30:4; Ezekiel 11:17; 36:24; 37:21,25; 39:28). There is no clearer statement of this fact than in Psalm 89 with respect to the Davidic covenant:

> I [God] have made a covenant with My chosen; I have sworn to
> David My servant, I will establish your seed forever, and build up
> your throne to all generations...My lovingkindness I will keep

for him forever, and My covenant shall be confirmed to him. So I will establish his descendants forever, and his throne as the days of heaven (verses 3-4,28-29).

God then said,

> If his sons forsake My law and do not walk in My judgments, if they violate My statutes and do not keep My commandments, then I will punish their transgression with the rod and their iniquity with stripes. But I will not break off My lovingkindness from him, nor deal falsely in My faithfulness. My covenant I will not violate, nor will I alter the utterance of My lips. Once I have sworn by My holiness; I will not lie to David. His descendants shall endure forever…(verses 30-36).

In addition, God has guaranteed the fulfillment of the covenants to Israel not for their sake, but for the sake of His own reputation (Ezekiel 36:16-32). For this reason, Israel's present disobedience has not changed the past promises, for God has not changed, the chosen people (Israel) have not changed, and the chosen place (the land of Israel) has not changed. Final fulfillment for Israel will be within "God's kingdom program [which] was the outworking of His eternal and unconditional covenants with Israel."[8]

The Operation of the Biblical Covenants in the Present

All four biblical covenants are not only still in effect, but also still operative at the present time. The church does indeed have a relationship to these covenants, but it is not the relationship that is described by covenant theology. Today, Israel is a scattered nation but still a nation. Just as Israel remained distinct in Egypt, the Jewish people have remained distinct throughout the church age. No other nation that lost its national homeland and became dispersed for centuries has ever survived as a distinct entity. Rather, wherever those nations were scattered, they intermarried and disappeared into a melting pot. Not so with the Jews, whose distinctive history is still easily traceable. The fact that the Jews have continued to survive as a people—in spite of so many attempts to destroy them—shows that the Abrahamic covenant (inclusive of all the other covenants) is still operative.

The land covenant revealed that the land would be desolate (Isaiah 6:11; 33:8) and that a final worldwide regathering would follow a similarly worldwide dispersion (Deuteronomy 4:25-31; 30:1-9; Jeremiah 33:10-22; Ezekiel 36:3-24). While the final regathering is still future, the global scattering is a present fact and has been so since AD 70. Within the confines of the church age there has been no truly independent government in the land since AD 70 until recently. It has been overrun many times and ruled by many powers (Assyrians, Babylonians, Persians, Greeks, Romans, Byzantines, Arabs, Turks, and Britons), but always ruled from somewhere else, especially under Arab occupation (Baghdad, Cairo, Damascus, Amman, etc.).

Though the land was renamed *Palestine* by Hadrian in the second century AD, there never was a Palestinian state with a Palestinian government. The first time an independent government was set up in the land since AD 70 was in 1948 with the state of Israel. This modern return to the land is in keeping with the promise of the land covenant. Therefore, the history of the land of Israel reveals that the land promises have and are being fulfilled—demonstrating that the land covenant is still working itself out with the chosen people. Never in history has Israel possessed, dwelt in, and settled in all of the Promised Land. However, the land covenant guarantees that someday it will (Ezekiel 37:25-26; 45:1-8; 47:13-23).

The Davidic covenant (2 Samuel 7:8-16) offered four eternal promises: a house (verses 11,16), a throne (verses 8,13,16), a kingdom (verses 12,16), and a descendant (verses 12,13,14-15). The fact that Yeshua the Messiah, "the son of David" (Matthew 1:1; Luke 1:32; cf. Revelation 5:5), is David's eternal descendant and is now seated on a throne at the right hand of God (Psalm 110:1) shows that this covenant is still functioning. Messiah is not currently ruling from the Davidic throne over the physical kingdom of Israel (note that the throne of David was on earth and the throne of God is in heaven), but the very fact Messiah has yet to sit upon the throne of David to rule over Israel confirms that the status of the chosen people has been maintained.

As for the promised kingdom, God stated this provision in 2 Samuel

7:10: "I will also appoint a place for My people Israel and will plant them, that they may live in their own place and not be disturbed again, nor will the wicked afflict them any more as formerly." It is evident from Israel's present experience in the Middle East conflict that this promise has not yet been fulfilled but will be in the future (Jeremiah 33:14-17,19-22). Therefore, this covenant must remain in operation until its fulfillment.

The new covenant (Jeremiah 31:31–33:26) was made between God and Israel as the means to the fulfillment of the covenantal promises.[9] The major feature of this covenant was Israel's national salvation, inclusive of every individual Jew. This covenant was signed and sealed by the shedding of Yeshua the Messiah's blood. While this provided the basis for individual Jewish salvation, the national salvation of Israel awaits a future fulfillment, with Israel's national repentance and acceptance of Yeshua when He comes to bring national redemption and restoration (Zechariah 12:10–13:1,8-9; 14:4; Acts 3:19-21; Romans 11:25-27). While the church has a relationship to this covenant, this is a uniquely Jewish covenant and therefore can only be fulfilled by a future national salvation of Israel. However, its present outworking, witnessed in the individual salvation of a Jewish remnant and their indwelling by the Holy Spirit within the church (Romans 1:16-17; 9:27-29; 11:1-5; 10: Acts 2:1-4), gives assurance that the promised national salvation (Ezekiel 36:24-32) will take place.

In addition, the fact that the Abrahamic covenant is still operational is confirmed by the fact that the blessings and curses promised in Genesis 12:3 continue to be experienced by the world's nations based on their relationship to Israel. Those who have opposed or oppressed Israel have fallen, and those who have harbored and protected Israel have risen. This ongoing blessing or judgment of the nations affirms the continual functioning of the Abrahamic covenant during this era of the new covenant.

Still the Chosen People

Some have been confused by the fact that the Jewish people are in partial possession of the Promised Land yet are not in a spiritual relationship with God, per the conditions stated within the covenants. This confusion is removed when we recognize that the prophets spoke of two international returns: the first a regathering in unbelief in preparation for judgment (Ezekiel 20:33-38; 22:17-22) during the tribulation (Matthew 24:15-21), which will be followed by a second regathering in faith in preparation for the blessings of the messianic age (Isaiah 11:11-12; Ezekiel 36:22-24). The restoration of the Jewish state is a fulfillment of the prophecies that spoke of a regathering in unbelief in preparation for judgment. The fact that prophecies are being fulfilled with the modern state of Israel shows that Israel continues to remain God's chosen people.

As we have seen, the biblical covenants contained two types of promises: physical and spiritual. The physical promises were, and still are, limited to Israel and will be fulfilled only by Israel, which is an aspect of chosenness. Another aspect of chosenness is that the spiritual blessings of these covenants would be mediated by Israel to the Gentile world. By faith, Gentiles can become partakers of the Jews' spiritual blessings, but they are not taker-overs, as replacement theology teaches. All the spiritual benefits are now being shared by the church (comprised of both Jews and Gentiles), but the still-future fulfillment of these covenants with regard to Israel indicates they remain in operation today and Israel is still the chosen people.

In the final analysis, despite Israel's present discipline and the problems posed by the Middle East conflict, Israel continues to be the chosen people because the world has not yet experienced the international peace, prosperity, and blessing that the Jewish people were chosen to bring to mankind (Isaiah 2:2-4; 60:5-14; Zechariah 8:23).

CHAPTER 16
READER RESPONSE

What Should We Think About the Jews as a Chosen People?

WHAT DO *YOU* THINK?

I agree with the author on

I disagree with the author because

What was news to me?

How does this change the way I think about the Jews as a chosen people?

What Should We Think About Jews Who Become Christians?

DAVID BRICKNER

Despite the historic antagonism between churches and synagogues, many thousands of Jews through the ages have become Christians. How does this affect them as Jews, especially those who may be citizens of the Jewish State? What is the status of Jews who accept Jesus as their Messiah and Lord, and how do the Jewish and Christian communities relate to them?

You cannot be Jewish and believe in Jesus!"
I can't count the number of times that statement has been directed toward me by my fellow Jews—sometimes with a tone of dismissiveness and at other times in anger, but almost always it is intended as an insult. For most Jews, the idea of Jews for Jesus makes about as much sense as vegetarians for meat! How did this attitude come about, and how should we think about Jews becoming Christians today?

Jewish Believers in Jesus from an Historical Perspective

The first people ever to be called Christians were the Jewish disciples of Jesus, who were part of the early church in Antioch (Acts 11:26). Jesus and His disciples were clearly born into a Jewish world and lived their lives as Jews. The entire New Testament was written by Jews, even though some argue that Luke was a Gentile.[1] The early church was an entirely Jewish church. The most natural candidates for becoming Christians were the Jewish people. As C.S. Lewis wrote, "In a sense the converted Jew is the only normal human being in the world…Everyone else is, from one point of view, a special case, dealt with under emergency regulations."[2]

During the beginning years of church history, the attitude that Jewish religious leaders had toward Jews who became Christians was not that they weren't Jewish, but rather, that they were simply wrong to believe that Jesus was the Messiah. Some Jewish leaders held views characterized by that of Gamaliel, who counseled tolerance toward the Jewish church in Jerusalem (Acts 5:34-39).

It wasn't until the late first and early second century AD, when Jewish believers in Jesus refused to take part in the Jewish rebellion against Rome, that this attitude of tolerance began to change. When Jerusalem came under siege by the Romans in the first century, many Jewish believers in Jesus saw this as a fulfillment of Jesus' warning in the Olivet Discourse and followed His admonition to "flee to the mountains" (Matthew 24:16).[3] Then when the leader of a second-century revolt, Simon bar Kokhba, was proclaimed to be the Messiah by a leading rabbi of the day, Jewish followers of Jesus again withdrew their support of this second revolt against Rome. The resulting split has never been repaired, though some have argued that the split occurred more gradually. A malediction against Jews who believed in Jesus was added to early synagogue liturgy,[4] and Jewish believers were also castigated in the early rabbinic literature known as the Talmud.[5] But even here the tendency was merely to call early Jewish Christians *minim* or *apikorus*, or "heretic."[6] Jewish leaders did not deny the early believer's Jewish identity, they simply denounced them as bad Jews for believing in Jesus.

It was the fourth-century church that most forcibly declared, "You can't be Jewish and believe in Jesus." This was a result of anti-Semitism that had found its way into the church, leading Emperor Constantine—at the Council of Nicaea in AD 325—to disallow Jewish Christians from observing Jewish practices such as Sabbath-keeping and Passover.[7] Prior to this council there were Jewish believers who held prominent positions of leadership within the church, including some who were bishops.[8] Over time, however, the number of Jewish believers in church leadership diminished because of the growing anti-Jewish sentiments in the church.

Despite this, all through church history there have been examples of Jewish Christians who continued to live out their faith in Jesus while maintaining their Jewish identity.[9] Sadly, their influence has been stained and undermined by the many examples of Jewish "converts" to Christianity who renounced their Jewishness and even imbibed the anti-Semitism prevalent within the church. Several such individuals, especially in the Middle Ages, gladly participated in so-called "disputations" with Jewish leaders.[10] These disputations amounted to forced theological debates held in public where "the fix was in" and the outcomes often resulted in the severe persecution of entire Jewish communities. This only served to widen the gulf between Jews and Jewish believers. "Jews cannot believe in Jesus" became the dominant refrain in the Jewish community.

The arc of history began to change in the nineteenth century with the rise of what came to be known as the Hebrew-Christian movement. Although this hyphenated term *Hebrew-Christian* may seem archaic and has mostly fallen out of use, it enabled Jewish believers to affirm their Jewish identity, and gradually, they became more widely accepted in the Jewish community as a result of the Enlightenment.[11] This renewed acceptance was itself a direct result of the success of the modern missions movement. The successful effort by missionaries to evangelize Jews led to a greater sympathy within the church in Europe and America, and Jewish converts were even encouraged to share their personal stories and participate in Jewish missionary efforts.[12] Christians in Great Britain especially began to promote the idea of a Jewish return to Palestine as part of a prophetic movement of God, and this too led to greater tolerance toward those Hebrew Christians who wanted to maintain some degree of Jewish identity.[13]

My own family story grew out of this time in history. In the middle of the nineteenth century, my great-great-grandfather, Levy Yitzhach Glaser, was the chief hasidic (ultraorthodox) rabbi of Zhitomir, a city in the Ukraine. His daughter, Esther, and eventually his wife and other family members became followers of Jesus. Their story was documented in a book entitled *The Romantic Career of a Twice-Born Jewess*. Esther became a missionary with the London Society for Promoting Christianity Amongst the Jews, serving first in Odessa, then in London, and eventually in Toronto. These family members continued to maintain their Jewish identity through the decades.

After Grandfather Fred graduated from the very first Jewish studies program at Moody Bible Institute in Chicago in the late 1920s, he started a ministry in Detroit called Israel's Remnant. He also started what was known as First Hebrew-Christian Church of Detroit. It was during a service at this church that my orthodox Jewish father responded to an invitation to receive Christ. I had the privilege of being raised in a home where I learned about my Jewish identity in light of faith that Jesus is the promised Messiah. We celebrated both Jewish and Christian holidays. I raised my children in that same context, and my son is raising his children that way as well. With my grandchildren, that makes seven generations of Jewish believers in Jesus on my mother's side, probably the longest lineage of Jewish believers I know of today.

Jewish Believers in Jesus from a Biblical Perspective

Understanding the 2,000-year-old history of Jewish believers in Jesus is helpful when it comes to answering the question about what we should think about Jews becoming Christians. But what is even more helpful is understanding what the Bible has to say about this. It speaks very much in favor of Jews becoming Christians.

The entire enterprise of Christianity is inconceivable apart from Jews becoming Christians, and the effort to bring the gospel to the Jewish people lies at the center of the New Testament instructions on missions. When Jesus sent out His disciples two by two, the very first "missionaries," He instructed them, "Go nowhere among the Gentiles and enter no town of the Samaritans, but go rather to the lost sheep of the house of Israel" (Matthew 10:5-6 esv). It was not until after Christ's death, burial, and resurrection and just prior to His ascension that the orders were changed for Jesus' disciples: "You will receive power when the Holy Spirit has come upon you, and you will be my witnesses in Jerusalem and in all Judea and Samaria, and to the end of the earth" (Acts 1:8 esv). The good news of Jesus Christ was to be proclaimed throughout the world, but notice that this effort, according to Jesus, was to begin in Jerusalem and Judea. How sad that for much of the history of Christianity this beginning point has been neglected, forgotten, and even called into question by various Christian denominations and leaders.

But the greatest Christian leader after Jesus did not forget, neglect, or call into question Jews becoming Christians. The apostle Paul, in his letter to the Romans, declared, "I am not ashamed of the gospel, for it is the power of God for salvation to everyone who believes, to the Jew first and also to the Greek [Gentile]" (Romans 1:16 ESV). In a sense, Paul was simply restating Jesus' words from Acts 1:8. His use of "first" was not merely a comment on history but a statement of priority. Jews becoming Christians must remain a priority of gospel proclamation.

Paul lived out that conviction in his own life and missionary journeys. Follow travels through the book of Acts and you will see that in almost every city he visited, the first place he preached was in the local synagogue (Acts 13:14; 14:1; 16:13-16; 17:1,10; 18:4,19,26; 19:18; 22:19). Even though he was called to be an apostle to the Gentiles, Paul maintained his commitment toward calling Jews to become Christians. In fact, there is likely no one in history who was more passionate about Jews becoming Christians than Paul.

Later in the book of Romans Paul made this astounding statement:

> I am speaking the truth in Christ—I am not lying; my conscience bears me witness in the Holy Spirit—that I have great sorrow and unceasing anguish in my heart. For I could wish that I myself were accursed and cut off from Christ for the sake of my brothers, my kinsmen according to the flesh…Brothers, my heart's desire and prayer to God for them is that they may be saved (Romans 9:1-4; 10:1 ESV).

As much as I love the Jewish people and have dedicated my life to bringing the gospel to them, I can hardly say with integrity that "I could wish that I myself were accursed and cut off from Christ" for the sake of their salvation.

While I imagine most followers of Jesus might have a hard time sharing the depth of passion Paul expressed, all who read and believe these Bible verses must clearly care deeply about Jews becoming Christians. In obedience to the Scriptures, every Christian should want to tell Jewish people about Jesus.

"But," you may say, "even if I wanted Jews to become Christians, why should I care whether or not they maintain their identity as Jews? Why don't they just call themselves a Christian and be done with it?"

The Bible addresses this. In 1 Corinthians 7, Paul said his "rule in all the churches" (verse 7 ESV) is that if you were Jewish when you became a believer, then you should remain a Jew, and if you were a Gentile when you became a believer, you shouldn't try to become a Jew. "Remain as you were called" was his instruction to believers. Paul lived that same rule for himself and his colleagues. He continued to celebrate the Jewish holidays (Acts 20:16). When he was in Jerusalem, he worshipped in the Temple (Acts 21:26-30; 22:17; 24:12,18; 25:8). And he instructed his closest disciple, Timothy, to be circumcised, even though Timothy had only one Jewish parent (Acts 16:3).[14]

As a Christian, Paul continued to identify as a Jew, saying, "I myself am an Israelite, a descendant of Abraham, a member of the tribe of Benjamin" (Romans 11:1). He actually declared that Jews who believe in Jesus are in fact "a remnant, chosen by grace" (verse 5). That word "remnant" is rich in meaning, a theological term that you can trace all throughout the Bible. The word is used 89 times in Scripture, and the first time it is used is when Joseph is explaining to his brothers how God took what they intended for evil and turned it for good, "to preserve for you a remnant on the earth" (Genesis 45:7 ESV).

Remnant theology speaks of God's commitment to the perpetuity and flourishing of the Jewish people. In the New Testament, Paul took that idea and applied it to Jewish believers in Jesus. In order for a remnant to stay a remnant it has to be visible, and God intends for Jewish believers to remain visibly and continuously a remnant of the Jewish people, a sign of His grace and continued love for them. In fact, Paul said it is God's intention that not just a remnant of Jews become followers of Jesus; rather, God ultimately intends that all Jewish people will become followers of Christ. In Romans 9–11, Paul went to great lengths to explain how even though most Jewish people did not believe in Jesus, he was hopeful all that would change one day: "A partial hardening has come upon Israel, until the fullness of the Gentiles has come in. And in this way all Israel will be saved" (Romans 11:25-26 ESV). If Paul was hopeful about Jews becoming Christians back then, so should we remain hopeful today.

Jewish Believers in Jesus Today

So how is it going? What progress has been made with regard to Jewish people becoming Christians? In one sense things are getting better than ever. I mentioned earlier the rise of the Hebrew-Christian movement in the nineteenth century, which was a significant bright spot after a very long, dark 15 centuries with little to show. And the number of Jewish people coming to Christ continues to increase. While we cannot be certain of just how many Jewish believers there are worldwide, some have offered estimates ranging from 200,000 all the way to as many as a million.[15] I myself lean toward the more conservative figure. But even if you go with a higher number, that is a precious few when you consider there are approximately 14 million Jews around the globe.

Still, with this growth, the remnant has become more visible than ever before. Jewish believers have asserted their faith and identity more than ever. The Hebrew-Christian movement has grown into what is now known as the messianic Jewish movement, which began in the latter part of the twentieth century. Many thousands of Jewish people came to Christ in the 1970s, most of them in North America. These Jews, many of whom were young activist types with a vibrant faith, were eager to maintain their identity as Jews. It was during this time that the Jews for Jesus ministry began.

Before the messianic Jewish movement begin, rabbis could easily say Jews don't believe in Jesus. But the rapid growth and visibility of this Jewish remnant made it difficult for Jewish leaders to proclaim that Jews don't believe in Jesus. More and more, they had to argue for *why* Jews shouldn't believe in Him.

It was also during the early 1970s that the organization known as the Hebrew Christian Alliance changed its name to the Messianic Jewish Alliance.[16] The name change reflected the growth of the movement as well as a greater commitment to Jewish life and practice. At the same time a messianic congregational movement began to flourish. Jewish believers formed their own culturally Jewish expressions of faith in Christ with Jewish liturgy and practice at the center of their worship services.

Some of these developments have not been without problems. For example, some in the messianic Jewish community would find difficulty with the very title of this chapter. They might say that Jews *shouldn't* become Christians. The Jewish community views the term *Christian* as being synonymous with *non-Jewish*, and they contend *Christian* should not be used to describe Jews who believe in Jesus.

While the desire to maintain a Jewish identity is both commendable and biblical, this aversion to the word *Christian* among some messianic Jews can become a wedge within the body of Christ, creating confusion and hurt and raising charges of "neo-Galatianism," or going back under the law. And in some instances, that charge could be well-founded. When Jews become Christians, their Jewishness should never become more important than their "Jesusness." The Scriptures do tell us that Jews and Gentiles in the church constitute "one new man" (Ephesians 2:15), and anything that goes against that supernatural reality in Christ is problematic at best. But, as professor Paul Pierson has said of new spiritual movements, "every movement is less than perfect and often messy at the edges."[17]

Yes, the modern-day messianic movement can at times be quite messy, but there is no doubt that the visibility and the Jewish communal footprint of Jesus-believing Jews has helped create a climate of faith that has continued to influence Jewish people for the sake of Christ. In fact, an even more recent move of the Holy Spirit that began in the 1990s is occurring even now among Russian-speaking Jews. With the fall of the Iron Curtain, tens of thousands of Jews in the former Soviet Union began coming to faith in Jesus. Jews for Jesus and Jewish Voice Ministries, along with many others from the messianic congregational movement, were able to take part in bringing the gospel to these Russian-speaking Jews, many of whom have made their way to Israel and built up the small body of Christ there. At Jews for Jesus, we have seen that even in Israel the greatest openness to the gospel is found within the large Russian immigrant community now residing there. What's more, there are now more Russian-speaking Jews in Israel than there are in the entire former Soviet Union. That gives many of us hope for a further movement of the Holy Spirit among Jews in Israel as well.

Right now there may be as many as 20,000 Jewish believers living in Israel,[18] and the majority are made up of immigrants from America,

Europe, and the Soviet Union. We do see more and more native-born Israelis coming to faith in Christ, and yet Israelis remain largely gospel-resistant among the secular majority and especially in the religious community. That is why those Jews who become Christians are often ostracized and persecuted for their faith. In fact, it's because the religious Jews control certain aspects of the government—such as the ministry of the interior—that Jewish believers are regularly denied the right to immigrate and become citizens.[19] Sometimes Jesus-believing Israeli citizens are even threatened with having their citizenship revoked.

Still, much has changed for the better for Jewish believers in Israel and elsewhere. Even in North America, negative attitudes toward Jewish believers in Jesus have started to change. In 2016, Jews for Jesus worked with the Barna Group to conduct a survey of Jewish millennials in North America. This survey indicated that there is a greater openness to Jesus among members of this age group than in previous generations.[20] This confirmed an earlier Pew Research Center study indicating that some 34 percent of Jews believe it is possible to be both Jewish and a Christian[21]—quite a change from the early 1970s and before. Much of this may be in part due to the relatively high rate of intermarriage among Jews outside of Israel, a phenomenon that has enabled more and more Jews to be exposed to Christianity. It has also opened the door for greater ministry to Jewish-Gentile couples.

We should remain hopeful, then, about Jews becoming Christians, and the future looks bright. Back in the 1850s theologian Charles Hodge wrote, "As the rejection of the Jews was not total, so neither is it final...Because if the rejection of the Jews has been a source of blessing, much more will their restoration be the means of good."[22] That good is built into the very architecture of the coming New Jerusalem. On her gates will be written the names of the 12 tribes of Israel, and on her foundation stones the names of the 12 apostles (Revelation 21:12,14). Jews and Christians will dwell together in God's kingdom for all eternity because of their unity found in Jesus. One new man—such a heavenly vision!

What Should We Think About Jews Who Become Christians?

WHAT DO *YOU* THINK?

I agree with the author on

I disagree with the author because

What was news to me?

How does this change the way I think about Jews who become Christians?

18

What Should We Think About Palestinian Christians?

PAUL WILKINSON

In recent times, opposition within the church to the alleged Israeli occupation has been spearheaded by those who refer to themselves as Palestinian Christians. Their personal testimonies and outspoken resistance to Israeli government policy have greatly influenced the way many evangelicals in the West perceive the conflict. Who are these Palestinian Christians, do they speak with one voice, and how should we respond?

I have had no thought of sparing your book...With yourself the case is somewhat different. Not that I can distinguish, as some do, between a book and its author. If the book is a guilty one, its author is guilty of it. But there is another feeling [that] arises as to the author, which does not as to the book. To the book I can measure out, without a pang, unmingled feelings of disgust and contempt; to the author I could not...I do mourn...But I write that you may at least feel that my attacking your book is as far as possible from bitterness toward you...I am not dealing with you about it, but with it before God and my reader.[1]

The guilty party was Francis William Newman (1805–1897),[2] the offending book was *Phases of Faith* (1850), and the prosecutor was John Nelson Darby (1800–1882), the Anglo-Irish founder of the Plymouth Brethren and a man many Palestinian Christians love to hate. What is the reason for their hatred? During the nineteenth century, Darby had played a pivotal role, especially in the United States, in restoring to the church the biblical truth concerning Israel and the second coming of Jesus.[3] What was it that compelled Darby to write to Newman in this manner? Anguish of heart over Newman, but also anguish of spirit over the flock of Christ, which needed protecting from those who "denied and dishonoured"[4] the Lord.

Darby's denunciation of Newman's work was checked by a genuine concern for the man who had once tutored in his sister's home in Dublin. The way in which Darby handled the matter is instructive, and it is pertinent to this chapter. In addressing the question regarding how we should think about Palestinian Christians, we will consider three case studies. These will illustrate the main theological positions held by Palestinian Christians, and keep Darby's words in mind when appraising those positions. We will begin with the man who has done arguably more than any other Palestinian clergyman to recruit Western Christians to the anti-Israel cause.

Study 1: Naim Ateek and Palestinian Liberation Theology

In April 2004, I attended the fifth International Sabeel Conference in Jerusalem. I was there as an observer, having recently commenced my doctorate on John Nelson Darby and Christian Zionism.[5] The program included a visit to the Temple Mount, access to the Dome of the Rock, and a meeting in Ramallah with Yasser Arafat, chairman of the Palestine Liberation Organization (PLO). The man behind the conference was Naim Stifan Ateek, a Palestinian Episcopal priest and founder of Sabeel—otherwise known as the Palestinian Ecumenical Liberation Theology Center in Jerusalem. Sabeel is an official partner with the Church of Scotland and the Presbyterian Church (USA).

Known as "the Desmond Tutu of Palestine,"[6] Ateek is vitriolic in his denunciation of Israel as an apartheid state. To that scurrilous accusation is added the charge of occupation, ethnic cleansing, war crimes, and the violation of international law. He is equally hostile toward premillennial/ dispensational Christians (Christian Zionists) who stand with Israel based on a literal interpretation of the Bible. Ateek is incensed at the way Christian Zionists link the establishment of the modern state of Israel to Old Testament prophecy, and counters by asserting that Israel's rebirth was a catastrophe, a Zionist crime aided and abetted by Western colonialists, "a sin against God and humanity,"[7] and "a seismic tremor of enormous magnitude that has shaken the very foundation"[8] of Palestinian Christianity. Fired by these convictions, he launched Sabeel in 1993 "to make the gospel relevant to Palestinian Christians"[9]—a telling statement.

Ateek began to articulate his liberation theology during his graduate studies at the Church Divinity School of the Pacific in Berkeley, California; he received his doctorate from San Francisco Theological Seminary. His theology is essentially a "Palestinianized" version of Latin American Roman Catholic liberation theology, which emerged in the 1960s with Marxist overtones and an overriding emphasis on social justice for the poor and oppressed. The spark that ignited Sabeel was the first Palestinian Intifada, or uprising, which broke out in 1987 and gave rise to Hamas. Since its founding, Sabeel has partnered with Christian nongovernmental organizations and church denominations and thereby gained a major foothold within mainstream Protestantism and the evangelical church. Sabeel's tenth international conference, held in 2017, was headlined, "Jesus Christ Liberator, Then and Now: Facing the Legacy of Injustice." Friends of Sabeel chapters have been established around the world, including Friends of Sabeel North America (FOSNA), which is based in Portland, Oregon.

Ateek is a liberal, ecumenical, interfaith Protestant who rejects the historicity of biblical books such as Jonah, denounces certain Old Testament authors as racist, and claims that much of the Old Testament is irrelevant to Palestinians and without authority. He claims that from Genesis to Malachi, much of the text is exclusive, racist, xenophobic, and genocidal, and serves only to reflect an early primitive understanding of God as tribal ("Holy One *of Israel*"). He considers the Joshua narrative of the Israelites' entry into Canaan to be especially problematic. He asserts that Jesus' first coming rendered Jerusalem and the land of Israel theologically redundant, and he downplays the second coming, believing that the church is called to build God's kingdom on earth now. The following excerpts capture the essence of Ateek's theology:

> Palestinian liberation theology focuses on the humanity of Jesus of Nazareth, who was also a Palestinian living under an occupation...The experience of Palestinian Christians who live today in oppressive conditions under the Israeli occupation are quite similar to the experience of Jesus and his followers under the Roman occupation...It seems to many of us that Jesus is on the cross again with thousands of crucified Palestinians around him...The Israeli government crucifixion system is operating daily...It is the occupation that is evil and violent. It is apartheid in its ugliest form.[10]

> For most Palestinian Christians, as for many other Arab Christians, their view of the Bible, especially the Hebrew Scriptures, or Old Testament, has been adversely affected by the creation of the State of Israel...For Palestinian Christians, the core question that takes priority over all others is whether what is being read in the Bible is the Word of *God* to them and whether it reflects the nature, will, and purpose of *God* for them.[11]

> Isaiah uses language that today we would consider narrow and racist...This exclusivist text [Isaiah 61:5-6—please look it up] is unacceptable today, whether it has to do with God or people or land. It must be de-Zionized...In fact, without the New Testament, many parts of the Old Testament are, in today's language, Zionist and racist...The New Testament does not only reinterpret the Old Testament, it de-Zionizes it.[12]

> We stand particularly in the line of the theology of the book of Jonah, the first Palestinian liberation theologian, which we see as the climax of the theology of the Old Testament, and which dismantles the theology of exclusivism and racism of his day...Could it have possibly been written by a woman liberation

theologian who cut across every religious taboo? For us Palestinian Christians, it is our spiritual and theological lifeline. Thank God for Jonah![13]

Ultimately, we must build the New Jerusalem here and now.[14]

Only the Lord knows how many Sabeelites are true believers, but Ateek's liberation theology and liberal approach to the Bible, coupled with his ecumenical/interfaith exploits, contravene the Christian faith at every level. Palestinian Christians who have been swayed by this theology need to be warned that Sabeel (an Arabic word meaning "way") is not teaching God's way and urged to come out of this movement that is deceiving them, damaging Israel, and dishonoring Jesus.

Study 2: Salim Munayer, Munther Isaac, and "Checkpoint" Evangelicalism

In March 2012, I attended the second Christ at the Checkpoint conference in Bethlehem. This increasingly popular biennial conference is hosted by Bethlehem Bible College, an interdenominational Palestinian evangelical school that was founded in 1979. During the conference I was accosted by two of its organizers, Salim Munayer and Munther Isaac, who expressed indignation at what I had been writing and presenting on the subject of Christian Palestinianism.[15]

Munayer and Isaac, along with many of their Bethlehem Bible College colleagues, studied theology in the United States. They did so at institutions that fall lamentably short in their biblical understanding of Israel; some, in fact, are known for their pro-Palestinian stance. The schools they attended include Fresno Pacific University Biblical Seminary (formerly Mennonite Brethren Biblical Seminary, Fresno, CA), Asbury Theological Seminary (Wilmore, KY), Gordon-Conwell Theological Seminary (Hamilton, MA), Church Divinity School of the Pacific (Berkeley, CA), San Francisco Theological Seminary (San Anselmo, CA), Fuller Theological Seminary (Pasadena, CA), Wheaton College (Wheaton, IL), and Westminster Theological Seminary (Glenside, PA).

Fuller, Wheaton, and Westminster are particularly noteworthy, either for their direct participation in anti-Israel activism (Fuller and Wheaton), or for their underlying Reformed theology (Westminster). This theology stems from the creeds and confessions that were drawn up during the Protestant Reformation, and does not allow for Israel's national restoration and Christ's physical return as king to Jerusalem.[16] This helps explain why it holds sway over many Checkpoint evangelicals, whose writings are full of references to Reformed theologians such as O. Palmer Robertson, David Holwerda, and their leading American Checkpoint advocate, Gary Burge.

The prolific writings of the renowned British New Testament scholar N.T. Wright and the American Old Testament scholar Walter Brueggemann—both of whom have condemned the state of Israel and abhor Christian Zionism—also feature prominently in Checkpoint writings. When presenting the history of the modern state of Israel and the Palestinian conflict, Munayer and Isaac are also among those who appeal to the dubious authority of revisionist Israeli academics such as Benny Morris, Tom Segev, Shlomo Sand, and Ilan Pappé. These men are known collectively as New Historians because they have challenged and revised the traditional account of Israel's modern history.

The R Word

Salim Munayer is the founder and director of Musalaha, a ministry of reconciliation to Israelis and Palestinians. He is also a professor at Bethlehem Bible College. Munther Isaac is an ordained minister within the Evangelical Lutheran Church in Jordan and the Holy Land. He is also the academic dean at Bethlehem Bible College, director of Christ at the Checkpoint, and a member of Musalaha's board. In contrast to Naim Ateek, both are evangelicals and neither subscribe to liberation theology. Having said that, they interpret Scripture passages pertaining to Israel in much the same way as Ateek does, they share Ateek's basic political convictions, and they endorse his view that the so-called occupation is "a sin against God and humanity."[17] Munayer and Isaac have also collaborated with Ateek on writing projects and at conferences. Ateek was a speaker at the first Christ at the Checkpoint conference in 2010, while Isaac spoke at the ninth International Sabeel Conference in 2013, which celebrated 25 years of Palestinian liberation theology.

One of the most conspicuous aspects of Checkpoint theology is its vocabulary. Whenever the thorny issue of Bible prophecy is addressed, words such as *redefine, reinterpret,* and *reconstitute* are frequently used. These theologically loaded *r* words are synonymous with the aforementioned N.T. Wright. Munther Isaac lists among his favorite books "anything N.T. Wright writes."[18] Munayer and Isaac both draw heavily upon Wright when arguing that Christ came to redefine and reinterpret the meaning of *Israel, people of God, chosen,* and *Promised Land.* As the following excerpts illustrate, their central thesis is that the promises given to Abraham and the Jewish people have now been expanded and universalized in Christ:

Salim Munayer

> God redefines the boundaries of identity around Messiah followers…This enlarges and reinterprets the family of God, following God's original intention to expand the eschatological kingdom of Israel to include the nations.[19]

> The land is a gift that has been promised to all people…It is perhaps wise to rethink our traditional interpretation of the promises God made to Abraham…The arrival of Jesus made this [land] promise available to all…God's promise has been fulfilled through Jesus, and our understanding of it has shifted from the narrowly defined land of Canaan to the whole world…We find evidence of the universalization of the promises when Jesus tells his disciples that they are to be his witnesses "in Jerusalem, and in all Judea and Samaria, and to the end of the earth" (Acts 1:8)…When we remember the universal nature of God's promise, it is clear: The land flowing with milk and honey is not Canaan…it is a future return to the garden as the fulfillment of God's promises.[20]

Munther Isaac

> Jesus restored Israel and fulfilled the promises of the OT, including the land…The land has thus been universalized in

Christ...Jesus relives the story of Israel...Jesus is the *only legitimate recipient* of the Abrahamic promises...Jesus has become Israel...The coming of Jesus has redefined what it means to be Israel...The church today, consisting of Jews and Gentiles, thus *inherits the story of Israel*...A new Israel is formed...and the covenant has been redefined or renewed...The time of the kingdom is *now*...The presence of the church today as God's viceregent eliminates the necessity and the possibility of a future Israelite kingdom. The role of Israel has been absorbed first in Christ, and through him in the church...The story of Israel, therefore, has reached its climax.[21]

In other words, the Israel we thought we knew from the Old Testament—Patriarchs, people, covenants, land, holy city, Temple, prophecies, exile, restoration, and future messianic kingdom—has expired!

A natural, literal, and consistent reading of Scripture will never yield this conclusion; it can only be drawn by imposing a certain theological system upon the biblical text. As previously noted, one of the dominant systems of thought being used in the church to eradicate Israel is Reformed Theology, which is rooted in the allegorical, amillennial teachings of some of the church fathers, most notably Augustine of Hippo (AD 354–430). According to the definition given by the Greek philosopher Heracleitus, allegory is "saying one thing, and meaning something other than what is said."[22] This is how Checkpoint evangelicals handle God's Word.

With all this in mind, then, can believers who stand with Israel truly fellowship with Palestinian Christians like Munayer and Isaac? According to the international messianic community, they cannot. In February 2012, the Messianic Jewish Alliance of America, the Union of Messianic Jewish Congregations, the International Messianic Jewish Alliance, and the International Alliance of Messianic Congregations and Synagogues issued a joint statement objecting to "the anti-Israel and, indeed, unbiblical nature of the Christ at the Checkpoint conference soon to be held in Bethlehem."[23] They were also deeply concerned that a few of their members were not only planning to attend but had also accepted invitations to speak. Here is an excerpt from their statement:

The Messianic Jewish community has noted the growing opposition to Zionism and the state of Israel within some elements of
the Evangelical Christian world…Equally troubling, this opposition is often linked to a resurgent supersessionism [replace-
ment theology]…This theology, which has led historically to
anti-Semitism and the tragic oppression of the Jewish people,
appears to permeate this entire conference.[24]

The problem with Palestinian Checkpoint evangelicalism is systemic.
Its underlying theology of Israel is unbiblical, and its political involve-
ment in the global anti-Israel crusade is deplorable. In his 1839 sermon
"The Mind of Christ Respecting the Jews," the eminent Church of England clergyman and evangelical leader Edward Bickersteth (1786–1850)
denounced any theology that robs the Jews of their promised inheritance
as "most hateful to God."[25] If that is so, what should our response be?

Study 3: Naim Khoury and Arab Christian Zionism

The testimonies coming out of Israel in recent years make one fact very
clear: In the midst of incessant conflict, God is changing lives. Israeli Jews,
Israeli Arabs, and Arabs living in the designated Palestinian areas are coming to know Jesus Christ as their Lord and Savior—all glory to God! In the
case of Palestinian/Arab converts, some of them are not only being reconciled to the Jewish people, but also to Israel. I became aware of this in 2008
when I was warmly received in Haifa by pastor Najeeb Atteih and his wife,
Elizabeth, who were previously unknown to me. Najeeb is an Israeli Arab
and Elizabeth is of Armenian descent. Their ministry of reconciliation is
to all who pass through the doors of their evangelical church and book-
shop, without discrimination—and they have a biblical understanding of
Israel! The same is true of another Arab pastor and family who minister in
a different part of the land.

Naim Khoury is the Arab Israeli pastor of the First Baptist Church
of Bethlehem, and the founder of Holy Land Missions (HLM), which
serves the struggling Arab Christian community. His son, Steven, is pastor
of Calvary Baptist Church in Jerusalem and executive director of HLM.
In a 2015 interview with *Israel Today*, Naim was asked for his opinion of

Christ at the Checkpoint. He gave the following informative and forth-right response:

> I do not participate in that and I am against it...They are wolves
> in sheep's clothing who are playing politics. And for me, as an
> evangelical Bible-believing Christian standing with the whole
> Word of God, I don't believe that I should be involved politically.
> The Bible, the whole Bible, meaning the Old Testament and the
> New Testament, is the real answer to our situation...There is no
> need to say "Christ at the Checkpoint." That's politics. That's
> not biblical...A few years ago, I did a study and discovered that
> most of the Palestinian Christians and churches are basing their
> positions on Replacement Theology...Israel is not perfect. No
> nation is. But that does not mean I should deny the basic tenets
> of my faith concerning the Word of God.[26]

When asked whether he believed the establishment of the modern
state of Israel had anything to do with the Bible, Khoury was emphatic:

> Oh yes. Biblically, there is no doubt about it. I have to accept it
> because you cannot accept part of the Bible and deny the rest.
> I believe in the whole Bible as the infallible, inspired Word of
> God. And this is my answer to those who don't accept the State
> of Israel or who use Replacement Theology to say the Church
> has replaced Israel.[27]

Many Arab believers and pastors are paying a heavy price for their
faithfulness to God's Word and His people; Pastor Khoury has received
death threats, and his church has been fire-bombed numerous times. His
interview is insightful and encouraging, but his closing remarks are wor-thy of particular attention:

> You cannot love the Jews and hate the Arabs. And, you cannot
> love the Arabs and hate the Jews. Yeshua died for both people,
> and He loves both people. May God open your eyes and hearts
> to the fact that there are Palestinian Arabs who love Jesus and
> love Israel, and they are taking a stand and paying a price to
> preach the Word of God in this land.[28]

The Call to Be Heavenly Minded

Despite insisting that the land they call Israel-Palestine is theologically redundant, Palestinian Christians in general—we thank God for the exceptions—spend an inordinate amount of time, energy, prayer, *and* money fighting for it! They seem oblivious to the apostle Paul's exhortation that, as believers, no matter where we live on earth, "our citizenship is in heaven, from which we also eagerly wait for a Savior, the Lord Jesus Christ" (Philippians 3:20-21).

We close with another important "warning" from the nineteenth-century evangelical Edward Bickersteth. This time his words are quoted as a reminder to us that doctrine alone, however noble and lofty (even concerning Israel and the second coming of Jesus), is of little value if it serves only to inform the mind and never touches the heart:

> O how easy it is to be filled with the interest of a great and exciting truth, and to maintain it intellectually and scripturally; and yet unless the Holy Spirit use it for our sanctification, bringing it home to the conscience, and by his inward teaching and energy making it really mighty to touch the heart and quicken the life— the interest may but blind the mind, destroy spiritual sensibility, and leave us more hardened and unimpressible...God give then to us who know and believe his faithfulness to the literal Israel, and expect their restoration with all its accompanying momentous events, grace to be sensible of this danger, and to live in the spirit of humility, watchfulness, and holy obedience. May we ever bear in mind that *knowledge puffeth up, but charity edifieth*, and hence seek especially to be filled with love to our differing brethren.[29]

CHAPTER 18
READER RESPONSE

What Should We Think About Palestinian Christians?

WHAT DO *YOU* THINK?

I agree with the author on

I disagree with the author because

What was news to me?

How does this change the way I think about Palestinian Christians?

Afterword:
Why We Should Think
More About Israel

RANDALL PRICE

In this book a number of controversial questions have been raised, facts presented, and a challenge issued as to how the reader should think about Israel. In order to appraise this data, it is important to know how to think about the issues and claims, weighing theological viewpoints, political revisionism, and even sentimentalism to come to an objective conclusion as well as to a proper course of action.

We are grateful that you have come this far with us! The topics we have considered together are at the front line of our society yet are uneasy to discuss because the various viewpoints are polarizing and the people who hold to them are passionate. As an old Israeli joke goes, "In Israel, pessimists say, 'Oy vey, things couldn't get any worse,' and optimists say, 'Oh yes they can!'" What we want to do in this conclusion is to look not at the problems, but the solutions. While we can offer no solution for resolving conflicts that have multifaceted causes and are bound to unchanging devotion to religion and culture, we can offer objective (as possible) guidelines to resolve the problems of misinformation and misunderstanding about Israel. As we do this, the intention is not to think about Israel in terms of more information, but to think about Israel with more understanding and with a desire for justice and compassion (terms that are frequently denied to Israel in the public forum). In other words, how can we think more *properly* about Israel in light of the mixed messages we receive—many of which come not only from the mainstream media, but also the evangelical church?

Thinking More About Israel Requires a Proper Interpretation

In this book we have argued for separating fact from fiction based on a biblical worldview. We are aware that not all our readers may be convinced of this approach, but let us consider for a moment how one's political affiliations and views may be affected by the lack of a religious orientation. American Jewish writer, intellectual, and scholar Will Herberg made the uneasy transition from Communist to conservative based on his perspective of how a departure from religious values can affect civilization. Based on a lifetime of ideological struggle, he wrote this in his 1951 work *Judaism and Modern Man*:

> The moral principles of Western civilization are, in fact, all derived from the tradition rooted in Scripture and have vital meaning only in the context of that tradition. The attempt made in recent decades by secularist thinkers to disengage these values from their religious context, in the assurance that they could live a life of their own as "humanistic" ethic, has resulted in our "cut-flower culture." Cut flowers retain their original beauty and fragrance, but only so long as they retain the vitality that they have drawn from their now severed roots; after that is exhausted, they wither and die. So with freedom, brotherhood, justice and personal dignity the values that form the moral foundation of our civilization. Without the life-giving power of the faith out of which they have sprung, they possess neither meaning nor vitality.[1]

Israel as a people and a nation has its origins in the Bible. It cannot be explained in history apart from this religious background, or rather, without God. Therefore, whatever our worldview, in order to properly interpret Israel, we must at some point adopt a biblical worldview. As Herberg has further stated,

> Hebraic thought, therefore, starts not with self-sufficient nature or reason…but with the will of God…Long ago, Josephus,

who undertook the task of interpreting the Jewish outlook to the Greek world, put the matter in succinct and pregnant form. "Moses," he said, "did not make religion a part of virtue [i.e., ethics], but he saw and ordained the virtues to be a part of religion...for all our actions and our words have a reference to piety towards God."[2]

This viewpoint is the opposite of the secular, humanistic, postmodern perspective that currently dominates the thinking toward Israel found in our educational institutions, foreign policy, and the media. It has also affected the Jewish people, resulting in an abandonment of historic faith positions within Judaism and producing a secular government in Israel. British Orthodox rabbi and theologian Jonathan Sacks writes, "I believe that at a certain point in history Jews lost their faith in God and placed their trust in man. That has been the story of Western Civilization as a whole, but it happened to the Jews more suddenly and poignantly than to anyone else."[3]

A survey of the beliefs of American Jews revealed

> the most common answer at roughly 50 percent was "a commitment to social equality," followed by support for Israel, at 20 percent. "Religious observance," the closest quality to something like belief, was cited as the most important quality of Judaism only 17 percent of the time...And when asked whether Jews of any kind believed in God, 18 percent said they did not. Forty percent said they believed in an impersonal God, while 26 percent said they believe in a God they saw as "a person with whom one can have a relationship."[4]

Herberg again offers wisdom in an explanation for this lack of religious conviction:

> The fact of the matter seems to be that the modern unbeliever refuses to believe for the same basic reason that the unbelievers of all ages have refused: the biblical word is a decisive challenge to his pretensions to self-sufficiency and to all the strategies that he has devised to sustain them. Modern man is ready to "accept"

revelation if that revelation is identified with his own intellectual discovery or poetical intuition. But with the revelation that comes from beyond to shatter his self-sufficiency, to expose the dereliction of his life and to call him to a radical transformation of the heart, with that revelation he will have nothing to do.[5]

It has been said, "When men stop believing in God they don't believe in nothing; they believe in anything."[6] Such a plurality of ideas centered in social action seems to characterize the social and political outlook of Jews as well as others in today's society. Yet the concept of Israel requires belief in the biblical definition of a chosen people designed to represent God to the world (both in their experience of discipline and blessing) and whose support as a people and a nation derives not from their character or conduct, but is based on the divine program supporting them in their role to bring about universal peace and prosperity to this planet under the rule of God through His Messiah. Starting with this proper interpretation, we can offer to Israel the understanding it most needs in an age when it is most misunderstood.

Thinking More About Israel Requires Political Intervention

Proper thinking requires proper action. Some readers of this book may have been among those who have opposed Israel because of the influence of a professor, pastor, media reports, or the BDS movement and therefore have acted personally and politically against the modern state of Israel and, as a consequence, against the Jewish people. But if we feel constrained to act on the behalf of others to bring about justice and compassion, why not do so for Israel, which stands more than many others in need of such intervention? After all, it was Israel who, through the revelation given to them, introduced these concepts to the world. As Thomas Cahill writes:

> Unbelievers might wish to stop for a moment and consider how completely God—this Jewish God of justice and compassion—undergirds all our values and that it is just possible that human effort without this God is doomed to certain failure. Humanity's most extravagant dreams are articulated by the Jewish prophets. In Isaiah's vision, true faith is no longer confined to one nation,

but "all the nations" stream to the House of YHWH "that He may teach us his ways" and that we learn to beat [our] swords into plowshares." All who share this outrageous dream of universal brotherhood, peace, and justice, who dream the dreams and see visions of the great prophets, must bring themselves to contemplate the possibility that without God there is no justice.[7]

This is an often-unstated reason the United States has one of the most pro-Israel foreign policies in the world. While the United States recognizes Israel is the only democracy in the Middle East and appreciates the strategic intelligence benefit of gathering terror information from the region that an alliance with Israel affords, it is the moral and spiritual values shared by both nations as a result of our Judeo-Christian heritage that have guided our leaders to regard Israel above other nations. Our appeal for support for Israel, which involves political action on behalf of Israel and the Jewish people in accord with biblical principles and concerns, does not disregard concern for the needs of other peoples, but it argues that Israel should not be marginalized. Rather, in harmony with the biblical priority of bringing the good news of salvation through Messiah "to the Jew first" (Romans 1:16), actions on behalf of Israel should have a priority in our mission to bring about justice and compassion. Because Israel is the most targeted and vilified nation on university campuses today, it is only just that informed voices speak out in its support to balance the scale of justice.

In seeking places where our voices might be heard, we have too often assumed that the typical arenas of power—such as academic institutions and political parties—will provide the platform for social change. Herberg, however, reminds that such social avenues have more often than not been a source of corruption rather than change:

> The far-reaching power of sin through its embodiment in the structures and institutions of society is a basic aspect of the influence of the past upon the present that makes for the continuity of history. It accounts for the plight in which men find themselves at any point in the course of events, but it does not relieve them of responsibility for their actions... The tragic predicament

of men in history is that the iniquity which we do and for which we are responsible is only too often something we have had to choose because the historical situation offered us no course of action that was altogether free from evil.[8]

A better course of action might be to find an association with an institution or organization whose political policies are sourced in Scripture rather than a sinful society whose track record of social change is less than ideal. There are many pro-Israel organizations that operate from a biblical worldview and provide a means for education and political action in support of Israel on university campuses and other venues nationwide. There are also many churches that have a proper view of Israel and advocate on its behalf. Look for these opportunities to learn, and then exercise your freedom to unite your voice with others.

Thinking More About Israel Requires Prayerful Intercession

While we hope you have been challenged to think more about Israel as a result of the presentations in this book, we realize that some readers may still hold religious and cultural stereotypes about the Jewish people and Zionists in particular. These views may have been developed over a lifetime and become so governed by family and society that it is not possible to have a part in public support for the Jewish state as suggested above. However, if you are among those who claim a personal relationship with God and respect the authority of His Word and adopt the biblical worldview mentioned at the beginning of this chapter, then you can pray for Israel. How should you pray? Here are two ways that we can pray for Israel today:

Pray for Israel's Spiritual Salvation

Israel as a nation has the same social sins as any society and these can be significantly exacerbated by the tensions Israelis and Jews experience worldwide on a regular basis. While many of the stories of abuse under occupation may not be accurately presented, we do not suggest that none may not be. Israel is in its promised land today as a result of God's covenantal promise, but it is also suffering in this context for the same reason. National Israel is under divine discipline for its abandonment of faith in the God of Abraham, Isaac, and Jacob and for its rejection of its Messiah, Yeshua, whom God sent 2,000 years ago. As the apostle Paul considered this rejection, which would soon be met with the destruction of Jerusalem and the Temple, he declared, "My heart's desire and my prayer to God for them is for their salvation" (Romans 10:1). This is in harmony with what God reveals concerning His plan for Israel. There is coming a day when He will remove its spiritual hardness of heart and move the nation to repentance toward the Savior (Yeshua) that He sent and who is returning to bring redemption and restoration (Romans 11:25-27) so that, as the chosen people, they can fulfill their calling to bless the world.

Some may blame the unfathomable horrors of the Holocaust that have made them unable to accept a God who would allow such evil to engulf so many. For others, it has been the influence of other worldviews such as Communism and Socialism, which operate in dependence on man without need of God. Yet others have become disenchanted with the religion of Judaism because it has not brought about any change in their condition or that of the world. As Mordecai Kaplan has observed, "Before the beginning of the nineteenth century all Jews regarded Judaism as a privilege; since then most Jews have come to regard it as a burden."[9] Thus, praying for Israel's turning to God must include prayer for its turning from humanism, as well as anything else that has been sought to fill the spiritual vacuum left in their lives.

For those religious Jews who have maintained their Judaism, there is also a need, as the apostle Paul noted in the words that immediately follow his appeal for prayer on their behalf, for they "have a zeal for God—but not in accordance with knowledge. For not knowing about God's righteousness and seeking to establish their own, they did not subject themselves to the righteousness of God. For Christ is the end of the law for righteousness to everyone who believes" (Romans 10:2-4).

Therefore, Israel, as a collective of sinful Jewish souls, needs those who already believe to pray that they, in turn, might also believe. If we want to see greater justice and compassion demonstrated in the Middle East conflict, it will happen when change takes place from within. As witnessed in the testimony of believing Jews who have reached out to Palestinian and Arab believers to find unity in their common faith, it *is* possible to attain a measure of peace (and reconciliation) between national enemies once personal peace is obtained from a relationship with God (Romans 5:1; 12:18; Ephesians 2:14; Colossians 1:20; Hebrews 12:14).

Pray for Israel's Physical Survival

Anti-Semitism is an unreasoning attitude that has infected people on a global scale. It has been the cause of untold persecution and suffering for the Jewish people through the ages and, rather than diminishing in our pluralistic age of professed tolerance, it has increased. Whether or not anti-Semitism is claimed (it is usually denied) as the basis for action against the Jewish people and the state of Israel, it is a motivating factor that is usually veiled by religious or political rhetoric.

This can be witnessed on a regular basis in the United Nations, where disproportionate numbers of votes are cast to condemn Israel while ignoring vastly greater instances of occupation and aggression in the Middle East and other parts of the world. As the new anti-Semitism has focused on Israel as a nation, there has been an unrelenting succession of attacks on it from its declared enemies. Countries with nuclear arsenals or ambitions repeatedly call for the destruction of Israel. Terrorism within the Jewish state and against Jews worldwide is justified on account of "defending" those said to be occupied by Israel. It is an incontestable fact that the greatest physical threat facing modern Israel is that of survival.

God, in His Word, has a plan for Israel's future and has demonstrated in history that He can and has preserved it through every attempt to remove it from the map of the Middle East and from the memory of mankind. Part of that plan includes Israel living within its land in peace and security: "They will no longer be a prey to the nations...but they will live securely, and no one will make them afraid" (Ezekiel 34:28). This basic need for "peace and security" (within recognized borders) is one of the nonnegotiables for Israel in the peace process. Prayer for national Israel within its land is in concert with God's will and therefore should be an activity that we, as believers, are willing to do.

A final reason we should think more about Israel is because in the end it will be Israel, as redeemed and restored by God, that will lead a redeemed world to the realization of its hopes and dreams in the kingdom of God. As Herberg has stated:

Hebraic eschatology thus solves the problem of history in the only way it can be solved, by finding its meaning not in the premature completions that man in his pretensions tries to force upon it, but in the judgment and fulfillment toward which it is directed by the hand of God...when all is said and done, the biblical view of history is not a philosophy of history but a gospel of salvation. It tells us how and why we have gotten into this dreadful plight of sinful existence. It brings to us a shattering sense of the human predicament, yet forbids us to despair, for it assures us that in the very midst of the tragedy and frustrations of the historical process, the divine power is at work, redeeming temporal existence and leading it forward to fulfillment in a "new age" in which life will at last realize all its potentialities and be transfigured in the fulness of the love of God. Such is the word of Hebraic eschatology; it is a word that can be really apprehended only in faith.[10]

The new world for which all mankind aspires, and those of true faith acquire, is part of a process that started and ends with Israel. Despite its present failure in this regard, the God of Israel is not finished with the nation, and the best is yet to come.

Above the entrance to the main building on the campus of the University of Texas is a stone inscription that reads, "You shall know the truth, and the truth shall make you free." Most of the students on campus who daily observe that statement have no idea of its source, but assume it refers to the educational process as a means to free-thinking and thus to the liberation of society. They might be surprised to learn that its source is the Bible—John 8:32.

Moreover, the students would be even more surprised to learn that its meaning qualifies truth, making it not dependent upon a worldly institution, but centered in a divine person, for the rest of the biblical text reads: "If the Son makes you free, you will be free indeed" (John 8:36). May we who recognize this fact, as well as those presented in this book, come to know the meaning of the words of the Son, Israel's Messiah, and come to respect Israel for what God intended it to be, His chosen vessel to separate fact from fiction so that the world might know His truth and be truly free.

APPENDIX A

Interview with Israeli Pastor on Relations with Arabs and Arab Christians

In September 2018, Randall Price conducted an interview with Meno Kalisher, pastor of the Jerusalem Assembly House of Redemption. Pastor Kalisher, the son of Holocaust survivor Zvi Kalisher, who escaped from the Warsaw Ghetto and came to Israel under the British Mandate, planted his congregation in the city 20 years ago and is now planting a second congregation. Throughout his ministry, he has sought to reach out to Arab believers and find a common ground for worship together despite the political views that continue to divide Jews and Arabs.

While the reconciliation work Pastor Kalisher engages in is necessarily secret to protect Arab believers who would be subject to persecution or worse for alleged "collaboration" with Israel, he has said, "We *must* do this for the sake of the next generation of Christians in this country—we *must!*" He shares about his experience growing up in Jerusalem with Arabs and the problems both face in the midst of conflict. He also describes how the situation in Israel changed with the Palestinian Intifada, and how Arab Christians view their Jewish counterparts. His comments provide a real-world perspective on relations between those who struggle to share their faith in the midst of the Middle East conflict.

Price: In talking about Israel-Arab relations, we have to go back to before 1948. I understand that a lot of the pogroms came in the 1920s and after, and Haj Amin al-Husseini was behind stirring up the local Arab community against Jews as part of the final solution in Palestine. Can you talk about this so people will have some historical understanding of what has happened?

Kalisher: When you say the name Haj Amin al-Husseini, it's like saying "Hitler" because this man was the Muslim Arab Hitler. The difference between the two is that the European Hitler had the ability and the tools to fulfill his idea, and the Arab Hitler Haj Amin al-Husseini didn't have the means and the tools—he simply had a plan. But both of them had the same target, the same idea, and the same final solution to end the Jewish people.

Haj Amin al-Husseini was motivated by religious hatred. He understood the Qur'an and his Islamic religion, and he simply followed it as a faithful Muslim. He was very faithful to Islam and tried to apply it in a practical way, exactly as it says. And from his point of view, killing the Jews was being a good Muslim.

Price: Why would Muslims, or why would the Qur'an, tell Arabs to treat Jews this way?

Kalisher: The canonical Hadith compiled by al-Bukhari says that "when you find a Jew behind the stone or behind the tree, kill him. Even the stone will say to the tree, 'There is a Jew behind me—come and kill him'" (*Sahih Bukhari* 4:52:176). This is also featured prominently in the Hamas Covenant, article 7.

Mohammad didn't have a good experience with the Jews because they didn't agree with him and did not follow his ideas. His solution was to get rid of whoever did not agree with him. Therefore, the moment Muslims accept the authority of the Qur'an they are obligated to follow the direction of their Prophet.

Price: Let's move to the Declaration of the state of Israel and relations between Jews and Arabs as a result. Start at 1948 and explain what happened—why Jews and Arabs had problems back then.

Kalisher: By 1948 there was a big influx of Jewish people coming into Israel after the Holocaust. As more Jewish people came to Israel, the local Arab community realized that the land—which they believed was theirs—was becoming increasingly occupied by these new Jewish immigrants who were settling in cities, building, getting stronger. They truly feared that as more Jews came they would lose what they had because they felt there was no place for Jews that came and lived on *their* land. Jewish immigration caused enmity, and the Arabs fought against it.

Don't forget that during that time the Arabs weren't called Palestinians in that sense; they were only called Arabs who were under the influence of Jordan or Egypt or other countries that were the forces in our land. Before 1948, there was also the British Mandate. The British managed the area, but they didn't try to control things between Arabs and Jews; they just wanted to keep the peace and to prevent riots. I cannot blame them, but that's what they wanted.

If you ask Jewish people from that era about this, they'll tell you that the British favored the Arabs over the Jews. The Jewish people coming out of Eastern Europe and Arab lands realized they had no other land to go to but the land of Israel. Many believed that this is the promised land and that this is the place God assigned for them. They truly wanted to live together with the Arab community that was here, and the Israeli government was happy with the British-drawn borders of the new state that they were given. The ones who started the conflict immediately after the declaration of independence were the Egyptians. Jews had no choice but to try to defend themselves. The Middle East conflict began in 1948 when Egypt and Jordan attacked Israel, and ever since, we have been at war.

Price: How has that affected daily life between Jews and Arabs?

Kalisher: There has always been enmity, but until the Palestinian Intifada that began in 1987 there was no fear factor. The Arabs were working everywhere in the country and there was not much terror activity. I'm not saying there was none, but Jews were among Arabs and Arabs were among Jews. You went to buy groceries in Arab cities, they came anywhere and everywhere to work in companies (specifically building companies) and so on.

I remember every Shabbat, every Saturday, we used to go to the Old City [of Jerusalem]. Once every few weeks we would take the Arab bus to Bethlehem to buy whatever we wanted. There was total freedom to do so— there were no checkpoints. When the Intifada started, that stopped. There was a huge rise in terror activity such that if anyone went to Bethlehem as before it would have been suicidal. I can tell you that I haven't gone to Bethlehem like that since 1987. I can count on two hands the times in the last thirty years that I have gone to the Old City just to enjoy it. It is very uncomfortable; you see the hatred in the eyes of everyone there. It's very unpleasant.

Price: If someone says that's the result of Israeli occupation, how do you reply?

Kalisher: First, I would say that we do not live in a perfect world. If you ask a person who believes in God and you ask a secular person, you will most likely get two different answers. I'll give you both. If you ask a secular Jewish person, from his point of view, the Bible means nothing—totally nothing. There is no authority whatsoever in the Bible. So he may come to the conclusion that we Jewish people suffer as a result of occupying the place of the Arabs. He would say that because we were a little bit stronger than the inhabitants that we stole their place. He would say it's wrong and we need to ask forgiveness and to share the land with them in a fair way in order to live together.

From the viewpoint of a person who believes the Bible is truth—and I believe the Bible is truth—the returning of Jewish people to the land of Israel is the fulfillment of the biblical prophecy. It's the fulfillment of God's plan. God promised through the mouth of the prophets, such as in Ezekiel 37, that we would dwell in this land—this that is the land God promised to Abraham and his descendants. Joshua believed this promise and gave us the borders of this land. Therefore, our returning to this place is fulfilling God's commandments, God's prophecies, God's covenants, and God's promises. I don't believe that we stole anyone's land.

However, when the Israeli [settlers] take the top of a hill in this country, what happens? An Arab will appear and say, "It belongs to me." The Israeli will say, "If it belongs to you, please show us papers, show us anything to prove that it belongs to you." He will say, "I don't have a paper, but I can tell you that in the last one hundred years my goats and sheep were eating on this hill." If I were to come with this kind of answer, you know very well that the courts would not help me. Many of the cases are exactly like this. [The Arabs] don't have any proof, except the claim "Israel occupied their land."

Another case is when a city is developed or needs to be built, and a hill claimed by an Arab is in the middle. The Israeli government respects his claim and tells the owner, "We brought an appraiser and know the value of your property. We can pay you or give you a different place." But the Muslim authorities tell these Arabs, "If you sell the ground [to Israel] we will kill you." So it's the death penalty by Muslims to any Arab who sells the ground to Jewish owners. Even if the government tells the owner, "Here is one million dollars"—and they want to give it because it is a law in Israel—the Arab says, "I don't want it" or runs away.

It is an inescapable situation because a country will grow, and if a hill is in the way of a highway the government has to take it, but is willing to pay for it. This applies to everyone the same. When Israeli settlers take a hill that belongs to an Arab and the Arab goes to the Israeli Supreme Court with his [ownership] paper, the court orders the government to remove the Israeli settlers and their houses and to give it back to the Arab person.

Again, we're not living in a perfect world, but in 1948 and 1967 it was not Israel that started the war—Israel's survival was threatened. When we defended ourselves, overcame our enemies, and took their territories, they ran away! Afterward these same enemies came and said, "You took my land; give it back!" But did we start the war? So there are a lot of problems as a result of this bad situation, but there is a court in Israel and if something belongs to you, then go to court. Prove it, and you'll get it back.

Price: The media has published stories saying that the Israeli government tears down people's houses, cuts branches off of their olive trees, does a lot of abusive things to try to drive Arabs from their land. Is any of this true? How do you understand it?

Kalisher: There are situations, very sad situations, where bad people take their own initiative and do awful things. It happens on both sides. Arabs will burn fields and forests; every year we have it happen. Both sides are doing things like this and it's devilish. Usually they blame settlers for doing such things, but there are bad apples on both sides. On the Israeli side some people express their hatred by cutting olive trees or burning them or trying to hurt innocent people. It's very sad. But it is totally false to say that the Israeli government has initiated such things.

Now concerning destroying houses. I'm an Israeli and I live in an apartment building in the middle of north Jerusalem, but it took me twelve years to get a license to build an office under my living room. So I understand the difficult situation of getting permits in this country. Yet I know it's much harder for an Arab person in some villages to receive a license to build. It's a sad situation, and I wish it would improve. Because of this, many Arabs build without a license and they build in places the government has planned for future cities or main roads. The Arabs receive warnings not to build there, but they still do. So the government has no choice but to come—after court approval—with a tractor and destroy what was built without a license.

Now, no one can take away anyone's house unless the supreme court permits it. The Arab will say to the court, "I understand, but you don't give me a choice. I want a license, but it takes forty years to get a license!" That's the problem, and I wish and pray that the situation will improve. I wish the Israeli government would share their city plans with the Arab villages so people can know where it is possible for Arabs to build without future problems. It's bureaucracy, a sad situation.

Price: What does the Bible say about Jews and Arabs together?

Kalisher: The Bible tells us that in the past, in the present, and in the future (and also in the millennium) that the foreigner will always dwell with us. We were foreigners in Egypt, so we need to remember how it is to be a foreigner. I do believe that Israel should give foreigners in their midst a lot of care, but frankly, a lot is being done and people are either not aware of it or don't want to hear about it. If you ask an Israeli Arab, "Where do you want to live—in the Palestinian Authority or in Israel?," you will not have to wait more than half a second to hear, "I prefer to live in Israel." When you point out, "You're suffering in Israel—why do you want to live in Israel?," the Arab will often tell you, "In Israel it's much better. The social services and everything else are much better."

Our problem is that the Arabs demand the rights of a citizen but don't want to give what a citizen is supposed to give to his country. They hate it; they are tolerant toward terrorism; they don't serve in the army—although I understand their problem with that. They don't want to serve in hospitals or schools or anywhere else. They give nothing [in return] to the country where they receive the benefits of a citizen. There are a few Arabs who are wonderful and exemplary, but unfortunately I'm talking about the majority.

So what God demands biblically is to take care of the foreigner—to respect him, to love him, to be there for him because he will always be with us. It is wrong, it is devilish, to try to push away the foreigner in our land if he was born here and has citizenship. As a citizen, he is entitled to everything I am entitled to—no difference whatsoever. But he should be willing to accept the responsibilities of a citizen and not just receive the benefits.

Price: What about Arab Christians? They read and follow the same Bible, so why is it so difficult for them to get along with Jewish believers? What theological problems are keeping Arab pastors and Jewish pastors and Arab Christians and Jewish Christians from coming together?

Kalisher: I'll try to be as objective as possible and present both sides in a truthful, loving way. Both sides are not perfect, both sides many times will elevate nationalism before submitting to Christ and the Word of God. What happens is that most of the Jewish believers (I would say 99.9 percent of them) believe that God has a program and a plan for the people of Israel in the land of Israel—that God chose our people, the descendants of Abraham, Isaac, and Jacob, to be a kingdom of priests in the land of Israel within the borders specified in the Bible. This will be fulfilled literally in the millennium.

If you go to Arab Christians, belief is divided. Most hold to replacement theology and only a minority agree with messianic Jews about the Bible. Fellowship with this minority of Arab pastors who believe that God still has a plan for Israel and reject replacement theology is much easier than with Arab pastors who hold to replacement theology. However, in recent years, we have tried to create channels of speaking and fellowshipping between Israeli pastors and Arab pastors who hold to replacement theology. We know that we see God's plan for Israel in a different way, but we try to focus on portions of our ministry together. Sometimes they will call Israel "the occupied territories," or say, "Your independence day is my *Nabkah* ('disaster day')." But we try to overcome this vocabulary, humble ourselves before Christ Jesus, and fellowship, meet together, and bring the churches together to praise God. We try. It's something that while I'm speaking to you is in process.

Some may say, "How can you sit together?" But people from the other side will say the same to Arab pastors. Yet for the sake of Christ, for the sake of His name, for the sake of the next generation—that they will grow to be more united in faith in Jesus; and they will be more able to listen to one another and to submit themselves to the authority of the Word of God—we meet together to try to elevate one another before the Lord, to learn to love one another, and to participate in some ministry of evangelism and so on to exercise what God expects us to do.

Price: Who organizes these meetings? Where do they take place?

Kalisher: The last meetings were in Germany. The next meeting will be in Israel. We invited the youth group of an Arab church, and they invited us. We want to do more of that. We want our children to grow, to pray for one another. We know that politics will continue the conflict until the Lord returns. We have to work at unity, and we can for His name's sake.

Price: I think that's something people need to know more about. Can you tell us about how long these meetings have been going on, and how successful they are?

Kalisher: There were plans in place before, but the actual meeting happened in May 2017. The second meeting was July 2018. Both groups have their own ideas about what the Bible says, so I'm not going to a meeting with the mindset that I'll convince the other person. I'm not coming to fight; I'm coming to know the person, to really listen and get to know the person, to learn to be friends, and as friends we can study together, we can go over God's Word together. It will take time. I don't know how much time, but I know by doing this that our children will not grow up seeing the Arab believers as enemies, but as brothers and sisters in the Lord.

Price: That's what people need to hear. Are these meetings publicized or are they secret?

Kalisher: Let's put it this way: We are not announcing what we do. We prefer that people would see the success, God willing, through the lives, through the mutual unity of ministry that we try to come up with together. That means seeing and tasting the fruit rather than speaking too much. So we prefer to do it underground. But if you want it? Join us.

Price: From the Palestinian or Arab side are those participants afraid of any government or Muslim reaction?

Kalisher: When Christian Arabs hug Jews with love they might be considered collaborators, so yes, I'm sure that they're taking a risk to do so.

Price: I know that Israeli and Arab youth have tried to do camps and other things together. How has that worked out?

Kalisher: There is an Arab organization with some Jewish believers in it and they take Jews and Arabs to camps in order to bring them closer to one another. Years ago we sent some of our youth and they retuned telling us that they felt very bad because it was very nationalistic. The Arab kids blamed the Jewish kids and called them occupiers, and because they were serving in the army, they told them they were bad guys. So we did not do anything more with this organization. However, in our last meeting we mentioned this experience, and I hope that the leaders of that organization took our words to heart and understand that if they want to bring the two together, they need to learn to look to Christ and not at nationalism. And I say this for both sides.

Price: That's what I wanted to know. That's what is happening in Israel, and the focus of this book is Israel. What more do you think should be said about Arab-Jewish relations to those who aren't aware of what is going on?

Kalisher: People need to know that we are not enemies. We pray for our Christian Arab brethren. Yes, our doctrines are not identical, but also many churches in America and other countries do not have identical doctrines and you don't consider yourselves enemies. I believe what we need to do more is to pray for one another. As a local church, we participate and donate and invest in evangelism to Muslims. As for me, when I see a Christian, I don't see an Arab or Israeli—I see a Christian. I see a born-again child of God. I don't make the Arab or Israeli distinction. That's how we educate our next generation—I'm happy with what we have now, and I will be glad to do more with Arab churches in the future. It can be done. I know some of them pretty well by now; they are good friends. I enjoy fellowship with them and even though they have different doctrines concerning Israel, that does not mean they hate me or hate Israel. But you can only come to this conclusion after sitting together and praying and sharing heart to heart.

Dialogue on Thinking About Israel

The following four-part dialogue between David Brickner of Jews for Jesus and John Piper of Desiring God Ministries originally appeared on the Christianity Today website in June 2012 and is used here with permission.

Do Jews Have a Divine Right to Israel's Land?
DAVID BRICKNER

*P*art one of a conversation between John Piper and Jews for Jesus *head David Brickner.*

Do Jews have a divine right to the Promised Land? Are American pastors dismissive of Arab Christians in Israel? Should Christians treat the Israeli-Palestinian dispute differently than other conflicts? As pastor of Bethlehem Baptist Church in Minneapolis, John Piper has been addressing these contentious questions for years. After he began informally discussing them with David Brickner, executive director of Jews for Jesus, *we invited them to share some of their discussion with our readers. We begin today with Brickner's response to some of Piper's recent writings and sermons, and will continue tomorrow with Piper's response.*

Dear John,

It is an honor to dialogue with you on the important and timely subject of Israel/Palestine, the land and the people. I am deeply aware of your uncompromising commitment to the cause of Christ among all peoples, including the Jewish people. The opportunities you have consistently extended to Jews for Jesus to share our ministry with the family at Beth-lehem Baptist Church—and the way you have stood your ground in sup-porting Jewish evangelism, even after receiving considerable pressure from Jewish community leaders—speak volumes. There can be no doubt that what we share in common is far greater than the areas where we may disagree.

Yet, if I understand your views regarding the modern state of Israel and its current conflict with its neighbors correctly, I do have some real concerns—particularly in light of the current political climate (the U.N. vote on Palestinian statehood) as well as a growing trend among certain Christian polemicists against Israel (see Gary Burge and Stephen Sizer). I believe our exchange will demonstrate to readers that, despite the heated arguments that occur at the poles of the Christian positions on these issues, there is a broad middle ground where the majority of us can stand and exchange our views in an irenic and thought-provoking way.

I have recently reread your article for *World Magazine* (May 11, 2002), along with sermons you preached at Bethlehem Baptist Church in November 2002 and March 2004, and more recently a blog from March 2011. I'll begin this exchange on the basis of those writings.

I appreciate your clear statement of belief in God's continuing pur-poses for ethnic Israel. I also note that you affirm, "God promised to Israel the presently disputed land from the time of Abraham onward." And yet there seems to be a "disconnect" between those statements and your com-ments regarding the present-day situation as well as the future. As I see it, this disconnect occurs at two important points.

First, you say that because the majority of Jews do not believe in Jesus they have broken covenant with God and have no divine claim at this time to the land God promised them.

Second, you say that the future of the land promised to Israel becomes subsumed under the promise of God that all believers will "inherit the land...because the entire new heavens and new earth will be ours."

I believe that these views can potentially undermine Christian confi-dence in the ongoing election of Israel based upon the Abrahamic cove-nant and give encouragement to those who have adopted a supersessionist position toward Israel today. (*Editors' note: supersessionism teaches that the church has replaced Israel in God's covenants and plans.*)

I agree with you that Israel does not currently enjoy a *divine right* to the Land. But I would argue that it has never been by divine right but rather by *divine mercy* that Israel has dwelt in the Land. God blessed Abraham in the land he had promised him though Abraham at times acted in unbelief, at times had to fight for his land, and at one point even paid for his land (and in the end never even possessed all the land that was promised him). Similarly, for much of the biblical record, Israel lived in the Land while rebellious and breaking the Mosaic covenant. Yet God was merciful and allowed Israel to remain in the Land despite her unbelief. He did this because of his gracious promise to Abraham and his descendants. Why could God not act the same in our present-day situation?

While God declared that his judgment upon Israel for her unbelief would include removal from the Land, he also promised he would re-gather his people to that land, not based on divine right but again as a result of his mercy. Could God in his mercy allow Israel to be re-gathered to the Land although in unbelief? I believe he could. In fact, it would appear the Scripture implies that Israel will indeed be back in the Land in unbelief prior to the return of Christ (see Ezekiel 37; Zechariah 12; Romans 11).

Could present-day Israel be uprooted once again from the Land because of her unbelief? I would have to say yes, though I hope not. There is a growing remnant of believers in Jesus in the land of Israel, and God has consistently extended mercy on behalf of the remnant of his people. Paul makes much of the theology of the remnant in asserting that God has not forsaken his people. The church can rejoice in that ever-increasing remnant, with all the ramifications it holds for the modern and future state of Israel. As you have noted, "these privileges belong fully and savingly to an elect remnant of Israel now."

The future of ethnic Israel is indeed bright; just as God has promised, "all Israel will be saved. As it is written: the deliverer will come from Zion...." But surely that bright future must also include the fulfillment of the specific land promises God has made to Abraham and his descendants as well. To imagine that God's very specific promises are subsumed in his wider promise that all believers will inherit the new heavens and earth makes it seem as though God is reinterpreting his original promise so as to effectively make its original meaning null.

Imagine if I had offered your grandfather a beautiful home in Minneapolis and told him very specifically that it was not only for him, but for his descendants. After you move in, I inform you that some time in the future I will be renovating the entire city and you will have a much bigger and better house. Of course, you will share the city with many others as well. And in the meanwhile, several neighbors are moving into the original house I promised your grandfather. Probably you would find either my ability to remember my promises, or my intention of keeping them, somewhat lacking. It seems to me that subsuming God's past and precise promises into his wider, future promises reflects similarly on God's memory or intentions of promise-keeping.

As to the issue of how Christians should understand the current conflict between Israel and the Palestinians, I agree with you that Israel "should seek a peaceful settlement not based on present divine right, but on principles of justice, mercy, and practical feasibility." Israel's government is secular and should be evaluated by the same standards as any other secular government. There has been injustice and suffering on both sides of the conflict, and we are called to care for all those who are suffering. At the same time we must avoid the common practice today of drawing a moral equivalence between acts of terrorism against citizens and the efforts of a government to defend its people and territory.

Most importantly, I absolutely agree with you that "the Christian plea in the Middle East to Palestinians and Jews is: 'Believe in the Lord Jesus, and you will be saved.'" The only hope for peace was born in the Middle East, our wonderful Messiah Y'shua. God loves Israelis and Palestinians equally. Indeed, when Arabs and Jews can say to one another, "I love you in Jesus' name," the world will truly see the reconciling power of the gospel. Through the proclamation of the gospel there today we are beginning to see this happening, to the praise of his grace.

Your Jewish brother in him,

David Brickner

How to Treat a Rebellious Israel
JOHN PIPER

Part two of a conversation between John Piper and Jews for Jesus *head David Brickner.*

Dear David,

Thank you for taking this happy initiative. I am eager to discuss Israel and the Promised Land with you. I love Jews for Jesus. Your leadership, and Moishe Rosen's before you, have been for me a cause for continual thanksgiving. "To the Jew first, and also to the Greek" (Rom. 1:16) has never ceased to carry weight with me. I pray we will never lose Paul's passion in Romans 10:1: "My heart's desire and prayer to God for them is that they may be saved."

We both agree that the way God chose to bring all the nations under the sway of King Jesus is astonishing. After sketching it, Paul praised God, "How unsearchable are his judgments and how inscrutable his ways!" (Rom. 11:33).

- First, God chose Israel. "The Lord your God has chosen you to be a people for his treasured possession, out of all the peoples who are on the face of the earth" (Deut. 7:6).

- Then, for 2,000 years, he focused his saving work mainly on Israel, "allowing all the nations to walk in their own ways" (Acts 14:16).

- Then he sent Jesus, the Messiah, to Israel, knowing they would crucify him, so that the Gentiles might "receive mercy because of their [Israel's] disobedience" (Rom. 11:30).

- And then, lest we Gentiles think we are the end of the story, Paul told us that Israel "has now been disobedient in order that by the mercy shown to you [Gentiles] they [Israel] also may now receive mercy" (Rom. 11:31).

- And the point of it all? To show that "from him and through him and to him are all things. To him be glory forever. Amen" (Rom. 11:36).

What was Paul's response to this flabbergasting way of saving the world? *Unsearchable! Inscrutable!* "Who has known the mind of the Lord, or who has been his counselor?" (Rom. 11:34).

So, you are right. I believe God has a future for ethnic Israel. And we agree this is not because there are two tracks to glory or two different covenants of grace. Rather, corporate Israel will be saved in the end because she will be grafted back into the same covenant tree with all of us wild olive branches (Rom. 11:16-24). Both Jews and Gentiles become heirs of the promise of Abraham in the same way: "If you are Christ's, then you are Abraham's offspring, heirs according to promise" (Gal. 3:29).

So I am persuaded with J. C. Ryle that Israel, as a people, will someday be converted to the Messiah and saved:

> They are kept separate that they may finally be saved, converted and restored to their own land. They are reserved and preserved, in order that God may show in them as on a platform, to angels and men, how greatly he hates sin, and yet how greatly he can forgive, and how greatly he can convert. Never will that be realized as it will in that day when "all Israel shall be saved." (*Are You Ready for the End of Time?* pp. 137-138)

Moreover, I also believe the promise of the Land to this redeemed ethnic Israel is both conditional and irrevocable. *Irrevocable* means they will finally have it as a special dwelling place when the Deliverer comes from Zion and banishes ungodliness from Jacob (Rom. 11:26).

The Land is part of God's everlasting covenant with Israel. "He confirmed to Jacob as...an *everlasting covenant*, saying, 'To you I will give the land of Canaan'" (Ps. 105:10-11). "All the land that you see I will give to you and to your offspring *forever*" (Gen. 13:15). "I will give to you and to your offspring...the land of your sojournings...for an *everlasting possession*" (Gen. 17:8).

But this irrevocable covenant promise is also *conditional*. The obedience that comes from faith is the condition. Here's the logic of the covenant promise: "I have chosen him [Abraham], that he may command his children and his household after him to keep the way of the Lord by doing righteousness and justice, *so that* the Lord may bring to Abraham what he has promised him" (Gen. 18:19). They are to keep the way of the Lord, *so that* the promises will count for them.

Abraham was justified by faith (Gen. 15:6), but his obedience, for example on Mount Moriah, confirmed his covenant standing and was the condition of the final promise: "In your offspring shall all the nations of the earth be blessed, *because* you have obeyed my voice [in offering Isaac]" (Gen. 22:18; cf. 26:4-5). Similarly, God spoke this condition to Israel at Mount Sinai: "If you will indeed obey my voice and keep my covenant, you shall be my treasured possession among all peoples" (Ex. 19:5).

Thus, when Israel broke her covenant in protracted disobedience, God, after much mercy, brought judgments on her, including eviction from the Promised Land. "The king of Assyria carried the Israelites…because they did not obey the voice of the Lord their God but transgressed his covenant" (2 Kings 18:11-12). "Because you sinned against the Lord and did not obey his voice, this thing has come upon you" (Jer. 40:3; cf. Deut. 28:45; Ps. 78:56-61).

Today, Israel as a nation is a covenant-breaking people—they are rejecting their Messiah, Jesus. In this condition of unbelief and disobedience, she has no "divine right" to the Land of Promise. This does not mean that other nations have the right to molest her. She still has human rights among nations. Nations that gloated over Israel's divine discipline were punished by God (Isa. 10:5-13).

Therefore, the Christian plea in the Middle East to Palestinians and Jews is: "Believe on the Lord Jesus, and you will be saved" (Acts 16:31). And until that great day when Jesus-trusting Israel will inherit the Land without lifting sword or gun, the rights of nations should be decided by the principles of compassionate and public justice, not claims to national divine right or status.

You point out that "it has never been by *divine right* but rather by *divine mercy* that Israel has dwelt in the Land." I totally agree. It has *always* been by divine mercy that Israel has dwelt in the Land. She has never *merited* it as a right. I wasn't thinking of "divine right" in contrast to "divine mercy," but in contrast to "human right." That is, Israel *may* have a human right to the Land, even while she has no divine right to it. That is, in negotiations with other nations, covenant-breaking Israel cannot say, "God has given us a right to this land *presently* in our state of unbelief and disobedience." While Israel rejects Jesus as her Messiah, neither God's mercy nor his justice offers compelling warrant for her possessing the Land.

You say, "God was merciful and allowed Israel to remain in the Land despite her unbelief....Why could God not act the same in our present-day situation?" I answer: He not only can. He is. Israel is in the Land. And it is all mercy. All I am saying with the term "no divine right" is that the promise of God that Israel will someday rightfully possess the Land carries no leverage among the nations while she is rejecting her Messiah.

With regard to the final inheritance of the Land, you suggest that my handling of the promise to Israel "effectively makes its original meaning null." The reason is that I said,

> Jewish believers in Jesus and Gentile believers will inherit the Land. And the easiest way to see this is to see that we will inherit the world which includes the Land. Jewish Christians and Gentile Christians will not quibble over the real estate of the Promised Land because the entire new heavens and the new earth will be ours. 1 Corinthians 3:21–23: "All things are yours, whether Paul or Apollos or Cephas or the world or life or death or the present or the future—all are yours, and you are Christ's, and Christ is God's." All followers of Christ, and only followers of Christ, will inherit the earth, including the Land.

Does this way of seeing things nullify the promise that God will give Israel the Land? I don't think so. Israel will get no less than promised because the Gentiles get more than imagined. For all I know, in the millennium and in the new earth redeemed and glorified ethnic Israel will locate mainly in the new Palestine. But she will also own the world, and no saint will begrudge her emigration, or any Gentile's immigration.

In the present situation in Israel, I agree with your wise counsel: "we must avoid...drawing a moral equivalence between acts of terrorism against citizens and the efforts of a government to defend its people and territory."

My prayer is that the good news of Jesus, the crucified and risen Messiah, would flood Jewish communities around the world, that the veil would be lifted, and that we would see a massive turning of Israel to the Lord Jesus. "For there is no distinction between Jew and Greek; for the same Lord is Lord of all, bestowing his riches on all who call on him. For 'everyone who calls on the name of the Lord will be saved'" (Rom. 10:12-13).

God Doesn't Keep Jews in a Pickle Jar
DAVID BRICKNER

This is part three of a four-part discussion between Bethlehem Baptist Church pastor John Piper and Jews for Jesus executive director David Brickner on the relationship and attitudes American Christians should have toward Israel.

Dear John,

Thank you for your insightful comments on a number of the issues brought up in my first letter to you, many with which I happily agree. We both uphold the need and priority of Jewish evangelism as integral to world mission. We both affirm the ongoing election of Israel (the Jewish people) and God's faithfulness to his covenant people and his promises. We both look forward to the second coming of Jesus and his glorious restoration of all things, including his people Israel. I do want to take issue with two of your comments before voicing my main concern.

To your assertion that the Abrahamic covenant is conditional, I will simply quote my friend and teacher Walter C. Kaiser Jr.: "Promise and blessing still precede the command to obey and to keep the commands of God. Obedience is no more a condition for Abraham than it is for the church living under the command 'If you obey my commands, you will remain in my love' (Jn. 15:10) or 'If you love me, you will obey what I command' (Jn. 14:15)."

Second, I read the context of 1 Corinthians 3 as primarily referring to boasting about different human leaders. It does an injustice to the text to take Paul's hyperbole to then relate to Israel's covenant promise concerning the Land. This results in minimizing the particularity of Israel's election in the midst of the universality of the nations' eschatological ingathering.

You are taking away with one hand what you give with the other—when Israel gets all, she actually gets nothing. (Regardless of whether she may, as you point out, end up in the land that was promised.)

However, these disagreements are secondary to my concern over an ongoing problem in the church today. Christians often have a great depth of theological understanding regarding Israel in the past. Many also have a keen interest and firm convictions regarding Israel in the future. Yet when it comes to present-day Israel it seems biblical thinking often takes a back seat to political expedience on both sides of the current conflict.

Christians today desperately need an informed theology concerning present-day Israel. I don't see where your recent response addressed my point concerning the remnant today and the implications of the growing number of Israeli believers in Jesus. Although I know you didn't intend this, your quote from Ryle that "they are reserved and preserved" makes it sound like we are in a pickle jar kept on a shelf somewhere! No. The apostle Paul insisted, "God has not rejected his people whom he foreknew." "Not rejected" does not mean he has shunted them off to the side for use at a later time. Israel today is marvelous evidence of God's continuing covenant faithfulness, his amazing sovereignty over world affairs, and the great power of his mercy despite human disobedience. The remnant in existence today is also "chosen by grace."

The birth of the modern state of Israel did not occur in a vacuum but sprang from the ashes of the Holocaust, where one third of the Jewish people were systematically annihilated simply because they were Jews. Evangelicals need to think more deeply about the implications of the Holocaust and its connection to Israel today. I believe Israel is in possession of the Land today by divine mercy, a mercy flowing out of the horrors of the Holocaust and to the ultimate defeat of all other efforts at Jewish genocide past and present. This can only be the hand of God in history despite Israel's current unbelief. Present day anti-Semitism is proof that Israel remains at the nexus of the cosmic conflict between God, who keeps his promises, and Satan, who wants to make God a liar. We shouldn't allow history to interpret the Bible, but we must allow the Bible to speak to recent and current history, not just ancient history and the future.

Unfortunately, the current posture of many evangelicals has been to jettison the overarching biblical picture of God's love for both Israel and the nations and to choose sides between Palestinians and Israelis, further fueling the present passions of pain and conflict. This is wrong.

Beginning with the household of faith, Christians must implore the people of the Land on behalf of Christ to be reconciled to God and then to one another. Christians need to formulate a full-orbed theology of reconciliation and Israel/Palestine can be the laboratory. As we apply biblical truth to the conflict today, the world will truly see the power of the gospel. To this end I know we both remain deeply committed. May our dialogue help encourage Christians to retake this biblical and gospel-centered middle ground. Let us believe in the ongoing promises of God to the Jewish people and re-double our efforts to proclaim this Good News to Israelis, Palestinians, and all humanity.

Your Jewish brother in Jesus,

David Brickner

Why Israel Exists "for the Palestinians"— And the Rest of the World
JOHN PIPER

This is the conclusion of a four-part discussion between Bethlehem Baptist Church pastor John Piper and Jews for Jesus executive director David Brickner on the relationship and attitudes American Christians should have toward Israel.

Dear David,

Let's get the relatively minor disagreements and misunderstandings out of the way, so we can celebrate the grand agreements.

I don't regard 1 Corinthians 3:21-23 as hyperbole the way you do. "*All things* are yours, whether Paul or Apollos or Cephas or the *world* or life or death or the present or the future—all are yours, and you are Christ's, and Christ is God's."

I think the Christian inheritance of all the created universe is the implication of our being "heirs of God and fellow heirs with Christ" (Rom. 8:17).

It's the point Jesus made in Matthew 5:5: "Blessed are the meek, for they shall inherit the earth." We will even judge angels (1 Cor. 6:3).

And it is remarkable that the "world" is the inheritance of the Christian Corinthians (1 Cor. 3:22) and the inheritance of Abraham and his offspring: "The promise to Abraham and his offspring that he would be heir of the *world* did not come through the law but through the righteousness of faith" (Rom. 4:13).

When I say that Abraham's inheritance is not only Israel, but the world, and that the Gentile Christian's inheritance is the world, including Israel, you say that I am "minimizing the particularity of Israel's election" and that I "take away with one hand what [I] give with the other."

I did say, and I do believe, that Israel, as a people, "will finally have [the Land] as a *special* dwelling place." By the word "special," I mean to preserve Israel's *particular* role in God's plan. But when I say Israel gets the world thrown in along with the Promised Land, I don't see why you say, "You are taking away with one hand what you give with the other." How is *adding* the world in any serious way a *subtracting*?

The only thing I take away is the "no trespassing" signs to those outside Israel, and the barbed wire on the borders for those inside. The Promised Land belongs to Israel in a special way, and belongs to all the "sons of Abraham" (Gal. 3:7) as well. God will honor the particularity of ethnic Israel's inheritance and the universality of spiritual Israel's inheritance. He will do it without taking anything good away from either. Surely it will not be true that "when Israel gets all, she actually gets nothing."

On the issue of the conditionality of the Abrahamic covenant, I agree with you that "obedience is no more a condition for Abraham than it is for the church." And I would simply add: *and no less.* All who belong to the visible church or to visible Israel, but who do not confirm their faith with obedience, will perish. To Israel and to the church, Jesus says, "Repent, and do the works you did at first. If not, I will come to you and remove your lampstand from its place, unless you repent" (Rev. 2:5). Final salvation is conditional for the church on the obedience that comes from faith, as for Israel. No more, no less.

But let us celebrate our common convictions about the wonder of present-day Israel both the nation and the remnant. I'm sorry that Ryle's language proved misleading, namely, that present day Israel is "reserved and preserved" for a great future destiny. Neither he nor I imply that Israel is "in a pickle jar kept on a shelf somewhere." Both he and I agree with you that on the way to this future destiny (of conversion and inheritance), Israel is a "marvelous evidence of God's continuing covenant faithfulness." Yes. Amen!

On the 60th anniversary of the birth of the modern state of Israel (May 7, 2008), I celebrated the astonishing apologetical power of the sheer existence of Israel. I drew attention to Anne Rice, the vampire novelist who some years ago turned from 30 years of atheism because of Israel. Even her more recent misgivings about institutional Christianity don't nullify the validity of her discovery. She said, "I stumbled upon a mystery without a solution, a mystery so immense that I gave up trying to find an explanation because the whole mystery defied belief. The mystery was the survival of the Jews....It was this mystery that drew me back to God."

God's purposes for Israel are not on hold. They are active daily. He is moving in this world with sovereign power over all nations in order to accomplish his saving purposes for Jew and Gentile. "As regards the gospel, they [Israel] are enemies of God for your [the Gentiles] sake. But as regards election, they are beloved for the sake of their forefathers. For the gifts and the calling of God are irrevocable" (Rom. 11:28-29).

To give this a sharp and radical point, this means that the people of Israel exist today, as they are, "for the sake of" the Palestinians. For the sake of Iranians, Egyptians, Jordanians, Lebanese, Syrians, Americans. And woe to us (Arab or American) Gentiles, if we become arrogant toward Israel, failing to see in her both the root of our salvation and the truth about our condemnation.

"Whatever the law says it speaks to those who are under the law [Israel], so that every mouth may be stopped [all Gentiles], and the whole world may be held accountable to God" (Rom. 3:19). So let all the Gentile world take heed: "Do not be arrogant toward the [unbelieving Jewish] branches. If you are, remember it is not you [Gentiles] who support the root [of Abraham's promise], but the root that supports you" (Rom. 11:18).

And as for the remnant—the gloriously ever-increasing remnant—of Jesus-receiving Israel, yes, these too are evidence of God's covenant keeping faithfulness with all Israel. As Paul says in Romans 11:1-2: "Has God rejected his people? By no means! For I myself am an Israelite.... God has not rejected his people whom he foreknew."

Both unbelieving Israel and believing Israel are the work of God's mercy this very day. Both point to Jesus, crucified and risen, as the only hope of the world. Israel—at enmity with her God and reconciled to her God—are at the center of world history. Each witnesses in her own way to Savior of the world, Jesus Christ.

So yes, David, yes, I am with you: "Let us believe in the ongoing promises of God to the Jewish people and re-double our efforts to proclaim this Good News to Israelis, Palestinians, and all humanity."

Your brother, indeed,

John Piper

Scripture Index

Genesis

1:27	120
3	212
3:15	24, 80, 169, 212
5:1-31	212
6:10	161
9:6	120
9:26	212
11	200
11:1-9	212
11:10-26	212
12	187, 189
12:1-3	24, 58, 59, 69, 71, 76, 80, 212, 224, 225, 227, 233
12:7	41, 59, 212
12:10-20	214
13:14-15	41, 70, 72, 229, 284
13:14-17	59, 212
14:18	87
14:22-23	77
15	189, 214
15:1-6	69, 218, 285
15:1-17	71
15:1-21	58, 59, 60, 71
15:2	72
15:7-21	60, 212
15:8	72
15:9-17	213
15:10	70
15:13-16	230
15:17-21	70
15:18-21	26, 41, 60, 213, 216, 230
16:2-6	59
17	189, 218
17:7,13,19	60, 72, 80, 130, 214, 229
17:8	41, 72, 80, 130, 213, 216, 229
17:9-14	77
17:14	73
17:18	59, 212, 284
17:19	212, 229
18:19	225, 285
20:7	59
21:10-11	59
21:25-33	208, 230
22	189
22:1-2,9	98
22:10-14	98
22:16-17	59, 227, 285
25:21-23	191
27	214
28:1	41
28:10-22	214
28:12-13	60
37:25	80
42:18	59
45:7	242
49:8-10	24
50:24	60

Exodus

2:24	215
3:6-10	225
9:16	25
15:17	88, 98
15:18	230
19:5	217, 220, 285
19:6	61, 217, 220, 225, 226
20–31	59
22:21	64
23:9	64
23:31	230
25:8	102
25:21-22	88
32:13	229

Subject and Person Index

Notes

Preface: What Should We Think About This Book?—Randall Price

1. "Israel: An Archaeological Journey," *Biblical Archaeology Spotlight* (September 7, 2018), accessed at biblicalarchaeology.org/dm?id=8D4097D384BAC0A032DF265 94D33D866B787DDAA31E6F94A.

2. Mike Evans, "Donald Trump, 'Holy Ground,'" CBN News (September 2, 2018): 2, accessed at http://www1.cbn.com/cbnnews/us/2018/september/donald-trump-ndash-holy-ground.

3. On this matter see Maurice M. Roumani, *The Case of the Jews from Arab Countries: A Neglected Issue* (Jerusalem: Alpha Press, 1975) and "The Forgotten Refugees" in Paul R. Wilkinson, *Israel Betrayed: The Rise of Christian Palestinianism* (San Antonio, TX: Ariel Ministries, 2018), 285-292.

4. Aviel Schneider, "Nobody Talks About the Second Nakba," *Israel Today* 225 (September 2018): 6-7.

5. Joseph Klein, "World Silent as ISIS Slaughters Palestinians," *Frontpage Magazine*, (April 9, 2015), accessed at http://www.freerepublic.com/focus/news/3277382/posts?page=1.

6. For further information on this problem see Arsen Ostrovsky, "The Online Intifada—Social Media and Incitement" in Alex Ryvchin, ed., *The Anti-Israel Agenda: Inside the Political War on the Jewish State* (Jerusalem: Gefen Publishing, 2017), 185-204.

Introduction: Why Should We Think About Israel?—Mark L. Bailey

1. Gerald R. McDermott, *Israel Matters: Why Christians Must Think Differently About the People and the Land* (Grand Rapids, MI: Baker Publishing Group, 2017), 46.

2. "Why Did God Choose Israel?" accessed September 9, 2018. https://www.onefor israel.org/bible-based-teaching-from-israel/why-did-god-choose-israel.

3. "The Balfour Declaration," accessed September 10, 2018, https://sourcebooks.ford ham.edu/mod/balfour.asp, emphasis added.

4. For the survey results and summary, see Darrell L. Bock and Mitch Glaser, eds., *Israel, the Church, and the Middle East* (Grand Rapids, MI: Kregel Publications, 2018), 228-56.

5. Bock and Glaser, eds., *Israel, the Church, and the Middle East,* 230.

6. Michael J. Vlach, *Has the Church Replaced Israel?* (Nashville, TN: B&H Publishing Group, 2014), 12.

7. See Scot McKnight's 12 arguments against supersessionism. Scot McKnight, "Supersessionism Is Not Biblical," accessed September 10, 2018, http://www.patheos.com/blogs/jesuscreed/2012/05/07/supersessionism-is-not-biblical. Other chapters in this volume by Oliver Melnick, Darrell Bock, Tim Sigler, and Seth Postell will address these tensions and offer some helpful reasons we need to think better and clearer on these issues.

8. Bock and Glaser, eds., *Israel, the Church, and the Middle East,* 231.

9. Leviticus 26:33; Deuteronomy 4:25-28; 28:58-68; 1 Kings 14:15; Nehemiah 1:8; Psalms 44:11; 106:27; Jeremiah 9:16; 16:15; 18:17; 23:8; 30:11; Lamentations 4:16; Ezekiel 5:10; 11:16; 12:15; 20:23; 22:15; 36:19; Zechariah 2:6; 7:14; 10:9.

10. Deuteronomy 4:29-30; 30:4; Isaiah 11:11-12; 27:12; 43:5; 54:7; 56:8; Jeremiah 29:14; 31:8,10; 32:37; Ezekiel 11:17; 20:34,41; 28:25; 34:13; 36:24; 37:21; 39:27-28; Zephaniah 3:20.

Chapter 1: What Should We Think About the Zionist Movement?—Thomas Ice

1. "Zionism," *Encyclopedia Judaica*, vol. 16 (Jerusalem: Keter Publishing House Ltd., c. 1971), 1032.

2. "Zionism," *Encyclopedia Britannica*, Internet edition, https://www.britannica.com/topic/Zionism.

3. Rufus Learsi, *Fulfillment: The Epic Story of Zionism* (New York: The World Publishing Company, 1951), 40.

4. Learsi, *Fulfillment*, 409.

5. Learsi, *Fulfillment*, 41-45.

6. Walter LaQueur, *A History of Zionism: From the French Revolution to the Establishment of the State of Israel* (New York: Schocken Books, 1972, 2003), 40.

7. Benjamin Netanyahu, *A Place Among the Nations: Israel and the World* (New York: Bantam Books, 1993), 8.

8. "Anti-Semitism," *Encyclopedia Judaica*, vol. 3, 87.

9. "Anti-Semitism," *Encyclopedia Judaica*, vol. 3, 99.

10. See Isaiah 11:11-12; 18:7; 27:12-13; 29:1,8; 44; 60:8-21; 66:18-22; Jeremiah 3:17-18; 11:10-11; 23:3-6; 29:14; 30:7,10; 31:2,10,31-34; 33:4-16; 50:19; Ezekiel 11:17; 20:33-37; 22:19-22; 28:25; 36:23-24,38; 37:21-22; 39:28; Daniel 2:41-45; 7:24-28; 12:1; Hosea 3:4-5; 14:4-8; Joel 3:20-21; Amos 9:9,11-15; Obadiah 15-21; Micah 2:12; 3:9-10; 4:7,11-12; Nahum 2:1-2; Habakkuk 2:2-5; 3:3-19; Zephaniah 1:14-18; 2:1-3; 3:14-20; Haggai 2:4-9,20-23; Zechariah 7:7-8; 8:8; 10:6; 12:2-10; 13:8-9; 14:1,5,9; Malachi 3:6.

11. "At 70, Israel's Jewish population is 8.842 million, 43% of world Jewry," *The Times of Israel*, April 16, 2018, accessed August 9, 2018, https://www.timesofisrael.com/at-70-israels-population-is-8-842-million-43-of-world-jewry/.

12. "Population," *Encyclopedia Judaica*, vol. 9, 475.

13. Daniel Gruber, *The Church and the Jews: The Biblical Relationship* (Springfield, MO: General Council of the Assemblies of God, 1991), 301-302.

14. Andrew D. Robinson, *Israel Betrayed: Volume 1: The History of Replacement Theology* (San Antonio, TX: Ariel Ministries, 2018), 152.

15. Malcolm Hedding, "Christian Zionism," essay on the website of the International Christian Embassy Jerusalem, February 18, 2001, 4.

16. Carl F. Ehle Jr., "Prolegomena to Christian Zionism in America: The Views of Increase Mather and William E. Blackstone Concerning the Doctrine of the Restoration of Israel," PhD dissertation at New York University, 1977, 67, 80.

17. Ehle, "Prolegomena," abstract.

18. Gruber, *The Church and the Jews*, 299.

19. Michael J. Pragai, *Faith and Fulfillment: Christians and the Return to the Promised Land* (London: Vallentine, Mitchell, 1985), 10.

Chapter 2: What Should We Think About the Modern State of Israel?—Steven Charles Ger

1. For the sake of clarity of nomenclature, the terms *people of Israel, Jewish people, Jews, Jewish nation,* and *nation of Israel* all refer to the Jewish people in general and throughout history. When specifying the geographic homeland of the Jewish people, use of either *Israel* or *the land* is appropriate, and in reference to the modern state, *state of Israel. Israelites* should be employed only in reference to the Jewish people of the biblical era through from ninth-tenth century BC. *Israelis* should be exclusively employed in reference to the modern population of the state of Israel.

2. Genesis 12:1-3; 12:7; 13:14-17; 15:1-21; 17:1-21; 22:15-18 (not to mention Abraham's outright purchase of the field of Machpelah in Hebron (23:9-20).

3. Genesis 26:2-5.

4. Genesis 28:3-4,13-15; 35:9-13.

5. Genesis 47–Exodus 14.

6. As recounted throughout the narrative of the book bearing his name.

7. 2 Samuel 5:6–1 Kings 8:66.

8. The source of the term *Jews,* a more accurate description in light of Israel's having split into kingdoms north and south.

9. The Greeks conquered the Persians in 333 BC under the leadership of Alexander the Great. Upon Alexander's death in 323 BC, his kingdom was split into four parts and ruled by different dynasties. The Seleucid dynasty ruled the provinces of Syria and Judea.

10. Discussion of this revolution and the events that led to it is found in the books of 1 and 2 Maccabees. The victorious outcome is still annually celebrated by Jews as the Feast of Dedication, or Hanukkah.

11. This is the period that births the Jewish charitable practice of *halukkah,* which entails the raising of funds by the diaspora community to support their brethren in the land. This practice continued for centuries, intensifying during the Middle Ages and became particularly indispensable to the poverty-stricken Palestinian Jewish community's survival during the era of Ottoman rule. See Geoffrey Wigoder, ed., "Halukkah," in *The Encyclopedia of Judaism* (Jerusalem: Jerusalem Publishing House, 1989), 318.

12. In total, this would have represented more than a third and perhaps one-half of Judea's total population. See Flavius Josephus, *The Works of Josephus: Complete and Unabridged* (Peabody, MA: Hendrickson, 1996), *Wars.* VI, ix 3.

13. Historical estimates of the population in the Holy Land range from two to four million between the first and fifth centuries, with the Jewish population continuing to maintain the vast majority. See Jewish National Council, "First Memorandum: historical survey of the waves of the number and density of the population of ancient Palestine; presented to the United Nations in 1947 by Va'ad Leumi on Behalf of the Creation of a Jewish State" (PDF), accessed via http://cojs.org/the_land_of_israel_in_ancient-_medieval_and_early_modern_times-_1800_bce-1798/.

14. Second-century Roman historian Dio Cassius records the Roman destruction of 50 fortresses and 965 villages with 580,000 Jews killed, with the figure not counting additional collateral casualties of war. See *Encyclopedia Judaica* (Jerusalem: Keter, 1972) completed edition, vol. 4, "Bar Kokhba," 233.

15. The era of problematic Philistine aggression against the Israelites ranged from the early thirteenth through early sixth centuries BC. See sporadic encounters in Judges 3:3–2 Kings 18:8.

16. Based upon the high number of fourth- and fifth-century CE Jewish communities and synagogues that have been identified.

17. Abba Eban, *Heritage: Civilization and the Jews* (New York: Summit, 1984), 131-32.

18. See Jewish National Council, "Second Memorandum: historical survey of the Jewish population in Palestine from the fall of the Jewish state to the beginning of Zionist pioneering; presented to the United Nations in 1947 by Va'ad Leumi on Behalf of the Creation of a Jewish State" (PDF), accessed via http://cojs.org/the_land_of _israel_in_ancient-_medieval_and_early_modern_times-_1800_bce-1798/.

19. For a fascinating survey of centuries of Jewish immigration into Palestine, see Jewish National Council, "Third Memorandum: historical survey of the waves of Jewish immigration into Palestine from the Arab conquest to the first Zionist pioneers; presented to the United Nations in 1947 by Va'ad Leumi on Behalf of the Creation of a Jewish State" (PDF), accessed via http://cojs.org/the_land_of_israel_in_ancient- _medieval_and_early_modern_times-_1800_bce-1798/.

20. Mark Twain, *The Innocents Abroad* (Hartford, CT: American Publishing, 1879) 478- 608, Google eBook edition.

21. Twain, *The Innocents Abroad*, 607-608.

22. For a description of the estimated Jewish population of 15,000, see Jewish National Council, "Second Memorandum: historical survey of the Jewish population in Palestine from the fall of the Jewish state to the beginning of Zionist pioneering; presented to the United Nations in 1947 by Va'ad Leumi on Behalf of the Creation of a Jewish State" (PDF), accessed via http://cojs.org/the_land_of_israel_in_ancient- _medieval_and_early_modern_times-_1800_bce-1798/.

23. Martin Gilbert, *The Atlas of Jewish History* (New York: William Morrow, 1992), 29.

24. *Encyclopedia Judaica* (Jerusalem: Keter, 1972), completed edition, vol. 9, "Israel, State of (Population)," 472-74.

25. Caroline Glick, *The Israeli Solution: A One-State Plan for Peace in the Middle East* (New York: Crown, 2014), Kindle loc. 3689-3692.

26. Alan Dershowitz, *The Case for Israel* (Hoboken, NJ: John Wiley & Sons, 2003), Kindle ed., 19.

27. Dershowitz, *The Case for Israel*, 16.

28. Dershowitz, *The Case for Israel*, 25.

29. *Encyclopedia Judaica* (Jerusalem: Keter, 1972), completed edition, vol. 9, "Israel, State of (Aliyah, Absorption and Settlement)," 557.

30. Prof. Gideon M. Kressel and Dr. Reuven Aharoni, *Egyptian Emigres in the Levant of the 19th and 20th Centuries* (Jerusalem: Jerusalem Center for Public Affairs, March 20, 2013).

31. Joan Peters, *From Time Immemorial* (Chicago: J. Kap, 1984), 221-340, especially 255-256ff, where the exponential increase in the Arab population in the heaviest regions of Jewish settlement is discussed. See also Fred M. Gottheil, "The Smoking Gun: Arab Immigration into Palestine, 1922–1931," *Middle East Quarterly*, vol. 10:1, Winter 2003, accessed via https://www.meforum.org/articles/other/the-smoking- gun-arab-immigration-into-palestine, as well as Dershowitz, 26-28.

32. Daniel Gordis, *Israel: A Concise History of a Nation Reborn* (New York: HarperCollins, 2016), Kindle ed. 26-30.

33. Dershowitz, *The Case for Israel*, 37.

34. Or a mere ten percent of the territory for a homeland that had originally been promised in the Balfour Declaration.

35. Gordis, *Israel*, 146.

36. Peters, *From Time Immemorial*, 345-53.
37. Gordis, *Israel*, 198-201. The number of dispossessed Jewish refugees from Islamic countries forced to flee their homes and leave their possessions behind is numerically equivalent to the estimated 400,000 Palestinian Arabs who settled in refugee camps following the war of 1948–1949. The twentieth century, like most centuries prior, saw many such population transfers occur in multiple areas of the globe. The Palestinian Arabs are the only group in recorded history still classified as refugees after 70 years.
38. Ira Sheskin and Arnold Dashefsky, eds., *Jewish Population in the United States* (New York: Berman Institute, North American Jewish Data Bank, 2012), retrieved via http://www.jewishdatabank.org/Studies/downloadFile.cfm?FileID=2917.
39. "At 70, Israel's population is 8.842 million, 43% of world Jewry," *Times of Israel* (April 16, 2018), via https://www.timesofisrael.com/at-70-israels-population-is-8-842-million-43-of-world-jewry/.
40. Gordis, *Israel*, 199.

Chapter 3: What Should We Think About Christian Support for Israel?—Imad N. Shehadeh

1. Stanley Ellisen, *Who Owns the Land?* (Portland, OR: Multnomah Press, 1991), 186.

Chapter 4: What Should We Think About Israel's Right to the Land?—Walter C. Kaiser Jr.

1. For examples see Gary M. Burge, *Jesus and the Land: The New Testament Challenge to "Holy Land" Theology* (Grand Rapids, MI: Baker Academic, 2010), 33-35, 59.
2. Gerhard von Rad, *The Problem of the Hexateuch and Other Essays*, trans. E.W. Trueman Dicken (London: Oliver & Boyd, 1966), 79.
3. Gerald McDermott, *Israel Matters: Why Christians Must Think Differently About the People and the Land* (Grand Rapids, MI: Brazos Press, 2017), 49.
4. This Abraham covenant is often referred among the Jewish people as the "covenant between the parts" (Hebrew, *Brit bein ha-Betarim*).
5. For more details on this theme in the Bible, see Walter C. Kaiser, Jr., *The Promise-Plan of God: A Biblical Theology of the Old and New Testaments* (Grand Rapids, MI: Zondervan, 2008).
6. Gary M. Burge, *Whose Land? Whose Promise? What Christians Are Not Being Told About Israel and the Palestinians* (Cleveland, OH: The Pilgrim Press, 2003), 72, 78.
7. Abraham understood and accepted the content of messianic revelation revealed to that point (beginning in Genesis 3:15) when he "believed God" (Genesis 15:6) prior to this ritual declaration of God's covenant faithfulness. For more on this point see Walter C. Kaiser Jr., "Is It the Case that Christ Is the Same Object of Faith in the Old Testament? (Genesis 15:1-6)," *JETS* 55/2 (2012): 291-98.
8. The symbolic interpretation of the Old Testament was first made by the Alexandrian Jewish philosopher-theologian Philo (d. AD 50), thereby weaving the theme of the land into everything that was said about the future.
9. Ronald Youngblood points to multiple texts that could conceivably indicate the Abrahamic covenant had conditions attached to it (Genesis 12:1; 17:1,9-14; 22:16; 26:5). Ronald Youngblood, "The Abrahamic Covenant: Conditional or Unconditional?" in *The Living and Active Word of God: Studies in Honor of Samuel J. Schultz*, eds. Morris Inch and Ronald Youngblood (Winona Lake, IN., Eisenbrauns, 1983), 31-46.
10. For example, David Noel Freedman interprets the failure to perform the condition

of circumcision (Genesis 17) as exclusion from the covenant community. D.N. Freedman, "Divine Commitment and Human Obligation," *Interpretation*, 18 (1964): 425.

11. N.T. Wright, *Jesus and the Victory of God* (London: SPCK, 1996), 446, 471.

12. N.T. Wright, *The New Testament and the People of God* (London: ASCK, 1992), 457-58.

13. Colin Chapman, *Whose Promised Land?* (Grand Rapids, MI: Baker, 2002), 172 (emphasis in the original). See my chapter 3 in Walter C. Kaiser Jr., *Jewish Christianity: Why Believing Jews and Gentiles Parted Ways in the Early Church* (Silverton, OR: Lampion Press, 2017), 37-49.

14. See Daniel Juster, *Passion for Israel: A Short History of the Evangelical Church's Commitment to the Jewish People and Israel* (Clarksville, MD: Lederer Books, 2012), chapter 1.

Chapter 5: What Should We Think About Jerusalem as the Capital of Israel?—Mitch Glaser

1. Randall Price, *Jerusalem in Prophecy: God's Stage for the Final Drama* (Eugene, OR: Harvest House Publishers, 1998), 78-79.

2. LifeWay Research, "Evangelical Attitudes towards Israel," 3.

3. Gary Burge, "You Can Be an Evangelical and Reject Trump's Jerusalem Decision" *The Atlantic* (December 6, 2017), https://flipboard.com/@flipboard/-you-can-be-an-evangelical-and-reject-tr/f-3c5d40d935%2Ftheatlantic.com.

4. Price, *Jerusalem in Prophecy*, 81.

5. The full text of the resolution can be accessed at: https://www.timesofisrael.com/full-text-of-new-unesco-resolution-on-occupied-palestine/.

6. Barak Ravid and Jack Khoury, "UNESCO Backs Motion Nullifying Jewish Ties to the Temple Mount," *Haartez* (October 13, 2016), http://www.haaretz.com/israel-news/1.747314.

7. United Nations Educational, Scientific and Cultural Organization, "Introducing UNESCO," http://en.unesco.org/about-us/introducing-unesco.

8. Irina Bokova, "Statement by the Director-General of UNESCO on the Old City of Jerusalem and Its Walls, a UNESCO World Heritage Site," UNESCOPRESS (October 14, 2016), http://www.unesco.org/new/en/media-services/single-view/news/statement_by_the_director_general_of_unesco_on_the_old_city/.

9. Soren Kern, "The Flap Over Israel's Nation-State Law," *Israel My Glory* 76:6 (November/December 2018), 7.

Chapter 6: What Should We Think About the Temple Mount?—Randall Price

1. "The Hashemite Kingdom of Jordan and the State of Palestine Status Report: The State of Conservation of the Old City of Jerusalem and Its Walls," presented to UNESCO World Heritage Centre, April 28, 2017.

2. "UN Confirms Denial of Jewish Connection to Temple Mount," *Israel Today* (October 26, 2016).

3. As cited by Eric Cline, *Jerusalem Besieged: From Ancient Canaan to Modern Israel* (Ann Arbor, MI: University of Michigan Press, 2004).

4. The biblical account is recognized as authoritative for religious Jews, but its historical account is largely accepted by secular scholars. For the historical documentation of the Temple outside of the Bible, see C.T.R. Hayward, *The Jewish Temple: A Non-Biblical Sourcebook* (London: Routledge, 1996).

5. F.M. Loewenberg, "Did Jews Abandon the Temple Mount?," *Middle East Quarterly* (Summer 2013): 37.

6. Rabbi Leibel Reznick, *The Mystery of Bar Kokhba: A Historical and Theological Investigation of the Last King of the Jews* (Lanham, MD: Jason Aronson, Inc., 1996), 77-79.

7. Jeffrey Brodd, "Julian the Apostate and His Plan to Rebuild the Temple," *Bible Review* 11:5 (October 1995): 38.

8. Moshe Dayan, *Moshe Dayan: The Story of My Life* (New York: William Morrow, 1976), 386-88.

9. For details see Randall Price, *The Battle for the Last Days Temple: Politics, Prophecy, and the Temple Mount* (Eugene, OR: Harvest House Publishers, 2004), 179-224.

10. For various views about the Temple movement see Motti Inbari, *Jewish Fundamentalism and the Temple Mount: Who Will Build the Third Temple?*, trans. Shaul Vardi (Albany, NY: State University of New York Press, 2009).

11. The oldest Arab sources are those of the ninth century historians Baladhuri, *Futuh* and Tabari, *Ta'rikh*. Compilations of Islamic history and tradition may also be found in *The Works of Kemal ed din ibn Abi Sheref* (1871), trans. Paul Lemming and Jelal ed din es Siyuti, *The History of the Temple* (1836), trans. Reverend J. Reynolds. See also E.H. Palmer, "History of the Haram Es Sherif," *Palestine Exploration Quarterly* (1870–1871).

12. Etgar Lefkovits, "Was the Aksa Mosque built over the remains of a Byzantine church?," *Jerusalem Post*, November 16, 2008; Leen Ritmeyer, "Third Jewish Mikveh and a Byzantine Mosaic Floor Discovered on the Temple Mount," Ritmeyer Archeological Design, November 17, 2008; *Israel Hayom* (Tel Aviv), June 29, 2012.

13. Specifically from the Anastasis Church dedicated to Christ and the Kathisma Church dedicated to Mary as the *Theotokos* ("God Bearer"), Rina Avner, "The Dome of the Rock in Light of the Development of Concentric Martyria in Jerusalem: Architecture and Architectural Iconography," *Muqarnas*, vol. 27 (Leiden, Netherlands: E.J. Brill, 2010): 31-49.

14. Statements against the Trinity (a defining doctrine of orthodox Christianity) such as "God is one and has no Son." For details on this view see S.D. Goiten, "Jerusalem During the Arab Period (638–1099)," *Yerushalayim* 4 (1953): 88-90.

15. Abu Jafar Muhammad al-Tabari, Ta'rihk I, 2405-6, as cited by Moshe Gil, "The Political History of Jerusalem During the Early Muslim Period" in *The History of Jerusalem: The Early Muslim Period 638–1099*, eds. Joshua Prawer and Haggai Ben-Shammai (Jerusalem: Yad Izhak Ben-Zvi, 1996), 8.

16. As cited in *Independent Media Review and Analysis*, December 25, 1996.

17. Interview with Sheikh Ekrima Sa'id Sabri, Offices of the Waqf, Jerusalem, October 1997.

18. For details of archaeological work related to the Temple Mount see Leen and Kathleen Ritmeyer, *Secrets of Jerusalem's Temple Mount* (Washington, DC: Biblical Archaeology Society, 1998) and *Jerusalem: The Temple Mount* (Jerusalem: Carta Jerusalem, Ltd., 2015).

19. The *New York Times*, Opinion letter, Jodi Magness, "The Temple Mount in Jerusalem" (October 12, 2015): A24. The letter was written in response to an earlier article in the *New York Times*: "Historical Certainty Proves Elusive at Jerusalem's Holiest Place" (October 9, 2015), in which Prof. Magness had been cited as an expert.

20. Katharina Galor and Hanswulf Bloedhorn, *The Archaeology of Jerusalem: From the Origins to the Ottomans* (New Haven, CT: Yale University Press, 2013), 36-37.

21. Irenaeus of Lyon, *Adversus Haereses* I, 26, 2.

22. Lorenzo Perrone, "Jerusalem, a City of Prayer in the Byzantine Era," *Proche-Orient Chrétien* 64 (2014), 5-30.

23. Aaron Klein, "Palestinian prof admits Arab denial of temples is baloney: Before Israel founded, 'Muslims would not have disputed connection Jews have,'" *World Net Daily* (December 20, 2009), https://www.wnd.com/2009/12/119 649/#gzKrJOimJKvhS3xd.99. See also https://www.thejc.com/news/israel/ arab-scholar-blasted-over-temple-mount-1.12840.

24. Moshe Gil, "The Political History of Jerusalem During the Early Muslim Period" in *The History of Jerusalem: The Early Muslim Period 638–1099*, eds. Joshua Prawer and Haggai Ben-Shammai (Jerusalem: Yad Izhak Ben-Zvi, 1996), 9.

25. Report of lecture by archaeologist Asaf Avraham, former director of the Jerusalem Walls National Park of the Parks Authority, in *The Jerusalem Connection* (March 17, 2017): 1.

26. *The Armenian History Attributed to Sebeos,* trans. R.W. Thomson, historical commentary by J. Howard-Johnston, assistance from T. Greenwood in *Translated Texts for Historians*, 2 vols. (Liverpool: Liverpool University Press, 1999).

27. Baladhuri, *Futuh*, 138, as cited by Moshe Gil, "The Political History of Jerusalem During the Early Muslim Period" in *The History of Jerusalem*, 7.

28. *A Brief Guide to the Al-Haram Al-Sharif, Jerusalem* (published by the Supreme Moslem Council, Jerusalem, 1935), 3. This statement remained unchanged in all subsequent editions of this guide until 1967.

Chapter 7: What Should We Think About Jewish and Arab Relations?—Tim M. Sigler

1. Wm. T. Young to Viscount Canning, January 13, 1842. Cited in Alan Dershowitz, *The Case for Israel* (Hoboken, NJ: John Wiley & Sons, 2003), 20.

2. "Former Jordanian PM Abdelsalam Al-Majali Defends Israel-Jordan Peace Treaty, Promises: If We Ever Become Stronger, We Will Take Haifa by Force" (August 18, 2018), clip no. 6737. Retrieved from https://www.memri.org/tv/former-jordanian -pm-majali-defends-israel-jordan-peace-if-we-become-stronger-we-will-take-haifa -by-force/transcript.

3. "Former Jordanian PM Abdelsalam Al-Majali Defends Israel-Jordan Peace Treaty."

4. David Saks, "Those biased against Israel complicit in Hamas propaganda," *News24* (May 29, 2018). Retrieved from https://www.news24.com/Columnists/Guest Column/those-biased-against-israel-complicit-in-hamas-propaganda-20180529.

5. Elder of Ziyon, "Did Arab States Really Promise to Push Jews Into the Sea? Yes!," *The Algemeiner* (February 20, 2014). Retrieved from https://www.algemeiner .com/2014/02/20/did-arab-states-really-promise-to-push-jews-into-the-sea-yes/.

6. See Resolutions of the Palestine National Council, July 1-17, 1968. U.S. Department of State. Retrieved from https://web.archive.org/web/20060106001731/http://www .state.gov/p/nea/rls/22573.htm.

7. *Daily Telegraph* (January 19, 1989).

8. Bootie Cosgrove-Mather, "The Father of Modern Terrorism," *National Review Online* (November 12, 2004). Retrieved from https://www.cbsnews.com/news/ the-father-of-modern-terrorism/.

9. See https://www.jewishvirtuallibrary.org/palestinian-maps-omitting-israel.

10. See https://www.newsweek.com/why-are-americans-paying-anti-semitic-text

books-479765. The Trump administration has recently announced that it is defunding UNRWA. See https://www.state.gov/r/pa/prs/ps/2018/08/285648.htm.

11. See http://www.palwatch.org/main.aspx?fi=92&doc_id=101.

12. See http://www.palwatch.org/main.aspx?fi=157&doc_id=26326.

13. See http://www.jewishpress.com/indepth/pa-summer-camps-teach-terror-and-martyrdom-death-to-kids/2017/09/04/. See also https://www.bridgesforpeace.com/article/can-no-peace-without-respect-life/.

14. See, for example, https://www.nytimes.com/2012/03/26/world/middleeast/israeli-supreme-court-orders-settlers-off-palestinian-land.html; and https://www.haaretz.com/israel-news/.premium-palestinians-can-seek-compensation-from-settlers-in-confiscated-land-case-court-says-1.5494863.

15. See http://articles.latimes.com/1996-02-27/local/me-40531_1_west-bank and https://www.jpost.com/Opinion/Abbas-and-Fatah-show-their-true-colors-in-Arabic-382071.

16. See http://www.palwatch.org/main.aspx?fi=449. See also https://www.jpost.com/Opinion/Abbas-and-Fatah-show-their-true-colors-in-Arabic-382071.

17. Judith Mendelsohn Rood, "The Palestinian Culture of Death." Retrieved from https://www.academia.edu/7792542/The_Palestinian_Culture_of_Death.

18. See https://www.yahoo.com/lifestyle/miss-iraq-family-reportedly-fled-country-took-selfie-miss-israel-191223504.html. Feminine self-expression is often shamed in the Arab world, at times with deadly consequences. See https://www.foxnews.com/world/instagram-model-and-beauty-queen-finalist-22-shot-dead-in-iraq.

19. See https://www.youtube.com/watch?v=8EDW88CBo-8&feature=youtu.be.

20. Benjamin Netanyahu, speech at the Knesset at the end of the 2006 Israel-Lebanon conflict (August 14, 2006).

21. See https://www.gatestoneinstitute.org/12103/palestinian-authority-corruption.

22. Bret Stephens, "Gaza's Miseries Have Palestinian Authors," *The New York Times* (May 16, 2018). Retrieved from https://www.nytimes.com/2018/05/16/opinion/gaza-palestinians-protests.html.

23. Tom Doyle, *Killing Christians: Living the Faith Where It's Not Safe to Believe* (Nashville, TN: W Publishing Group, 2015), xi.

24. See the testimony of a Muslim woman who hated the Jews and ended up falling in love with their king, Jesus. Retrieved from https://www.youtube.com/watch?v=wzfVAb4q8ZU.

25. Tom Doyle, *Dreams and Visions: Is Jesus Awakening the Muslim World?* (Nashville, TN: Thomas Nelson, 2012).

26. David Garrison, *A Wind in the House of Islam: How God Is Drawing Muslims Around the World to Faith in Jesus Christ* (Monument, CO: Wigtake Resources, 2014), 21.

27. Ariel Kahana, "Palestinians for Normalisation" (June 28, 2018). Retrieved from https://aijac.org.au/australia-israel-review/palestinians-for-normalisation/. See also https://blogs.timesofisrael.com/moderation-in-times-of-extremism-mohammed-dajani-daoudi/.

28. See https://www.independent.co.uk/news/world/middle-east/syria-conflict-latest-israel-deraa-assad-russia-putin-civil-war-a8444621.html, and https://www.ynetnews.com/articles/0,7340,L-5117904,00.html.

29. Judith Mendelsohn Rood, personal correspondence. See also Judith Mendelsohn Rood and Paul W. Rood, "The Testimony of the Nazarenes: Persecution of the

Followers of the Jewish Messiah Brings Jesus to the Foreground of the Middle East Conflict" (September 30, 2018). Retrieved from https://www.academia.edu/7870750/The_Testimony_of_the_Nazarenes_Persecution_of_the_Followers_of_the_Jewish_Messiah_Brings_Jesus_to_the_Foreground_of_the_Middle_East_Conflict. Another key resource on the historical, political, and spiritual background of the region is available from Joel C. Rosenberg, *Inside the Revolution: How the Followers of Jihad, Jefferson, and Jesus Are Battling to Dominate the Middle East and Transform the World* (Carol Stream, IL: Tyndale House, 2009).

30. Leland Ryken, James C. Wilhoit, Tremper Longman III, *Dictionary of Biblical Imagery* (Downers Grove, IL: InterVarsity, 2000), 632.

Chapter 8: What Should We Think About Israel's "Occupation"?—Paul Wilkinson

1. Ernst Frankenstein, *Justice for My People: The Jewish Case* (London: Nicholson & Watson, 1943), preface.
2. A quote from Ernst Frankenstein's son in an untitled manuscript from the archives of the Leo Baeck Institute, Center for Jewish History, New York, https://ia800507.us.archive.org/12/items/ernstfrankenstei1384unse/ernstfrankenstei1384unse.pdf.
3. Frankenstein, *Justice for My People*, 79.
4. Embrace the Middle East, "Embrace at Greenbelt 2013" (August 27, 2013), http://162.13.41.13/blog/embrace-greenbelt-2013.
5. World Council of Churches, "Statement on Israeli Settlements in the Occupied Palestinian Territory" (September 2, 2009), www.oikoumene.org.
6. In my latest book, *Israel Betrayed, Volume 2: The Rise of Christian Palestinianism* (San Antonio, TX: Ariel Ministries, 2018), I have comprehensively surveyed this burgeoning evangelical crusade against Israel, which I have labelled "Christian Palestinianism."
7. Ben White, *Cracks in the Wall: Beyond Apartheid in Israel/Palestine* (London: Pluto Press, 2018), 31.
8. Laura Payton, "Stephen Harper vows loyalty to Israel in speech to Knesset" (January 20, 2014), www.cbc.ca.
9. The name "West Bank" is written in quotation marks because it contravenes the biblical and historical record. Until the Jordanian forces illegally occupied this territory when attempting to destroy the newly established state of Israel, the territory was known by its biblical name Judea and Samaria. Jordan then changed the name to the West Bank.
10. Quoted in Efraim Karsh, *Arafat's War: The Man and His Battle for Israeli Conquest* (New York: Grove Press, 2003), 70-71.
11. Howard Grief, *The Legal Foundation and Borders of Israel Under International Law: A Treatise on Jewish Sovereignty over the Land of Israel* (Jerusalem: Mazo, 2013), 18.
12. Grief, *The Legal Foundation*, 34.
13. Jacques Gauthier, "From the 1917 Balfour Declaration to the Rebirth of Israel in 1948," http://jcpa.org/video/1917-balfour-declaration-rebirth-israel-1948/.
14. Quoted in Walter Laqueur and Barry Rubin, eds., *The Israel-Arab Reader: A Documentary History of the Middle East Conflict*, 7th ed. (London: Penguin Books, 2008), 19.
15. The Avalon Project, "The Palestine Mandate," http://avalon.law.yale.edu.
16. The Avalon Project, "The Palestine Mandate" (emphasis added).
17. The draft wording was "Palestine should be reconstituted as the national home of the Jewish people." This was approved by the British prime minister and the Foreign Office, but rejected by the war cabinet, which was ultimately responsible for the

declaration. One of the main objectors to the wording was Edwin Montagu, a Jewish member of the British government but not of the war cabinet, who was vehemently opposed to Zionism and the idea of a Jewish national home. "To Louis D. Brandeis, Washington (London, September 1917)," *The Letters and Papers of Chaim Weizmann, Volume VII, Series A, August 1914–November 1917*, ed. Leonard Stein (London: Oxford University Press, 1975), 505-506.

18. *The Letters and Papers of Chaim Weizmann, Volume I, Series B, August 1898–July 1931*, ed. Barnet Litvinoff (New Brunswick, NJ: Transaction Books, 1983), 290.

19. Judges 20:1; 1 Samuel 3:20; 2 Samuel 3:10; 17:11; 24:2,15.

20. The United States entered the war in 1917 without formally joining the Allies and was therefore an Associated Power. The US declared war on Germany, but not on the Ottoman Empire, seeking to remain as neutral as possible.

21. Grief, *The Legal Foundation*, 44.

22. Grief, *The Legal Foundation*, 36-37.

23. In 1936, the British government, under royal warrant, authorized an independent commission of inquiry into the disturbances in Palestine that had broken out in April 1936. The commission was led by William Wellesley (Earl Peel). Its ultimate objective was to determine whether or not the mandate was still viable.

24. *Palestine Royal Commission Report, Presented by the Secretary of State for the Colonies to Parliament by Command of His Majesty, July 1937* (London: His Majesty's Stationery Office, 1937), 24.

25. Quoted in Doreen Ingrams, *Palestine Papers 1917–1922: Seeds of Conflict* (London: John Murray, 1972), 174.

26. Jacques Gauthier, "The Jewish Claim to Jerusalem: The Case Under International Law," www.youtube.com/watch?v=VH5pD3yVH64.

27. The Avalon Project, "The Covenant of the League of Nations," http://avalon.law.yale.edu.

28. Grief, *The Legal Foundation*, 175-76.

29. Grief, *The Legal Foundation*, 38 (emphasis added).

30. In 1949, an armistice agreement was reached between Israel and Jordan, Syria, Egypt, and Lebanon, which officially ended hostilities. A demarcation line was drawn between Israel and its neighbors, which came to be known as "The Green Line" on account of the green pen used during negotiations. On the Arab side of the line was the "West Bank," East Jerusalem, Gaza, and the Golan Heights.

31. C.H. Spurgeon, *The Treasury of David, Volume One: Psalm I to LVII* (Peabody, MA: Hendrickson, 2005), 300.

32. For a comprehensive survey of replacement theology, see Andrew D. Robinson, *Israel Betrayed, Volume I: The History of Replacement Theology* (San Antonio, TX: Ariel Ministries, 2018).

33. MEMRI, "Kuwaiti Writer Abdullah Al-Hadlaq: Israel Is a Legitimate State, Not an Occupier," November 19, 2017, www.memri.org (emphasis added).

Chapter 9: What Should We Think About the Plight of the Palestinians?—Justin Kron

1. United Nations Relief and Works Agency for Palestine Refugees in the Near East.

2. See www.sfmew.org/wp-content/uploads/2016/04/JCPA-Background-Paper-on-Palestinian-Christians-7.3new-cover.pdf.

3. See www.theatlantic.com/international/archive/2012/11/kosher-jesus-messianic-jews-in-the-holy-land/265670/.

4. See www.nytimes.com/1997/05/12/world/arab-s-death-and-the-selling-of-land-to-jews.html.

5. A *fatwa* is a ruling on a point of Islamic law given by a recognized authority.

6. See uk.reuters.com/article/uk-palestinians-abbas-facebook/palestinian-journalist-gets-jail-term-for-abbas-insult-idUKBRE92R0UF20130328.

7. See www.aljazeera.com/news/middleeast/2014/08/hamas-kills-11-suspected-informers-israel-201482285624490268.html.

8. See www.nytimes.com/2014/08/23/world/middleeast/israel-gaza.html.

9. In his 2012 analysis and report "The Truth Behind the Palestinian Water Libels."

10. Nablus is located in the West Bank (Samaria). In the Hebrew Scriptures it is referred to as Shechem. In the New Testament it is Sychar.

11. See www.tabletmag.com/scroll/189519/did-netanyahu-put-anti-semitic-words-in-hezbollahs-mouth.

12. A collection of traditions containing sayings of the prophet Muhammad that, with accounts of his daily practice (the Sunna), constitute the major source of guidance for Muslims apart from the Koran.

13. See avalon.law.yale.edu/20th_century/hamas.asp.

14. See http://global100.adl.org/#country/west-bank-and-gaza/2014.

15. See www.timesofisrael.com/tires-slashed-hate-slogans-graffitied-in-latest-attack-on-palestinian-village/.

16. See www.bloomberg.com/view/articles/2016-07-01/the-palestinian-incentive-program-for-killing-jews.

17. See www.calevmyers.com/blog/2016/4/21/whered-all-the-money-go.

18. See www.gatestoneinstitute.org/3066/how-much-is-mahmoud-abbas-worth.

19. See www.algemeiner.com/2014/07/28/gazas-millionaires-and-billionaires-how-hamass-leaders-got-rich-quick/.

20. See www.cbsnews.com/news/arafats-billions/.

21. See https://data.worldbank.org/country/west-bank-and-gaza.

Chapter 10: What Should We Think About the Holocaust?—Michael L. Brown

1. For a now-classic study, see Raul Hilberg, *The Destruction of the European Jews* (New York: Holmes & Meier, 1985).

2. See https://www.history.com/this-day-in-history/babi-yar-massacre-begins.

3. Primo Levi, *Survival in Auschwitz*, trans. by Stuart Woolf (New York: Collier, 1961), 112.

4. Martin Rosenblum, as cited in Martin Gilbert, *The Holocaust: A History of the Jews During the Second World War* (New York: Henry Holt, 1985), 444.

5. See Robert Jay Lifton, *The Nazi Doctors: Medical Killing and the Psychology of Genocide* (New York: Basic Books, 1988).

6. See, e.g., "Antisemitism on rise across Europe 'in worst times since the Nazis,'" *The Guardian* (August 7, 2014), https://www.theguardian.com/society/2014/aug/07/antisemitism-rise-europe-worst-since-nazis.

7. Mandy Blumenthal, "'We no longer feel safe in Britain. Anti-Semitism is forcing us to leave our home,'" *The Telegraph* (July 22, 2018), https://www.telegraph.co.uk/women/life/no-longer-feel-safe-britain-anti-semitism-forcing-us-leave-home/.

8. Doree Lewak, "Anti-Semitism drove these Jews out of France" (February 24, 2018), https://nypost.com/2018/02/24/anti-semitism-drove-these-jews-out-of-france/.

9. Mona Charen, "70 years after Holocaust, Jews in Europe do not feel safe," *Chicago Sun Times* (April 26, 2018), https://chicago.suntimes.com/columnists/70-years-after-holocaust-jews-in-europe-do-not-feel-safe/.

10. Ben Cohen, "Anti-Semitism in France has moved 'from streets into homes,' says French Jewish leader," *World Israel News* (August 30, 2018), https://tinyurl.com/y7px7pml.

11. "Germany's Jews urged not to wear kippahs after attacks," *BBC News* (April 24, 2018), https://www.bbc.com/news/world-europe-43884075.

12. "Germany 'ashamed' over anti-Israel protests," *Times of Israel* (December 11, 2017), https://www.timesofisrael.com/germany-ashamed-over-anti-semitic-protests-against-israel/.

13. Joseph Abrams, "Protester Calls for Jews to 'Go Back to the Oven' at Anti-Israel Demonstration," *Fox News* (January 8, 2009), http://www.foxnews.com/story/2009/01/08/protester-calls-for-jews-to-go-back-to-oven-at-anti-israel-demonstration.html.

14. "The Killing Evolution," https://www.pbs.org/auschwitz/40-45/killing/.

15. See "2008 Mumbai Attacks," https://en.wikipedia.org/wiki/2008_Mumbai_attacks.

16. David Eliezrie, *The Secret of Chabad: Inside the World's Most Successful Jewish Movement* (New York: The Toby Press, 2015), Kindle loc. 183.

17. See, for example, Michael Bachner, "Jewish shrine in West Bank defaced with swastikas," *Times of Israel* (March 25, 2018), https://www.timesofisrael.com/jewish-shrine-in-west-bank-defaced-with-swastikas/.

18. Adam Kredo, "Iran-Backed Terror Group Claims Half-a-Million Missiles Aimed at Israel," *Free Beacon* (February 14, 2018), https://freebeacon.com/national-security/iran-backed-terror-group-claims-will-half-million-missiles-aimed-israel/.

19. Hayah Goldlist-Eichler, "40% of Israeli children in Gaza border town of Sderot suffer from anxiety, PTSD," *Jerusalem Post* (July 8, 2015), https://www.jpost.com/Israel-News/40-percent-of-Israeli-children-in-Gaza-border-town-of-Sderot-suffer-from-anxiety-PTSD-408306

20. See https://vimeo.com/263768606.

21. Efraim Karsh, *Palestine Betrayed* (New Haven, CT: Yale University Press, 2011).

22. Yossi Klein Halevi, *Letters to My Palestinian Neighbor* (New York: HarperCollins, 2018), 115.

23. See https://www.timesofisrael.com/iranian-official-threatens-to-destroy-israel-if-it-continues-childish-game/.

24. See http://palwatch.org/main.aspx?fi=974.

25. See https://askdrbrown.org/library/president-carter-aligns-himself-terrorists.

Chapter 11: What Should We Think About the New Anti-Semitism?—Olivier J. Melnick

1. Moshe Zimmermann, *Wilhelm Marr: The Patriarch of Antisemitism* (New York: Oxford University Press, 1986), 70-95.

2. Robert Chazan, *Medieval Stereotypes and Modern Antisemitism* (Los Angeles, CA: University of California Press, 1997), 126-27.

3. "Defining Anti-Semitism," US Dept. of State, accessed August 13, 2018, https://www.state.gov/s/rga/resources/267538.htm.

4. Gavin I. Langmuir, *Toward a Definition of Antisemitism* (Los Angeles, CA: University of California Press, 1990), 351-52.

5. Olivier J. Melnick, *End-Times Antisemitism: A New Chapter in the Longest Hatred* (Tustin, CA: Hope for Today Press, 2018), 37.

6. Jakob Jocz, *The Jewish People and Jesus Christ After Auschwitz* (Grand Rapids, MI: Baker Books, 1991), 8.

7. The term *church fathers* describes a body of early theologians and Christian leaders who, over a period of several centuries, upon the closing of the biblical record in the first century AD, organized, structured, and protected the Christian faith, then in its infancy.

8. Replacement theology, also known as supersessionism, is a theological position that presents the church as the ultimate fulfillment of the covenants God made with Israel. According to that theological position, the current church or body of Messiah is the "New Israel," forcing people to read "church" in the New Testament wherever it says "Israel."

9. Origen of Alexandria, *Contra Celsus*. as cited in Melnick, *End-Times Antisemitism: A New Chapter in the Longest Hatred*, 72.

10. Edward H. Flannery, *The Anguish of the Jews: Twenty-Three Centuries of Antisemitism* (New York: Paulist Press, 1985), 91-92.

11. Léon Poliakov, *The History of Antisemitism, Vol. 1: From the Time of Christ to the Court Jews* (Philadelphia, PA: University of Pennsylvania Press, 1955), 41-46.

12. Jeremy Cohen, *Christ Killers: The Jews and The Passion from the Bible to the Big Screen* (Oxford: University Press, 2007), 109-112.

13. William Nicholls, *Christian Antisemitism: A History of Hate* (Latham, MD: Jason Aaronson, Inc., 1995), 245-247.

14. Nicholls, *Christian Antisemitism*, 261-267.

15. Richard S. Levy, ed., *Antisemitism: A Historical Encyclopedia of Prejudice and Persecution,* vol. 2 (Santa Barbara, CA: ABC Clio, 2005), 552-53.

16. Michael R. Marrus, *The Holocaust in History* (New York: Meridian, 1987), 31-83.

17. Edward H. Flannery, *The Anguish of the Jews: Twenty-Three Centuries of Antisemitism* (New York: Paulist Press, 1985), 263-65.

18. Lucy S. Dawidowicz, *The War Against the Jews 1933-1945* (New York: Holt, Rinehart, and Winston, 1975), 41.

19. Raul Hilberg, *The Destruction of European Jews* (New York: Holmes & Meyer, 1985), 171-74.

20. Manfred Gerstenfeld, *The War of a Million Cuts: The Struggle Against the Delegitimization of Israel and the Jews, and the Growth of New Anti-Semitism* (New York: RVP Press, 2015), 36.

21. Gerstenfeld, *The War of a Million Cuts*, 318.

22. "Eugenics/Genetics." *Encyclopædia Britannica*, accessed August 17, 2018, https://www.britannica.com/science/eugenics-genetics.

23. Gerstenfeld, *The War of a Million Cuts*, 43.

24. Gerstenfeld, *The War of a Million Cuts*, 17.

25. Robert S. Wistrich, *A Lethal Obsession: Anti-Semitism from Antiquity to the Global Jihad* (New York: Random House, 2010), 785.

26. Alan Dershowitz, *The Case Against BDS: Why Singling Out Israel for Boycott Is Anti-Semitic and Anti-Peace* (New York: Post Hill Press, 2018), 9-10.

27. Shahar Azani, "Facing the Truth About BDS," *Campus Watch*, accessed on August 17, 2018, http://blogs.timesofisrael.com/facing-the-truth-about-bds/.

28. Pierre-André Taguieff, *Israël et la Question Juive* (Paris: Les Provinciales, 2011), 60-61.

29. Dershowitz, *The Case Against BDS*, 245-49.

30. Jackson Richman, "Terrorist-Sympathizer Speaks at George Washington University, Calls Zionists 'McCarthyites,'" *Campus Watch*, accessed on August 18, 2018, https://www.meforum.org/campus-watch/articles/2017/terroristsympathizer-speaks-at-george-washington-u.

31. Jonathan Marks, "Real Antisemitism on Campus," *Commentary*, accessed on August 18, 2018, https://www.commentarymagazine.com/anti-semitism/real-anti-semitism-on-campus/.

32. Tammi Rossman-Benjamin, *Anti Zionism on Campus: The University, Free Speech and BDS*, eds. Andrew Pessin and Doron S. Ben-Atar (Bloomington, IN: Indiana University Press, 2018), 312.

33. Max Samarov and Philippe Assouline, "Who is really behind the SJP organization?" *San Diego Jewish World*, June 2016, accessed August 20, 2018, http://www.sdjewishworld.com/2016/06/08/who-behind-sjp-organization/.

34. Christopher Holton, *The Muslim Brotherhood's Muslim Students' Association: What Americans Need to Know* (New York: Center for Security Policy, 2018), accessed on August 20, 2018, https://www.centerforsecuritypolicy.org/2018/04/29/the-muslim-brotherhoods-muslim-students-association-what-americans-need-to-know/.

35. Paul R. Wilkinson, *Understanding Christian Palestinianism: Charting the Rise of Evangelical Anti-Zionism* (Bend, OR: The Berean Call, 2016), 16-34.

36. Paul R. Wilkinson, *For Zion's Sake* (Nottingham, UK: Paternoster, 2007), 65. "Christian Palestinianism is an inverted mirror image of Christian Zionism. So that the Bible is seen to be Christian, not Jewish, the land of the Bible is Palestine not Israel, the Son of God is a Palestinian not a Jew, the Holocaust is resented not remembered, 1948 is a catastrophe not a miracle, the Jewish people are illegal occupiers not rightful owners, and biblical prophecy is a moral manifesto and not a signpost to the Second Coming."

37. The *Christ at the Checkpoint Manifesto* comprises 12 articles claiming a firm biblical foundation. Some of the articles are biblically justifiable while others depart from biblical truth. Yet a third kind dangerously mixes biblical truth and man-made fallacies, making it more difficult to discern where they depart from biblical truth. For a more detailed study of the Christ at the Checkpoint manifesto, see this author's *End-Times Antisemitism* (Tustin, CA: Hope for Today Press, 2018), 248-54.

38. There are many volumes one can read to learn about the history of anti-Semitism. This author recommends the following: Robert S. Wistrich, *A Lethal Obsession* (New York: Random House, 2010); Edward H. Flannery, *The Anguish of the Jews* (New York: Paulist Press, 1985); Léon Poliakov, *The History of Antisemitism, Volumes I-IV* (Philadelphia, PA: University of Pennsylvania Press, 1955); Gavin I. Langmuir, *Toward a Definition of Antisemitism* (Los Angeles, CA: University of California Press, 1990); Olivier J. Melnick, *End-Times Antisemitism* (Tustin, CA: Hope for Today Press, 2018).

39. BDS List, "Boycott these products to stop Israeli apartheid," accessed August 21, 2018. http://bdslist.org/.

Chapter 12: What Should We Think About the Boycott, Divestment, and Sanctions Movement?—Tuvya Zaretsky

1. Jena Martin and Karen E Bravo, *The Business and Human Rights Landscape: Moving Forward, Looking Back* (Cambridge: Cambridge University Press, 2016), 55-63.

2. See https://www.un.org/press/en/2012/ga11317.doc.htm.

3. The resolution was repealed in 1991; see https://www.nytimes.com/1991/12/17/world/un-repeals-its-75-resolution-equating-zionism-with-racism.html.

4. Tom Lantos, "The Durban Debacle: An Insider's View of the UN World Conference Against Racism" in *The Fletcher Forum of World Affairs*, vol. 26:1 (Winter/Spring 2002), 31-52, https://web.archive.org/web/20091103033200/http://fletcher.tufts.edu/forum/archives/pdfs/26-1pdfs/Lantos9.pdf.

5. Omar Barghouti, *Boycott, Divestment and Sanctions: The Global Struggle for Palestinian Rights* (Chicago, IL: Haymarket Books, 2011).

6. *World Conference Against Racism; NGO Forum Declaration.* Durban, South Africa, 3 September 2001. Section 418–426 "Palestinians and Palestine," https://i-p-o.org/racism-ngo-decl.htm.

7. S. Azani, "Facing the Truth About BDS," *The Times of Israel: The Blogs* (June 5, 2015). Retrieved from http://blogs.timesofisrael.com/facing-the-truth-about-bds/.

8. John Spritzler, "BDS needs to counterattack," *World Independent News* (February 11, 2014), https://web.archive.org/web/20150612184834/http:/www.scoop.co.nz/stories/WO1402/S00124/bds-needs-to-counterattack.htm.

9. Jonathan Kuttab, "And Now What? A Realistic Approach to the Current Impasse" (July 10, 2017), https://jonathankuttab.wordpress.com/2017/07/10/and-now-what-a-realistic-approach-to-the-current-impasse/.

10. Ali Mustafa, "Boycotts Work: An Interview with Omar Barghouti," *The Electronic Intifada* (May 31, 2009), https://electronicintifada.net/content/boycotts-work-interview-omar-barghouti/8263.

11. "Statement on Anti-BDS Legislation and Universities" in AAUP Updates (August 8, 2018), https://www.aaup.org/news/statement-anti-bds-legislation-and-universities#.W4x6MS2ZO1s.

12. Jesse M. Fried and Eugene Kontorovich, "Anti-Israeli Activists Subvert a Scholarly Group," *The Wall Street Journal* (December 3, 2017), https://www.wsj.com/articles/anti-israel-activists-subvert-a-scholarly-group-1512337924.

13. Jed Babbin with Herbert London, *The BDS War Against Israel: The Orwellian Campaign to Destroy Israel Through the Boycott, Divestment and Sanctions Movement* (New York: The London Center for Policy Research, 2014), x.

14. The United States Holocaust Museum and Memorial, "Protocols of the Elders of Zion," *Holocaust Encyclopedia,* https://encyclopedia.ushmm.org/content/en/article/protocols-of-the-elders-of-zion.

15. Rikki Hollander, "BDS, Academic/Cultural Boycott of Israel, and Omar Barghouti" in *CAMERA* (Committee for Accuracy in Middle East Reporting in America) (February 24, 2010), https://www.camera.org/article/bds-academic-cultural-boycott-of-israel-and-omar-barghouti/.

16. Gil Troy, "10 November 1975: Daniel Patrick Moynihan addresses the UN on Zionism" in *Oxford University Press's OUPblog* (November 10, 2012), https://blog.oup.com/2012/11/10-november-1975-daniel-patrick-moynihan-addresses-the-un-on-zionism/.

17. "SodaStream Leaves West Bank as CEO says boycott anti-Semitic and pointless,"

in *The Guardian* (September 3, 2015), https://www.theguardian.com/world/2015/sep/03/sodastream-leaves-west-bank-as-ceo-says-boycott-antisemitic-and-pointless.

18. Eschatology is the biblical study of last things, such as death, judgment, the destiny of the soul and of human beings.

19. Dexter Van Zile, "Profiting from Contempt" in *The Algemeiner* (January 30, 2014). https://www.algemeiner.com/2014/01/30/profiting-from-contempt/. I heard him present that position perhaps 20 years ago at a conference sponsored by a group called Evangelicals for Middle East Understanding (EMEU). I found the group was more about anti-Zionism than Middle East understanding.

20. *Kairos Palestine Document* at http://www.kairospalestine.ps/index.php/about-us/kairos-palestine-document.

21. Ryan Rodrick Beiler, "Christians urged to heed call for 'costly solidarity' with Palestine" in *The Electronic Intifada* (August 7, 2017), https://electronicintifada.net/blogs/ryan-rodrick-beiler/christians-urged-heed-call-costly-solidarity-palestine.

Chapter 13: What Should We Think About Replacement Theology?—Michael J. Vlach

1. Some prefer the title fulfillment theology, but the result is usually the same as what we identify as replacement theology. For a detailed explanation of replacement theology see Michael J. Vlach, *Has the Church Replaced Israel?: A Theological Evaluation* (Nashville, TN: B&H Academic, 2010).

2. George E. Ladd, "Revelation 20 and the Millennium," *Review and Expositor* 57 (1960): 167 (emphasis added).

3. David L. Larsen, *Jews Gentiles and the Church: A New Perspective on History and Prophecy* (Grand Rapids, MI: Discovery House Publishers, 1995), 72.

4. See Michael J. Vlach, *Has the Church Replaced Israel?* (Nashville, TN: B&H Academic, 2010), 55-57.

5. See Christopher J. Probst, *Demonizing the Jews: Luther and the Protestant Church in Nazi Germany* (Bloomington, IN: Indiana University Press, 2012).

6. Larsen, *Jews Gentiles and the Church*, 104.

7. For more, see Larsen's book *Jews Gentiles and the Church*.

8. Maggie Astor, "Anti-Semitic Incidents Surged 57 Percent in 2017, Report Finds" (February 17, 2018), https://www.nytimes.com/2018/02/27/us/anti-semitism-adl-report.html, accessed August 19, 2018.

9. Douglas J. Moo, *The Epistle to the Romans*, NICNT (Grand Rapids, MI: Eerdmans, 1996), 704.

10. Justin Martyr, *Dialogue with Trypho* 11, *The Ante-Nicene Fathers*, eds. Alexander Roberts and James Donaldson (Peabody, MA: Hendrickson, 1994) 1:200. Hereafter ANF.

11. Robert L. Saucy, *The Case for Progressive Dispensationalism: The Interface Between Dispensational & Non-Dispensational Theology* (Grand Rapids, MI: Zondervan, 1993), 212.

12. Clement, *The Instructor* 2.8, ANF 2:256.

13. Tertullian, *An Answer to the Jews* 1, ANF 3:152.

14. Jeffrey S. Siker, *Disinheriting the Jews: Abraham in Early Christian Controversy* (Louisville, KY: Westminster/John Knox, 1991), 195.

15. Siker, *Disinheriting the Jews*.

16. H. Wayne House, "The Church's Appropriation of Israel's Blessings" in *Israel, the Land and the People: An Evangelical Affirmation of God's Promises*, ed. H. Wayne House (Grand Rapids, MI: Kregel, 1998), 96.

17. Origen, *Commentary on the Gospel of Matthew* 19, ANF 9:507.

18. Jaroslav Pelikan, *The Emergence of the Catholic Tradition (100–600)*, vol. 1, The Christian Tradition: A History of the Development of Doctrine (Chicago, IL: University of Chicago Press, 1971), 81.

19. Pelikan, *The Emergence of the Catholic Tradition (100–600)*.

20. Tertullian, *An Answer to the Jews* 1, ANF 3:151.

21. See Iain H. Murray, *The Puritan Hope: Revival and the Interpretation of Prophecy* (Carlisle, PA: Banner of Truth, 1991); J. Van Den Berg, "Appendix III: The eschatological expectation of seventeenth-century Dutch Protestantism with regard to the Jewish people" in *Puritan Eschatology: 1600–1660*, ed. Peter Toon (Cambridge: James Clarke, 1970), 140.

22. William Watson, *Dispensationalism Before Darby: Seventeenth Century and Eighteenth Century English Apocalyptism* (Silverton, OR: Lampion Press, 2015).

23. Kendall Soulen, *The God of Israel and Christian Theology* (Minneapolis, MN: Fortress, 1996), x.

24. Soulen, *The God of Israel and Christian Theology*.

25. Robert Reymond, "The Traditional Covenantal View" in *Perspectives on Israel and the Church: Four Views*, ed. Chad O. Brand (Nashville, TN: B&H Academic, 2015), 48.

26. Bruce K. Waltke, "Kingdom Promises as Spiritual" in *Continuity and Discontinuity: Perspectives on the Relationship Between the Old and New Testaments*, ed. John S. Feinberg (Wheaton, IL: Crossway, 1988), 274.

27. "Support of Israel Wanes Among Younger Evangelicals" (December 4, 2017), https://lifewayresearch.com/2017/12/04/support-of-israel-among-younger-evangelicals/, accessed August 6, 2017.

28. "Support of Israel Wanes Among Younger Evangelicals."

29. "Support of Israel Wanes Among Younger Evangelicals."

30. "Support of Israel Wanes Among Younger Evangelicals."

31. "Support of Israel Wanes Among Younger Evangelicals."

32. Stephen Sizer, *Zion's Christian Soldiers: The Bible, Israel and the Church* (Nottingham, UK: InterVarsity, 2008), 16.

33. Sizer, *Zion's Christian Soldiers*, 17.

34. Sizer, *Zion's Christian Soldiers*, 36.

35. Sizer, *Zion's Christian Soldiers*, 27.

36. See Stephen R. Sizer, "An Alternative Theology of the Holy Land: A Critique of Christian Zionism," *Churchman* 113/2 (1999), http://archive.churchsociety.org/churchman/documents/cman_113_2_sizer.pdf, accessed August 16, 2018.

37. Gary Burge, *Jesus and the Land* (Grand Rapids, MI: Baker, 2010), 35 (emphasis mine).

38. N.T. Wright, *Jesus and the Victory of God* (London: SPCK Publishing, 1996), 471 (emphasis mine).

39. Wright, *Jesus and the Victory of God*, 131.

40. Wright, *Jesus and the Victory of God*, 241.

41. Wright, *Jesus and the Victory of God*, 349.

42. N.T. Wright, "The Holy Land Today" (n.d.), http://ntwrightpage.com/2016/04/05/the-holy-land-today/, accessed August 8, 2018.

43. N.T. Wright, "The Holy Land Today."

44. N.T. Wright, "Jerusalem in the New Testament" in *Jerusalem Past and Present in the Purposes of God*, ed. P.W.L. Walker (Cambridge: Tyndale House, 1992), 67, 70, 73-75.

45. J.C. Ryle, *Are You Ready for the End of Time?* (Fearn, Scotland: Christian Focus, 2001), 183.

Chapter 14: What Should We Think About the Role of the Jews in World History?—Jim Melnick

1. Paul Johnson, *The History of the Jews* (New York: Harper & Row, 1987), 2. "Writing a history of the Jews is almost like writing a history of the world, but from a highly peculiar angle of vision."

2. Jim Melnick, *Jewish Giftedness and World Redemption: The Calling of Israel* (Clarksville, MD: Messianic Jewish Publishers, 2017), 28-29; footnote 105, citing N. Berdyaev's *Smysl' istorii* ("The Meaning of History"), originally a series of lectures by Berdyaev in Moscow in 1920–1921.

3. One Jewish rabbi sees it this way: "Israel's repentance eventually leads not only to restoration for its sins but also catalyzes the nations to acknowledge God's hand in history. In Israel's punishment, the nations would see God's judgment. In Israel's restoration, they would also see God's mercy. As a consequence, they would recognize God's intervention, mercy, and power." Rabbi Juan Marcos Bejarano Gutierrez, *Tikkun Olam: A Jewish Approach for Redeeming the World* (Grand Prairie, TX: Yaron Publishing, 2017), 20.

4. Gutierrez further asserts that the "knowledge of God is spread among humanity ultimately by God himself *through* Israel's ongoing history [serving] as the medium" (*Tikkun Olam,* op. cit., 16).

5. Mike Moore, preface to John S. Ross, *Time for Favour: Scottish Missions to the Jews, 1838–1852* (Stoke-on-Trent, UK: Tentmaker Publications, 2011), 13.

6. Algernon J. Pollock, *The Amazing Jew* (London: The Central Bible Truth Depot, ca. 1935), 144, 7.

7. Kelvin Crombie, *Restoring Israel: 200 Years of the CMJ Story* (Christ Church, Jerusalem: Nicolayson's Ltd., 2008), Introduction, vi.

8. Mark Twain, "Concerning the Jews," *Harper's Magazine* (September 1899).

9. Dan Senor and Saul Singer, *Start-Up Nation: The Story of Israel's Economic Miracle* (New York: Twelve, 2009), 228.

10. Melnick, *Jewish Giftedness,* op. cit., ch. 7, "Jewish 'Drivenness' and Generosity," 131-38.

11. Thomas Cahill, *The Gifts of the Jews* (New York: Anchor Books, 1998), 3-4.

12. Melnick, *Jewish Giftedness,* 61.

13. Joseph Jacobs, *Jewish Contributions to Civilization: An Estimate* (Philadelphia, PA: The Conant Press, 1920), 49.

14. The seminal academic article on this topic was Veblen's 1919 essay in the *Political Science Quarterly,* "The Intellectual Pre-Eminence of Jews in Modern Europe," vol. 34, no. 1 (March 1919): 33-42.

15. Isaac Chotiner, "Richard Dawkins Interview: The Archbishop of Atheism," *The New Republic* (October 28, 2013), https://newrepublic.com/article/115339/richard-dawkins-interview-archbishop-atheism. Dawkins later reconfirmed this "stunning fact" of Jewish preeminence in *Brief Candle in the Dark: My Life in Science* (New York: HarperCollins, 2015), 249.

16. Dawkins, *Brief Candle in the Dark,* 249.

17. See my webpage "Jewish Genius and Excellence," https://jewishgiftedness.com/genius.html.

18. George Gilder, *The Israel Test* (New York: Encounter Books, 2012), 5.

19. As noted, *Ashkenazim* refers to European Jews and their descendants (excluding Spain and Portugal). *Sephardim* are defined as "the descendants of Jews who left Spain or Portugal after the 1492 expulsion" (https://www.jewishvirtuallibrary.org/sephardim). The *Mizrahim* (also known as Oriental Jews) are Jews who traditionally lived in the countries of the Middle East prior to the establishment of the state of Israel.

20. See, for example, Gregory Cochran, Jason Hardy, and Henry Harpending, "Natural History of Ashkenazi Intelligence," *Journal of Biosocial Science* 00, 1-35 (2005). The authors assert that "non-Ashkenazi Jews do not have high IQ test scores (Ortar, 1967), nor are they overrepresented in cognitively demanding fields. This is important in developing any causal explanation of Ashkenazi cognitive abilities: any such theory must explain high Ashkenazi IQ, the unusual structure of their cognitive abilities, and the lack of these traits among Sephardic and Oriental Jews," see at https://web.archive.org/web/20130911054719/http://harpending.humanevo.utah.edu/Documents/ashkiq.webpub.pdf (pp. 4-5). I believe these results would have been reversed had there been such a thing as IQ tests and measurements of creativity during the Sephardic "golden age" when it was the Ashkenazim who were being crushed: "It was only in modern times, when Jews were able to function outside their community, that Jewish creativity flourished." José Faur, *In the Shadow of History: Jews and Conversos at the Dawn of Modernity* (Albany, NY: State University of New York Press, 1992), 2.

21. Charles Murray, "Jewish Genius," *Commentary* (April 1, 2007), (http://www.commentarymagazine.com/articles/jewish-genius/; see also Melnick, *Jewish Giftedness,* 88.

22. Sephardic Jewish contributions today cannot compare with Ashkenazic contributions, but that was not always the case. Jewish philosopher Rebecca Goldstein has written that when the Sephardic Jews of Spain were "rising to lustrous prominence in the arts and sciences, the Jews of Christian northern Europe, the Ashkenazim, were pressed into squalid marginality or worse." Rebecca N. Goldstein, *Betraying Spinoza: The Renegade Jew Who Gave Us Modernity* (New York: Schocken Books, 2006), 94.

23. Steven L. Pease, *The Golden Age of Jewish Achievement* (Deucalion, 2009), 392.

24. Gilder, *The Israel Test*, 33.

25. Senor & Singer, *Start-Up Nation,* 158.

26. Robert Martin-Archard, *A Light to the Nations: A Study of the Old Testament Conception of Israel's Mission to the World* (London: Oliver and Boyd Ltd., 1962), 9 (ch. II, "The Missionary Message of the Deutero-Isaiah: Israel, A Light to the Nations"), citing the work of A. Lods (Paris, 1935).

27. Adolph Saphir, *Christ and Israel,* 107, from a May 18, 1868 sermon. See also Melnick, *Jewish Giftedness,* 170.

28. Louis Pollack, "The Survival of the Jewish People" in *Fingerprints on the Universe* (New York: Shaar Press, 2009), 157.

29. *Israel Today* cover, No. 197 (February 2016), www.israeltoday.co.il; editorial by Aviel Schneider, 2.

30. *Tikkun olam* ("repairing the world") is certainly a noble goal—all people of good will should want to make the world a better place. But when it becomes the *primary* driving force of one's worldview—as opposed to understanding that it is first *we* who are broken and in need of redemption, then things begin to go off track. We cannot fix the world ourselves. There is only one "Fixer," and that is Yeshua HaMashiach (Jesus the Messiah). The initial concept of *tikkun olam* originated in the Kabbalah, the

Jewish book of mysticism, which tried "to explain the moral history of the suffering world, and the role that the Jews were chosen to play in that moral history."

31. Daniel Gill in *I Am Jewish*, eds. Judea and Ruth Pearl (Woodstock, VT: Jewish Lights Publishing, 2004), 86.

32. J. Gutierrez, *Tikkun Olam*, op. cit., 6. Gutierrez adds that, in Jewish religious tradition, the "perfecting or improving [of] the world centers on the adulation of God as king over all the earth through the elimination of idolatry... The ultimate goal of Tikkun Olam then is to restore and return both Israel and humanity to the primeval knowledge of God as experienced initially in the creation and Gan Eden, i.e., the Garden Of Eden." Further, he says that "Jewish identity must have a purpose beyond self-preservation. It must be the vehicle through which the God of Israel is known throughout the earth" (11, 14, 42).

33. Dr. Michael Brown, *Our Hands Are Stained with Blood* (Shippensburg, PA: Destiny Image, 1992).

34. Charles Murray, *Human Accomplishment: The Pursuit of Excellence in the Arts and Sciences, 800 B.C. to 1850* (New York: HarperCollins, 2003), 275-277; see also Melnick, *Jewish Giftedness*, 50. Murray also cites historian of science George Sarton's finding that "95 of the 626 known scientists working everywhere in the world from [the years] 1150 to 1300 were Jews—15 percent of the total, far out of proportion" to their numbers in the world population (Murray, "Jewish Genius," *Commentary*, op. cit.).

35. Senor and Singer, *Start-Up Nation*, 11.

36. Senor and Singer, op. cit., 227.

37. Senor and Singer, *Start-Up Nation,* op. cit., 69, 100. One such unit is called *Talpiot*, which means "tall towers." According to author Jason Gerwitz, Talpiot graduates "stand at the forefront of several technologies still in the development stage..." (Jason Gewirtz, *Israel's Edge: The Story of the IDF's Most Elite Unit—Talpiot* (Jerusalem: Gefen Publishing House Ltd., 2016), 174. Further, "the combination of leadership experience and technical knowledge" that are found in Talpiot training "is ideal for creating new companies" (Senor and Singer, op. cit., 72).

38. Gilder, *The Israel Test*, 64.

39. Gilder, *The Israel Test*, 2.

40. George Gilder, "Choosing the Chosen People—Anti-Semitism is essentially hatred of capitalism and excellence," *National Review* (July 30, 2009).

41. Senor and Singer, op. cit., 126-128.

42. At a minimum, they "seemed to be facing, if not physical extinction, spiritual annihilation." See Gal Beckerman, *When They Come for Us, We'll Be Gone: The Epic Struggle to Save Soviet Jewry* (New York: Mariner Books, 2011), 41.

43. Melnick, *Jewish Giftedness*, 22.

44. Melnick, "An Introduction to Russian Jewish Ministry," *Mishkan,* special issue no. 69 (2011), 4-5. See also Dr. Mitch Glaser and Alan Shore, *Remnant and Renewal: The New Russian Messianic Movement* (New York: Chosen People Ministries, 2006).

45. Mitch Glaser, "A History of the Russian Messianic Congregational Conferences," *Mishkan,* Special Issue No. 69 (2011), 14.

46. Senor & Singer, op. cit., 227.

47. Dennis Mitzner, "Israel's desert city of Beersheba is turning into a cyber oasis," TechCrunch.com (March 20, 2016), https://techcrunch.com/2016/03/20/israels-desert-city-of-beersheba-is-turning-into-a-cybertech-oasis/.

48. Viva Sarah Press, "Beersheva goes cyber," Israel21c (August 3, 2015), https://www
.israel21c.org/beersheva-goes-cyber/.

49. Senor & Singer, op. cit., 212; see also *Jerusalem Post*, December 5, 2007; https://
www.jpost.com/Business/Business-News/Israel-leads-world-in-per-capita-scientists
-and-engineers; for 2016 statistics, see https://www.statista.com/statistics/264644/
ranking-of-oecd-countries-by-number-of-scientists-and-researchers/.

50. Gilder, *The Israel Test*, 2.

51. To keep up with some of the latest developments in Israeli high-tech, go to the
Israel21c.org website at: https://www.israel21c.org/topic/technology/.

52. For example, a persuasive case can be made, I believe, that, were it not for Hitler's
persecution of the Jews, nuclear weapons might never have been invented. Jewish
scientists were critical to the development of the bomb. Harvard professor Steven
Pinker agrees: "Quite possibly, had there been no Nazis," he writes, and, I would add,
no Nazi persecution of the Jews, "there would be no nukes." (see S. Pinker, *Enlightenment Now* [2018], 314). In *Pandora's Secrets: Nine Men and the Atomic Bomb* (2003),
author Brian VanDeMark wrote: "An irony of fate is that Hitler's actions removed
the one group of people who would have been able to provide him with the instrument for world dominance he so eagerly sought" (p. 15). For more on this story,
please see https://jewishgiftedness.com/planckandhitler.html.

Chapter 15: What Should We Think About Israel's Future?—Andy Woods

1. See the helpful map showing what was promised to the nation in the Abrahamic
covenant in comparison to what was attained in the conquest in Thomas L. Constable, "Notes on Numbers," 124, accessed August 13, 2018, http://www.soniclight.com.

2. John F. Walvoord, *The Millennial Kingdom: A Basic Text in Premillennial Theology*
(Findlay, OH: Dunham, 1959), 149-52.

3. J. Randall Price, *Jerusalem in Bible Prophecy: God's Stage for the Final Drama* (Eugene,
OR: Harvest House, 1998), 219-20; Arnold G. Fruchtenbaum, *Footsteps of the Messiah: A Study of the Sequence of Prophetic Events*, rev. ed. (Tustin, CA: Ariel, 2003),
102-103.

4. Arnold G. Fruchtenbaum, *Israelology: The Missing Link in Systematic Theology*, rev. ed.
(Tustin, CA: Ariel, 1994), 577.

5. Replacement theologians are those that argue that the church has permanently
replaced national Israel in the outworking of God's future purposes. Replacement
theology is also called supersessionism, since it maintains that the church has permanently superseded Israel.

6. Hank Hanegraaff, *The Apocalypse Code: Find Out What the Bible Really Says About the
End Times and Why It Matters* (Nashville, TN: Nelson, 2007), 52-53, 178-79.

7. See the helpful map showing what was promised to the nation in the Abrahamic
covenant in comparison to what was attained in the conquest in Constable, "Notes
on Numbers," 124.

8. Charles C. Ryrie, *The Ryrie Study Bible: New American Standard Bible* (Chicago:
Moody, 2012), 405.

9. Fruchtenbaum, *Israelology*, 521-22, 631-32.

10. John F. Walvoord, *Major Bible Prophecies: 37 Crucial Prophecies That Affect You Today*
(Grand Rapids, MI: Zondervan, 1991), 82.

11. Anthony Hoekema, *The Bible and the Future*, rev. ed. (Grand Rapids, MI: Eerdmans,
1979), 197-98.

12. Fruchtenbaum, *Israelology*, 186-88.

13. Fruchtenbaum, *Israelology*, 188.

14. Hans K. LaRondelle, *The Israel of God in Prophesy: Principles of Prophetic Interpretation* (Berrien Springs, MI: Andrews University, 1983), 110-11; Kenneth L. Gentry, "The Iceman Cometh! Mormonism Reigneth!," *Dispensationalism in Transition* 6, no. 1 (January 1993): 1.

15. S. Lewis Johnson, "Paul and the 'Israel of God': An Exegetical and Eschatological Case-Study," in *Essays in Honor of J. Dwight Pentecost*, ed. Stanley D. Toussaint and Charles H. Dyer (Chicago, IL: Moody, 1986), 181-96.

16. Fruchtenbaum, *Israelology*, 684-90.

17. See Justin Martyr, *Dialogue with Trypho*, 11; 123; 135.

18. Ernest de Witt Burton, *A Critical and Exegetical Commentary on the Epistle to the Galatians*, eds. Samuel Rolles Driver and Alfred Plummer and Charles Augustus Briggs, International Critical Commentary (Edinburgh: T. & T. Clark 1920), 358.

19. Bruce K. Waltke, "Kingdom Promises as Spiritual," in *Continuity and Discontinuity: Perspectives on the Relationship between the Old and New Testaments*, ed. John S. Feinberg (Wheaton, IL: Crossway, 1988), 273; Gary DeMar, *End Times Fiction: A Biblical Consideration of the Left Behind Theology* (Nashville, TN: Nelson, 2001), 203.

20. J. Randall Price, *The Temple and Bible Prophecy: A Definitive Look at Its Past, Present, and Future* (Eugene, OR: Harvest, 2005), 596-97.

21. That "the beloved city" in Revelation 20:9 refers to the city of Jerusalem as the millennial capitol, see Psalm 78:68 and 87:2. See also Robert L. Thomas, "A Classical Dispensationalist View of Revelation," in *Four Views on the Book of Revelation*, ed. C. Marvin Pate (Grand Rapids, MI: Zondervan, 1998), 207.

22. Kenneth L. Gentry, "A Preterist View of Revelation," in *Four Views on the Book of Revelation*, ed. C. Marvin Pate (Grand Rapids: Zondervan, 1998), 51-52.

23. Alva J. McClain, *The Greatness of the Kingdom: An Inductive Study of the Kingdom of God as Set Forth in the Scriptures* (Grand Rapids: Zondervan, 1959), 295-97.

24. Stanley D. Toussaint, *Behold the King: A Study of Matthew* (Portland, OR: Multnomah, 1980; reprint, Grand Rapids, Kregel, 2005), 15-18. Apparently, both Eusebius and Origen indicated that Matthew was written to those within Judaism who came to believe. See Eusebius, *Ecclesiastical History*, 3:24:6; 6:25:5.

Chapter 16: What Should We Think About the Jews as a Chosen People?—Arnold G. Fruchtenbaum

1. These statements have been excerpted and edited from the introduction of the updated blog of Rabbi Alan Lurie, "What Does It Mean that the Jews Are God's Chosen People?," *Huffington Post* (January 23, 2014), accessed at: https://www.huffingtonpost.com/rabbi-alan-lurie/jews-gods-chosen-people_b_1079821.html.

2. Jon D. Levenson, "Chosenness and Its Enemies," *Commentary Magazine* (December 1, 2008), accessed at: https://www.commentarymagazine.com/articles/chosenness-and-its-enemies/.

3. This action still required the individual to place their personal trust in the Person (God) and the promise of salvation (through the Messiah).

4. While circumcision of the flesh is a sign of one's membership in the elect nation, circumcision of the heart is a sign of individual salvation.

5. Author's translation to highlight the covenant name of God and its revealed meaning in the term "I AM" (see Exodus 3:14-15; 6:3).

6. Covenant theology uses a theological concept of covenant as a means of organizing the history of God's dealings with mankind under the themes of redemption,

works, and grace. Each of these "covenants," though not presented as such in Scripture, are said to best summarize the scriptural data with regards to a Christian theology. While covenant theology would agree that Christians (new covenant people) have replaced the Jews (old covenant people) as His chosen people, it would contend that this was not an abandonment of God's promises to Israel a fulfillment, since Christ established the church in organic continuity with Israel, not as a separate replacement entity. However, in its historical outworking, this concept of replacing national Israel with the church has led to Christian forms of anti-Semitism and some of the most egregious acts in history against the Jewish people. Historically this has been the view of the Eastern and Western Orthodox Churches as well as many Protestant denominations that had their roots in the Western (Roman Catholic) church. In modern times such churches have usually opposed Zionism and supported organized boycotts of the state of Israel.

7. In Romans 9:6 the context makes it clear that the discussion relates only to ethnic Jews. The teaching then is that those who have combined their fleshly lineage with faith in their Messiah are "spiritual Jews" as opposed to those who have not and are only "physical Jews." With respect to Rom. 11:26, S. Lewis Johnson Jr. has noted: "All Israel" does not mean every single Israelite; it means the nation as a whole. Just as every single Israelite did not reject the Lord Jesus, so every single Israelite shall not be saved. But the nation as a whole rejected Him and the nation as a whole shall be saved" *Commentary on Romans.* On Gal. 6:16 which confirms on the basis of grammar (Greek *kai* decisively means "and") that the phrase "the Israel of God" refers to believing Jews who are part of the church as distinct from the church as a whole, see S. Lewis Johnson Jr., "Paul and the 'Israel of God': An Exegetical and Eschatological Case-Study," in *Essays in Honor of J. Dwight Pentecost*, eds. Stanley D. Toussaint and Charles H. Dyer (Chicago: Moody Press, 1986), 188.

8. J. Dwight Pentecost, *Things to Come: A Study in Biblical Eschatology* (Grand Rapids, MI: Zondervan Publishing House, 1958), 9.

9. Additional passages dealing with the new covenant are Isaiah 55:3; 59:21; 61:8-9; Jeremiah 32:40; Ezekiel 16:60; 34:25-31; 37:26-28; and Romans 11:25-27.

Chapter 17: What Should We Think About Jews Who Become Christians?—David Brickner

1. For the case for Luke's Jewishness, see David L. Allen, *The Lukan Authorship of Hebrews*, NAC Studies in Bible & Theology (Nashville, TN: B&H Academic, 2010), 261-323.

2. C.S. Lewis, foreword to Joy Davidman, *Smoke on the Mountain: An Interpretation of the Ten Commandments* (Philadelphia, PA: Westminster Press, 1984), 7-8.

3. The fourth-century church historian Eusebius recorded that the Jewish-Christians had been warned by an oracle before the war to flee to Pella, a city of the Decapolis in the district of Perea (Eusebius, *Ecclesiastical History* 3, 5, 3); however, Epiphanius wrote that they went to Pella because Jesus had told them to leave Jerusalem (Epiphanius, *Panarion* 29,7,7-8; 30,2,7), although elsewhere he claimed an angel had warned them (Epiphanius, *On Weights and Measures* 15). The resident Jewish community who remained to fight against Rome thereafter regarded these Jewish-Christians as traitors who betrayed the nation at its greatest hour of need.

4. This malediction is known as the *Birkat Haminim*. See Oskar Skarsaune, *In the Shadow of the Temple: Jewish Influences on Early Christianity* (Downers Grove, IL: IVP Academic, 2002), 197-98.

5. See Richard Robinson, "Who Was a Jew?" in Kai Kjær-Hansen, ed., *Jewish Identity*

and Faith in Jesus (Jerusalem: Caspari Center, 1996), 33-40. Jesus Himself was also looked on unfavorably in the Talmud, see, e.g., Peter Schäfer, *Jesus in the Talmud* (Princeton, NJ; Oxford, UK: Princeton University Press, 2007).

6. A Jewish curse on heretics as the *Birkat haMinim* was added to the Eighteen Benedictions (Amidah) recited daily by Jews, probably as a means of outing Jewish believers in Jesus, for they would not pronounce a curse on themselves.

7. Louis Goldberg, *God, Torah, Messiah: The Messianic Jewish Theology of Dr. Louis Goldberg*, ed. Richard A. Robinson (San Francisco, CA: Purple Pomegranate Productions, 2009), 127-29.

8. Goldberg, *God, Torah, Messiah*, 721, n. 4.

9. For a substantial collection of biographies of Jewish believers in Jesus through 1909, see A. Bernstein, *Some Jewish Witnesses for Christ* (London: Operative Jewish Converts' Institution, 1909). Numerous biographies have been published in the twentieth and twenty-first centuries.

10. For a brief summary, see Joseph Telushkin, *Jewish Literacy: The Most Important Things to Know About the Jewish Religion, Its People, and Its History* (New York: William Morrow and Company, 1991), 187-189.

11. Yaacov Shavit, *The New Hebrew Nation: A Study in Israeli Heresy and Fantasy* (London: Frank Cass, 1987), xiv: "From the last quarter of the nineteenth century the term *Ivri* (Hebrew) became popular and widely used in the 'secular' Jewish national literature for describing the 'new Jew.'"

12. See Yaakov Ariel, *Evangelizing the Chosen People: Missions to the Jews in America, 1880–2000* (Chapel Hill, NC; London: The University of North Carolina Press, 2000).

13. See Michael R. Darby, *The Emergence of the Hebrew Christian Movement in Nineteenth-Century Britain* (Leiden; Boston: Brill, 2010).

14. Acts 16:1 (English Standard Version): "Paul came also to Derbe and to Lystra. A disciple was there, named Timothy, the son of a Jewish woman who was a believer, but his father was a Greek."

15. Numbers are notoriously hard to come by. See Renae Kooy and Wes Taber, "Survey of World Jewish Demographics" (Lausanne Consultation on Jewish Evangelism, 2015), 21, accessed September 4, 2018, http://www.lcje.net/10th%20International%20Conference%202015/2015%20Survey%20of%20World%20Jewish%20Demographics%20—%20Final.pdf. The authors cite the World Christian Database, which found 126,840 individuals in messianic congregations without distinguishing Jewish and Gentile attendees and not including Jewish believers in mainstream churches.

16. David Rudolph, "Messianic Judaism in Antiquity and in the Modern Era," in *Introduction to Messianic Judaism: Its Ecclesial Context and Biblical Foundations*, ed. David Rudolph and Joel Willitts (Grand Rapids, MI: Zondervan, 2013), 508-509, Kindle.

17. Jay Lorenzen, "Paul Pierson on Characteristics of Spiritual Movements," February 15, 2010, accessed September 4, 2018, http://onmovements.com/?p=663.

18. Lea Bendel, "How Has the Image of Messianic Jews in Israel Changed in the Last 37 Years?," *Mishkan: A Forum on the Gospel and the Jewish People* 76 (2016): 3-4, accessed September 4, 2018, http://www.caspari.com/wp-content/uploads/2016/12/Mishkan76.pdf.

19. Bendel, "Image of Messianic Jews," 20-23.

20. Barna Group, *Jewish Millennials: The Beliefs and Behaviors Shaping Young Jews in America* (Ventura, CA: Barna Group, 2017), 75-76, 78.

21. Pew Research Center, *A Portrait of Jewish Americans* (Washington, DC: Pew Research Center, 2013), 58. Also available at http://www.pewforum.org/2013/10/01/jewish -american-beliefs-attitudes-culture-survey/, accessed September 4, 2018.

22. Charles Hodge, *A Commentary on the Epistle to the Romans* (Edinburgh: Johnstone and Hunter, 1854), 338.

Chapter 18: What Should We Think About Palestinian Christians?—Paul Wilkinson

1. John Nelson Darby, "The Irrationalism of Infidelity: Being a Reply to 'Phases of Faith' (1853)," in *The Collected Writings of J.N. Darby*, ed. William Kelly, vol. 6 (Kingston-on-Thames: Stow Hill Bible & Tract Depot, n.d.), 1-2.

2. Newman was the younger brother of Cardinal John Henry Newman (1801–1890), an Anglican priest who left the Church of England to join the Roman Catholic priesthood. In 2010, he was beatified by Pope Benedict XVI.

3. Darby was the focus of my doctorate, first published in 2007 and later republished under the title *Understanding Christian Zionism: Israel's Place in the Purposes of God* (Bend, OR: The Berean Call, 2013).

4. Darby, "The Irrationalism of Infidelity," 1.

5. I shared my experience of the conference in a 2011 PowerPoint presentation, "Christian Palestinianism" (www.youtube.com/watch?v=osIx3tmvioY, beginning at frame 39:58).

6. Desmond Tutu is the Archbishop Emeritus of Cape Town, best known for his anti-Apartheid work in South Africa. He is the patron of Sabeel. (Friends of Sabeel North America, "Canon Naim Ateek," www.fosna.org.)

7. This phrase is used in a document released in December 2009 by Palestinian religious leaders entitled, "Kairos Palestine: A Moment of Truth—A Word of Faith, Hope, and Love from the Heart of Palestinian Suffering." Ateek was one of the architects of the document. (www.kairospalestine.ps/)

8. Naim Stifan Ateek, *Justice, and Only Justice: A Palestinian Theology of Liberation* (Maryknoll, NY: Orbis Books, 1990), 77.

9. Naim Stifan Ateek, *A Palestinian Christian Cry for Reconciliation* (Maryknoll, NY: Orbis Books, 2008), 13.

10. Ateek, *A Palestinian Christian Cry*, 11; Naim Ateek, "An Easter Message from Sabeel," April 6, 2001, www.sabeel.org; Naim Ateek, "The Massacre of the Innocents—A Christmas Reflection," *This Week in Palestine*, no. 32 (December 2000), www.pales tina-balsam.it.

11. Ateek, *Justice*, 77-79 (emphasis in original).

12. Ateek, *A Palestinian Christian Cry*, 56; Naim Ateek, "The Earth Is the Lord's: Land, Theology, and the Bible," in *The Land Cries Out: Theology of the Land in the Israeli-Palestinian Context*, ed. Salim Munayer and Lisa Loden (Eugene, OR: Cascade Books, 2012), 175, 178.

13. Naim Ateek, "The Theology of Sabeel—What We Believe," July 31, 2008, www .fosna.org; Ateek, *A Palestinian Christian Cry*, 71, 77.

14. Ateek, *A Palestinian Christian Cry*, 150.

15. A term I coined during my doctorate to represent all that is antithetical to Christian Zionism.

16. Fuller publicly endorses close cooperation with the Islamic world. In 2007, the seminary hosted the third Evangelical Christian-Muslim Dialogue Conference. Then president Richard Mouw, an open critic of Israel, was the keynote speaker. In 2016,

current president Mark Labberton was a speaker at the fourth "Christ at the Check-point" conference in Bethlehem.

17. Munther Isaac, *From Land to Lands, from Eden to the Renewed Earth: A Christ-Centered Biblical Theology of the Promised Land* (Carlisle, PA: Langham Monographs, 2015), 379.
18. Munther Isaac's blog, "About me," www.blogger.com.
19. Salim J. Munayer and Lisa Loden, *Through My Enemy's Eyes: Envisioning Reconciliation in Israel-Palestine* (Milton Keynes, UK: Paternoster, 2014), 207.
20. Salim Munayer, "Theology of the Land: From a Land of Strife to a Land of Reconciliation," in *The Land Cries Out*, 235, 246-248, 253.
21. Isaac, *From Land to Lands*, xv-xvi, 234-261, 291, 319-321.
22. Alister E. McGrath, *Christian Theology: An Introduction*, 2nd ed. (Oxford: Blackwell, 1997), 205.
23. UMJC, "Joint statement on 'Christ at the Checkpoint,'" February 17, 2012, www.umjc.org.
24. UMJC, "Joint statement on 'Christ at the Checkpoint.'"
25. Edward Bickersteth, "The Mind of Christ Respecting the Jews," in *The Restoration of the Jews to Their Own Land, in Connection with Their Future Conversion and the Final Blessedness of Our Earth*, 2nd ed. (London: R.B. Seeley and W. Burnside, 1841), 32-34.
26. Ryan Jones, "Bethlehem Pastor: There Are Palestinians Who Love Israel," *Israel Today*, January 2015, www.israeltoday.co.il.
27. Jones, "Bethlehem Pastor."
28. Jones, "Bethlehem Pastor."
29. Edward Bickersteth, "The Practical Use of the Doctrine," in *The Restoration of the Jews*, xciv-xcv (emphasis in original).

Afterword: Why We Should Think More About Israel—Randall Price
1. Will Herberg, *Judaism and Modern Man: An Interpretation of Jewish Religion* (New York: Harper & Row, 1951), 91-92.
2. Herberg, *Judaism and Modern Man*, 91.
3. Jonathan Sacks, *Radical Then, Radical Now: The Legacy of the World's Oldest Religion* (London: HarperCollins Publishers, 2001), 215.
4. Eric Herschthaf, "Are You There God? It's Us, The Jews: Can religion, especially Judaism, work if you don't believe in the Big Guy upstairs?" *The New York Jewish Week* (April 10, 2012).
5. Herberg, *Judaism and Modern Man*, 258.
6. Epigram from statements made by G.K. Chesterton in *The Oracle of the Dog* as codified by Emile Cammaerts.
7. Thomas Cahill, *The Gifts of the Jews: How a Tribe of Desert Nomads Changed the Way Everyone Thinks and Feels* (New York: Doubleday, 1998), 251-52.
8. Herberg, *Judaism and Modern Man*, 218.
9. Mordecai M. Kaplan, *Judaism as a Civilization* (New York: The Jewish Publication Society of America, 1981), 3.
10. Herberg, *Judaism and Modern Man*, 236.

Also by Randall Price

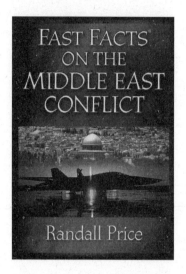

Fast Facts on the Middle East Crisis

The conflict in the Middle East raises many questions for Americans, Christians, and the world community. Randall Price, a bestselling author and expert in Middle Eastern studies, provides concise answers to those questions. In a practical Q-and-A format with maps, charts, and sidebars, this book unveils a fascinating timeline of the conflict development as it answers:

- Why is America involved?
- What are the common misconceptions about the conflict?
- How does the truth differ from the headlines?
- Is there a way to resolve this situation?

Price's knowledge of Israel, Islam, and the current controversies provides an insider's information in a quick-reference format. Readers will be able to understand the complex issues appearing in today's media reports.